Global Sustain

To the Legacy of Roy A. Rappaport

Global Sustainability and Communities of Practice

Edited by
Carl A. Maida
Sam Beck

berghahn
NEW YORK · OXFORD
www.berghahnbooks.com

Published in 2018 by
Berghahn Books
www.berghahnbooks.com

© 2018 Berghahn Books

Library of Congress Cataloging in Publication Data

A C.I.P. cataloging record is available from the Library of Congress
Library of Congress Cataloging in Publication Control Number:
2017055514

British Library Cataloguing in Publication Data

A catalogue record for this book is available from the British Library

ISBN 978-1-78533-844-1 hardback
ISBN 978-1-78533-845-8 paperback
ISBN 978-1-78533-846-4 ebook

Contents

Introduction: Towards Global Sustainability and Communities
of Practice   1
    Carl A. Maida and Sam Beck

Part 1: Sustaining the Countryside

1. Cultivating Sustainability Literacy and Public Engagement in
   Intag, Ecuador   23
       Linda D'Amico

2. Spaces for Transdisciplinary Dialogues on the Relationship
   between Local Communities and their Environment: The Case of
   a Rural Community in the Calchaqui Valley (Salta, Argentina)   43
       Marta Crivos, Maria Rosa Martinez, Laura Teves,
       Carolina Remorini

3. Affective Solidarities? Participating in and Witnessing Fair Trade
   and Women's Empowerment in Transnational Communities
   of Practice   60
       Debarati Sen

Part 2: Sustainable Urbanism

4. Plural Citizenship and Social Inclusion in Brazil's Urban
   Communities of Practice   75
       Carla Guerron Montero

5. The Role of Communities of Practice in Urban Rights Activism
   in Istanbul, Turkey   94
       Danielle V. Schoon and Funda Oral

6. Cultivating Civic Ecology: A Photovoice Study with Urban Gardeners
   in Lisbon, Portugal   109
       Krista Harper and Ana Isabel Afonso

7. Knowledge Production and Emancipatory Social Movements from
   the Heart of Globalized Hipsterdom, Williamsburg, Brooklyn   125
   Sam Beck

Part 3: Organizing for Sustainability

8. Knowing Sustainability: Building Communities of Practice through
   Project-Based Learning in Urban Ecology at High Tech High   151
   Carl A. Maida

9. Inventing Eco-Cycle A Social Enterprise Approach to
   Sustainability Education   174
   Sandy Smith-Nonini

10. Confronting Tyranny in a Public Health Agency: Crafting
    a 'Philosophy of Praxis' into a 'Community of Resistance'   190
    Brian McKenna

11. Local Trade and Exchange/Employment Systems (LETS)
    in Future Eco-sustainable Societies   207
    Richard Westra

Introduction

Global Sustainability and Communities of Practice

Carl A. Maida and Sam Beck

The community of practice originally denoted a group of people who share a craft or a profession (Lave and Wenger 1991); the concept has been expanded to indicate a process of collective learning within groups with a common concern or interest. As such, communities of practice are organisational forms that complement the current knowledge economy, which since the late twentieth century has witnessed revolutionary advances in information production and dissemination (Wenger 2000). A knowledge economy produces a reliance on shared information among social groups in-action. Communities of practice ensure greater engagement for sustainability by the public as local and global actors. It is a powerful paradigmatic construct that arose through the anthropological imagination (Lave 1988), providing a framework for 'thinking and learning in its social dimensions' (Wenger 2010a: 179). Etienne Wenger understands that this framework is enacted through a 'dual process of meaning making' (2010a: 180). This dual process exists in the interplay of ongoing participatory engagement that creates meaning in both the socially sustained dimensions and the physical and conceptual artefacts of these reified experiences.

Social engagement always has the potential of creating communities of practice as social groups come together, adhere to a common interpretation of the artefacts they create and perform actions in common. A community of practice thus provides a framework for understanding social learning in complex organisations, specifically the notion of 'knowing'. For novices and experts alike, knowing within a community of practice is based upon socially defined competence, or the ability to act and to be viewed as a competent member in both process and context (Argyris and Schon 1974). Belonging to a particular community is based upon engagement, imagination and alignment within a social learning system that supports and sustains members and the community itself, what Wenger refers to as a 'regime of competence' (Wenger 2010a: 184). Within a regime of competence, individuals have enhanced opportunities to operate above their personal resources, and approach challenging learning tasks without being overwhelmed because of their membership in a learning community.

Communities of practice are dynamic and provide the framework for social learning, because members: share a sense of joint enterprise, indicative of the level of *learning energy* within the community; interact on the basis of mutuality, which points to the depth of social capital generated by mutual engagement; and share a repertoire of resources, indicating the degree of participants' self-awareness (Lave and Wenger 1991).

This framework – of knowing, belonging and social learning through more informal styles characteristic of a community of practice – provides members with the skills to engage meaningfully in knowledge production, exchange and transformation in complex organisations by creating new ways of 'being in the world' with a common identity and membership (Wenger 2010b). Moreover, communities of practice are always in the making as meaning is ceaselessly being negotiated.

This book focuses on case-based chapters on communities of practice, within and beyond anthropological frameworks, to illustrate how participatory researchers, students, policy and community leaders, and the broader public, come to engage in community-based transformational sustainability research and practice. We also suggest here that when anthropologists participate in communities of practice, the skills, knowledge and values they bring into problem-solving processes provide enriched insights and enable anthropological knowledge to contribute to improving the lives of the most vulnerable in society.

Sustainability, Place and the Commons

The concept of sustainability holds that the social, economic and environmental factors within human communities must be viewed interactively and systematically. The Brundtland Report (World Commission on Environment and Development 1987) defines sustainable development as meeting the needs of the present without compromising the ability of future generations to meet their own needs. In 1996, an international group of practitioners and researchers met in Bellagio, Italy, to develop new ways to measure and assess progress towards sustainable development. The Bellagio Principles (1997) serve as guidelines for the whole of the assessment process, including the choice and design of indicators, their interpretation and communication of the results.

Although broadly conceived, the pursuit of sustainable development is pragmatically a local practice because every community has different needs and quality-of-life concerns. Despite local variation, the participation of ordinary citizens, or 'deliberative democracy', remains constant across the sustainable community movement (Hempel 1998). In rural areas undergoing rapid development and urban areas transformed by planning, clearance and renewal, new partnerships are forming on behalf of sustainable development (Chambers 2005; Chambers and Conway 1991; Conway and Barbier 2013). Residents, and state and non-governmental organisation experts, including academics, are partnering to design indicators and to monitor land, labour, housing, health and other quality-of-life concerns. Civic engagement by ordinary residents is essential as local people have practical experience and bring important intuitive insights and localised knowledge to the tasks of indicator design and monitoring. Jane Jacobs (1961) argued on behalf of such 'self-diversification', or neighbourhood transformation that reflects the vitality, mobility and aesthetic interests of its residents.

Delocalisation results when people become less affected with local concerns, especially in decisions about the management of common resources, and in their stance towards their neighbours who have been marginalised by consequences of global change (National Science Foundation 1995). Through its encounter with these displacements, the new ecological anthropology has come to view the community as embedded within larger systems at the regional, national and international levels, and to study the impact of a multi-tiered and globalising world on the locality (Burawoy et al. 2000; Gupta and Ferguson 1997; Kottak 1999; Marcus 1995; Oliver-Smith and Hoffman 1999; Wolf 2001). This recent paradigm recognises the importance of the state and cultural mediations in ecological processes at a time when local ethno-ecologies are being transformed by development, biodiversity conservation, environmentalism and the influence of non-governmental organisations (Brosius 1999; Escobar 1999).

Within political ecology, environmental justice research has addressed the ways poor communities organise to confront disproportionate, high and adverse environmental exposure (Harper and Rajan 2002; Pastor 2001, 2002). At the intersections of the social and the ecological, political ecology has helped to frame the narrative of social-ecological resilience (Peterson 2000), a *bridging concept* defined as 'the capacity of an urban region to absorb uncertain climatic stimuli and their effects so as to maintain the essential social and ecological functional and structural properties while undergoing change' (Beichler et al. 2014: 4). However, as with the design of sustainability indicators, many communities face challenges in developing their own resilience measures, notably because of limited time and resources; the lack of available data necessary to plan resilience-building efforts; and inadequate sharing of data among community stakeholders (National Academies of Sciences, Engineering, and Medicine 2017).

The concept of sustainable development, as framed by Michael Redclift (1987), links the transfer of capital, labour and natural resources within the global economic system. Through a comparative framework that situates the historical role of the environment within capitalist development, Redclift views resource exploitation and structural underdevelopment in the southern hemisphere as a consequence of environmental change in the industrialised northern hemisphere. With global change, localities throughout the world have undergone ecological crises, such as resource depletion, changes in land use, unequal resource allocation and biodiversity loss. The *Anthropocene* characterises the current geological age – a time when the human domination of nature is challenging our planetary boundaries, with consequent deforestation, pollution, climate change and species loss (Gibson and Venkateswar 2015). These conditions are frequently accompanied by anthropogenic hazards, such as emerging epidemic and persistent chronic diseases and chaotic environmental episodes, including drought, flooding and violent storms.

Since the industrial era, anthropogenic activities have become the major driver impacting on the Earth system; it is now exponentially worse. Complex environmental challenges, brought about by rapid and rapacious development, the voracious exploitation of both natural and human environments for profit, and the growth of human populations, together with the current technological revolution that has changed both lifestyles and social norms, call for a new approach to learning that facilitates interdisciplinary action on behalf of sustainability. Integrative science and education has shifted the emphasis towards actively using what learners know to explore, negotiate, interpret and create through collaborative activities across academic disciplines (Bruffee 1999) and on-the-ground practitioners. As a potentially disruptive innovation, collaborative learning challenges researchers, students and the public to acknowledge their roles as participants engaged in producing knowledge for change that integrates and synthesises data from diverse fields and experience into both whole-systems and political-economic process-oriented perspectives that move beyond normative and uncritical thinking to develop alternative well-grounded holistic approaches to improving the quality of life, especially for the vulnerable.

Woven throughout this transition is the narrative of sustainability, understood as focusing on the physical, sociocultural and institutional development practices that meet the needs of present users without compromising the ability of future generations to meet their own needs, particularly with regard to use and waste of natural resources (Maida 2007). To this end, sustainable practices support ecological, human and economic health and vitality, with the presumption that resources are finite, and should be used with a view to long-term priorities and consequences. However, cultivating sustainability literacy and public engagement on its behalf requires diverse perspectives, trans-generational timeframes and local-to-global connectivity. The need to promote participatory learning within a community of practice on behalf of sustainability literacy in the broader public is clear; however, few community-based approaches have been developed to date that integrate disciplines into a holistic perspective of Earth's natural and human systems.

Related to sustainability is the centuries-old controversy over how urbanisation and industrialisation affect the soil, water, air and other common resources. The debate pits those advocating for the local control of shared resources against proponents of centralised control of common holdings by state or corporate power – and this polarity has helped shape public policies and institutional arrangements. The 'tragedy of the commons' connotes, in part, the undesirable effects of population pressure on certain shared resources, especially commons, which originally refer to farming and grazing land, hunting and fishing areas, forests and places for the disposal of wastes to which all members of a society have access. These common-pool resources were enclosed and restricted in the face of exploitation by individuals or groups attempting to maximise their own gain (Agrawal 2003). Collective and shared use of such resources was ended through economic manipulation and outright violence transferring the use of such resources into the hands of private ownership for profit or the state in the age of capitalism.

Accompanying the neoliberal turn in contemporary capitalist development is an advanced form of extractive capitalism, including open pit mining and ocean overfishing, which displaces local communities and disrupts their regional economies. These practices continue to exploit longstanding common-pool resources through property rights and *financialisation* (Graeber 2011), conditions that give rise to the organic emergence of communities of practice to counter the incentives of global capital, including the debt economy and other moral hazards of globalisation (Federici 2014).

The literature on common-pool resources and common property has focused on environmental degradation, resource depletion and the impoverishment of populations. Scholars of the commons have offered the reinvention of community-based conservation as a corrective (Ostrom 2008). Bio-regionalists envision a more equitable relationship between human and natural systems through reorganising society around common ecosystems or bioregions and upon sustainable principles and self-management. Some have called for a 'recovery of the commons' as a means of regaining local community through peoples' direct involvement in the web of the natural resources and rearranging the relationships that people have with each other by collaborating across differences (Reid and Taylor 2010). This would come about through a revitalised sense of citizenship based upon shared governance around food, water, soil and energy, the release of human potentials, shared identity and common membership. Accompanying this push towards the reconstituting of the commons is the goal of creating the conditions for sustaining local cultures.

Such place-focused politics would become viable if local communities were rebuilt upon ecological principles rather than upon political or economic centralisation, principles of privatisation and profit making. Defining and securing a satisfactory quality of life for localities impacted by restrictions resulting from state- and market-based commodification of the natural and sociocultural commons, including public space and public health, is a key feature of the sustainability project. This emphasis on access to public goods expands the rhetoric and theory of the commons to include arenas not typically considered in current debates on common-pool resources. Sandy Smith-Nonini (2006: 235), for example, expands the concept of the commons to include medical and health services as a *health commons*, arguing that 'governments and societies have an obligation to collective social welfare, and that the health of populations should be maximized and thought of as a public good'.

Viewing the commodification of the urban commons by real-estate interests and other forms of private accumulation that drive capitalist urbanisation as contributing to the degradation of a city's land and labour resources, David Harvey (2012: 87) argues that 'if state-supplied public goods either decline or become a mere vehicle for private accumulation (as is happening to education), and if the state withdraws from their provision, then there is only one possible response, which is for populations to self-organize to provide their own commons'. Bonnie McCay (2002: 362) supports a cultural and historical approach as a way to contextualise these more institutional concerns surrounding the commons 'as ones about competition and collaboration among social entities; the embeddedness of individual and social action; and the historical, political, sociocultural, and ecological specificity of human-environment interactions and institutions'. By seeing these linked interactions as *situations*, we may get a better sense of the broader 'webs of significance or cultural "filters"' (McCay 2002: 393) through which people come to comprehend common-pool resource issues.

Life Politics and Restoration of the Commons

Citizen science bridges researchers and the lay public, across diverse populations and subpopulations, on behalf of sustainability (Bäckstrand 2003; Corburn 2005). Regarding the production or transfer of critical knowledge, citizen science is decidedly personal and interpersonal in style, enacted from the bottom up, most often at the local level, and based on relationship building (Bonney et al. 2009). It involves science initiated and carried out by citizens not trained to be professional scientists. These independent citizen perspectives, tied to local geographies, tend to be more holistic and serve as a corrective to normative science, in that they liberate citizens from the norms and specialised practices of professional disciplines. Early lay efforts to monitor common-pool resources and common property were carried out by users who depended upon a given resource for long-term sustenance. These efforts focused on meeting local and regional challenges of environmental degradation and resource depletion that threatened watersheds, fisheries and pasturage, with a goal of building consensus among users of a particular resource, and limiting the control over such resources by non-local entities. Initial interest in citizen science concerned ecological and environmental health sciences, as average citizens became more aware of the impact of science and technology on their personal lives and their community's quality of life (Brossard et al. 2005).

Citizen science remains effective to the degree that it relies upon standards and standardised procedures for measuring environmental impacts, and in this way bridges the gap between lay initiatives on behalf of democratising science and expert knowledge (Ottinger 2010). As an example, biomonitoring, or body-burden research, emerged in response to growing public demand for information about humans' exposure to chemicals in the environment (Morello-Frosch et al. 2005). Since then, community residents collaborating with environmental health scientists in universities and community-based organisations have monitored workplace toxins, air and water pollution, household lead, flame retardants in consumer products and environmental chemicals in breast milk (Morello-Frosch et al. 2009). On-the-ground data-collection techniques, such as 'ground-truthing', seek residents' knowledge to identify pollution sources located in their communities and verify compiled data derived from standardised risk-screening of environmental indicators (Heaney et al. 2007).

Anthony Giddens' (1991) notion of life politics, or those movements that challenge contradictions of capitalist growth and technological development through reflexive and existential means, is especially instructive. Without community-based institutions comprised of constituents caught up in these changes, considerable suffering and clearly less progress in meeting commons-destroying challenges may prevail. Social suffering, in this sense, is caused by disorders and inversions that threaten to destroy the sociocultural fabric of the modern world. Roy Rappaport (1994) understood this suffering as resulting from environmental degradation, population increase, warfare, globalisation, development and threats to cultural autonomy. At the community level, these typically manifest as social pathologies, including crime, environmental and mental illnesses, family dissolution and homelessness.

Expert and lay groups taking collective action on behalf of sustainability and maintenance of the commons view shifting organisational arrangements as examples of institutional bricolage, a patchwork of well-worn practices adapted to new conditions; hence, there is a sense of incremental tweaking or muddling through in carrying out necessary tasks. Bricolage denotes the construction or creation of a work, including an ideational or institutional structure, from whatever materials are at hand. These newer formations typically use ideas, tools and other forms of bricolage, borrowed from older institutional traditions, to craft strategies for survival and sustainability (Cleaver and de Koning 2015). The question of whether bricolage can be transformational remains unanswered, as there continues to be uneven distribution of power between the centre and the nascent, peripheral, community-based organisations forged as crisis formations and adaptations to extreme conditions, such as ecological threats to common-pool resources, and the risks and hazards of modernity.

The continued growth of these forms of social capital will require broader citizen access to electronically transmitted information and interactive communication technologies to stimulate interest in local affairs and participation in national policy dialogues. Nowhere is this more apparent than in the widening gap between information elites, such as scientists and policymakers, and the lay public with respect to knowledge about and access to computing and networked communication resources. The increasing access by laypersons to networked communication technologies has led to the formation of diverse lay interest groups, or 'virtual communities'. These may also be communities of practice, with frequently geographically dispersed individuals, linked together by interactive communication, who share a common concern. Similar to arenas sustained by scientific and policy elites, lay electronic networks engage and affiliate participants in spontaneous, but also considered, discussion and debate around clearly meaningful issues. Despite the substantial early apprehension of social scientists that computer-mediated communication would further isolate individuals and restrict their participation in the public sphere, alliances built electronically appear to strengthen social and civic ties, but also may blur many visually defined boundaries based on race, class, gender and disability. Electronic alliances can potentially sustain citizen participation within emerging federal arenas, such as consensus conferences and other forms of deliberative democracy that increasingly require the advice of laypersons in the development of scientific and technological policies (Worthington et al. 2011).

To this end, the task of reforming or restoring the commons in both rural and urban contexts is a challenge – an ecological, economic and equity-related challenge that involves a form of counter-hegemonic education and reflective and critical practices. Paulo Freire forwarded these practices to both promote collective action and social justice at the local level and obtain a clearer actionable understanding of the relationships individual groups have to power, providing the opportunity to rearrange such relationships by becoming literate about the power structure (Freire 1970).

Sustainability and Collaborative Anthropological Practice

Returning now to the community-based concerns of anthropologists engaged in sustainability research and practice, the operational framework of a community of practice is instructive. All communities of practice contain three structural elements: (1) domain, or the area of shared enquiry; (2) community, or the environment where relationships are built; and (3) practice, or the body of knowledge, methods, tools, cases and stories put into action. A community of practice, therefore, is comprised of individuals who share a common interest in a specific domain of knowledge (Lave 1996). They are engaged in sharing knowledge, developing expertise and solving problems within the specific area. Within communities of practice, local, regional, national and even global actors develop collaborative partnerships, on behalf of greater transparency in planning and implementing broad-based and inclusive sustainable practices.

As collaborative peer networks based upon a shared area of inquiry, communities of practice are, for the most part, voluntary and focused both on learning and on building capacity through collaborative relationships. They are engaged in sharing knowledge, developing expertise and solving problems. Communities of practice break down communication barriers through continuous exchange of knowledge in a more open and informal manner. In this way, they also operate as a knowledge commons, a shared social-ecological system that supports the flow of communication among members of collaborative practice communities (Hess and Ostrom 2006). However, to sustain a knowledge commons on behalf of local and global sustainability, communities of practice can work towards diminishing and making transparent the boundaries between the expert producers of such knowledge within the academic, public, non-profit and private sectors, by incorporating lay persons within them.

Translating anthropological research into action promotes better understanding, so that both experts and the lay public may meaningfully engage in informed dialogues about their common concerns for sustainable communities (Maida and Beck 2015). Collaborative methods, such as participatory action research, will ensure a more socially responsive sharing of anthropological knowledge across diverse sectors and constituencies. A critical anthropological approach also orients participants towards a deeper democratic lifeway creating the opportunity for 'environmental stewardship' and 'global citizenship', even at the local level.

The authors of this volume discuss in their chapters how networks of researchers, practitioners and experts communicate with a wider audience to translate sustainability concepts into terms broadly understood by the public, and how emergent communities of practice ensure greater engagement by the public, as citizens, activists and citizen scientists, locally, regionally, nationally and globally. The authors also address the ways that class, gender and ethnicity play a role in how these communities meet the challenges of global sustainability. As a result, dynamic and potent *regimes of competence* come into play within these chapters, and this concept is at once both synergistic and capable of bridging these discrete ethnographic cases into a narrative on the value of communities of practice in global sustainability.

Sustaining the Countryside

The first set of essays focus on the sustainability of local communities of practice in rural communities in the face of globalisation and its attendant changes. Linda D'Amico describes the ways rural women and men in the Ecuadorian Cloud Forests created regional and trans-regional institutions to develop and sustain effective environmental governance that offer examples of expanded social equity and adaptive resilience in the face of change. Marta

Crivos, María Rosa Martínez, Laura Teves and Carolina Remorini depict how intersectoral forums with governmental and nongovernmental actors and local residents helped bring about joint reflection on viability and sustainability of local and global practices and resources in a rural community in the Calchaqui Valley (Salta, Argentina). Debarati Sen examines how fair-trade-engendered solidarity practices in Darjeeling's tea plantations erase the complex history of workers' struggle with the state and established systems of power through collective bargaining, which, in turn, produce new kinds of transnational praxis affecting the plantation public sphere.

Sustainable Urbanism

The second set of essays look at how communities of practice can become paths towards sustainability in the urban context. Carla Guerrón Montero explores the relationships among state, culture and politics in the context of the largest educational project of social inclusion, local participation and citizenship in the Municipality of Camaçari, state of Bahia, north-eastern Brazil, in a community of practice where stakeholders are potentially producing a new way to understand what it means to be a modern Brazilian citizen. Krista Harper and Ana Isabel Afonso use ethnographic and Photovoice techniques to document how urban gardeners in Lisbon, Portugal cultivate the spirit of civic ecology while growing food in interstitial urban spaces. Danielle V. Schoon and Funda Oral examine a community of practice formed to advocate for spatial preservation of a neighbourhood and the cultural heritage of its Roman (Gypsy) residents in Istanbul, Turkey to argue that the challenges presented by rapid urbanisation in places like Istanbul require interdisciplinary action and collaboration. Sam Beck looks at the movement for affordable housing in Williamsburg, Brooklyn, where Latino residents created a community of practice and engaged in a struggle against displacement; for dignity, respect and self-determination; and for community sustainability by advocating for and achieving low- and moderate-income housing in a rapidly gentrifying community.

Organising for Sustainability

The third set of essays regard how communities of practice can help frame contemporary interventions in urban regions. Carl Maida describes a community of practice among high-school students and their adult mentors engaged in project-based learning that uses San Diego Bay as an outdoor laboratory to understand regional urban ecology with the goal of 'knowing sustainability'. Sandy Smith-Nonini discusses lessons learned from a social enterprise project – a non-profit co-op of upcycler crafters and vintage vendors – supporting sustainability education in central North Carolina. Brian McKenna provides a case of bureaucratic cooptation of a community of practice mobilised to confront local environmental health problems, specifically water and air pollution, and restaurant health, in mid-Michigan. A final theoretical essay by Richard Westra discusses how all communities of practice face questions relating to the material economic foundations of future sustainable societies concerning economic scale and the re-localising of production and consumption sundered by globalisation, and focuses on the local exchange and trading system as a foundation of rich, eco-sustainable community material life.

Together, the contributors to this volume explore communities of practice as a means to cultivate sustainability literacy and public engagement on its behalf, a task that requires diverse cultural perspectives, trans-generational timeframes and local-to-global connectedness.

Acknowledgements

We would like to thank the Organising Committee of the XVII World Conference of the International Union of Anthropological and Ethnological Sciences, held in Manchester, U.K. in August 2013, with the theme of Evolving Humanity, Emerging Worlds, for support of the session that would bring together the various authors in this volume for a day of presentations, discussions and conviviality. We are grateful to Brian McKenna and Bruce Woych for their critical reading of this introduction and their suggestions for revision. We are also grateful to Marion and Vivian Berghahn, and to Christine McCourt, for their support during the entire process of putting this volume together.

CARL A. MAIDA is a professor at the UCLA Institute of the Environment and Sustainability in the College of Letters and Science, where he teaches courses on action research methods and conducts community-based research on urban sustainability. His current research focuses on the ongoing dialogue between professional and lay knowledge in the areas of health, the quality of life and sustainability of urban communities, and on the larger national and global debates on access to public goods. He is a member of the UCLA Sustainability Committee. He is a Fellow of the American Association for the Advancement of Science, the American Anthropological Association and the Society for Applied Anthropology.

SAM BECK is Senior Lecturer at Cornell University where he directs the Urban Semester Program. He has dedicated himself in the last twenty years to an activist role as an anthropologist carrying out research in North Brooklyn. As such he is an active Executive Board member in local community-based organisations that insist on being recognised with dignity and respect and struggle for community sustainability. He is a member of the Vernon Avenue Project, Inc. and its spinoff Reconnect Industries, Churches United for Fair Housing, The Grand Street Boys and Brooklyn Legal Services A. He has received multiple awards for his community service work and as a teacher.

References

Agrawal, A. (2003), 'Sustainable Governance of Common-pool Resources: Context, Methods, and Politics', *Annual Review of Anthropology* 32: 243–262.

Argyris, C. and D. A. Schon (1974), *Theory in Practice: Increasing Professional Effectiveness* (San Francisco: Jossey-Bass).

Bäckstrand, K. (2003), 'Civic Science for Sustainability: Reframing the Role of Experts, Policy-makers and Citizens in Environmental Governance', *Global Environmental Politics* 3, no. 4: 24–41.

Beichler, S., S. Hasibovic, B. J. Davidse and S. Deppisch (2014), 'The Role Played by Social-ecological Resilience as a Method of Integration in Interdisciplinary Research', *Ecology and Society* 19, no. 3: 4. http://dx .doi.org/10.5751/ES-06583-190304

Bellagio Principles: Guidelines for the Practical Assessment of Progress Towards Sustainable Development (1997), (Winnipeg, Canada: International Institute for Sustainable Development).

Bonney, R., C. B. Cooper, J. Dickinson, S. Kelling, T. Phillips, K. V. Rosenberg and J. Shirk (2009), 'Citizen Science: A Developing Tool for Expanding Science Knowledge and Scientific Literacy', *BioScience* 59, no. 11: 977–984.

Brosius, J. P. (1999), 'Analyses and Interventions: Anthropological Engagements with Environmentalism', *Current Anthropology* 40, no. 3: 277–309.

Brossard, D., B. Lewenstein and R. Bonney (2005), 'Scientific Knowledge and Attitude Change: The Impact of a Citizen Science Project', *International Journal of Science Education* 27, no. 9: 1099–1121.

Bruffee, K. A. (1999), *Collaborative Learning: Higher Education, Interdependence, and the Authority of Knowledge,* 2nd ed. (Baltimore, MD: Johns Hopkins University Press).

Burawoy, M., J. A. Blum, S. George, Z. Gille and M. Thayer (2000), *Global Ethnography: Forces, Connections, and Imaginations in a Postmodern World* (Berkeley: University of California Press).

Chambers, R. (2005), *Ideas for Development* (London: Routledge).

Chambers, R. and G. R. Conway (1991), *Sustainable Rural Livelihoods: Practical Concepts for the 21st Century* (Institute of Development Studies, University of Sussex, Brighton, U.K.).

Cleaver, F. and J. de Koning (2015), 'Furthering Critical Institutionalism', *International Journal of the Commons* 9, no. 1: 1–18.

Conway, G. R. and E. B. Barbier (2013), *After the Green Revolution: Sustainable Agriculture for Development* (London: Routledge).

Corburn, J. (2005), *Street Science: Community Knowledge and Environmental Health Justice* (Cambridge, MA: MIT Press).

Escobar, A. (1999), 'After Nature: Steps to an Antiessentialist Political Ecology', *Current Anthropology* 40, no. 1: 1–30.

Federici, S. (2014), 'From Commoning to Debt: Financialization, Microcredit, and the Changing Architecture of Capital Accumulation', *The South Atlantic Quarterly* 113, no. 2: 231–244.

Freire, P. (1970), *Pedagogy of the Oppressed* (New York: Continuum).

Gibson, H. and S. Venkateswar (2015), 'Anthropological Engagement with the Anthropocene: A Critical Review', *Environment and Society: Advances in Research* 6, no. 1: 5–27.

Giddens, A. (1991), *Modernity and Self-identity: Self and Society in the Late Modern Age* (Stanford, CA: Stanford University Press).

Graeber, D. (2011), *Debt: The First Five Thousand Years* (Brooklyn, NY: Melville House).

Gupta, A. and J. Ferguson (eds) (1997), *Anthropological Locations: Boundaries and Grounds of a Field Science* (Berkeley: University of California Press).

Harper, K. and S. Ravi Rajan (2002), *International Environmental Justice: Building the Natural Assets of the World's Poor*. Political Economy Research Institute. International Natural Assets Conference Paper Series 12 (Amherst, MA: University of Massachusetts).

Harvey, D. (2012), 'The Creation of the Urban Commons', in *Rebel Cities: From the Right to the City to the Urban Revolution* (New York: Verso), 67–88.

Heaney, C. D., S. M. Wilson and O. R. Wilson (2007), 'The West End Revitalization Association's Community-owned and -Managed Research Model: Development, Implementation, and Action', *Progress in Community Health Partnerships: Research Education, and Action* 1, no. 4: 339–349.

Hempel, L. C. (1998), *Sustainable Communities: From Vision to Action* (Claremont, CA: Claremont Graduate University).

Hess, C. and E. Ostrom (eds) (2006), *Understanding Knowledge as a Commons: From Theory to Practice* (Cambridge, MA: MIT Press).

Jacobs, J. (1961), *The Death and Life of Great American Cities* (New York: Random House).

Kottak, C. P. (1999), 'The New Ecological Anthropology', *American Anthropologist* 101, no. 1: 22–35.

Lave, J. (1988), *Cognition in Practice* (New York: Cambridge University Press).

Lave, J. (1996), 'Teaching, as Learning, in Practice', *Mind, Culture, and Activity* 3, no. 3: 149–164.

Lave, J. and E. Wenger (1991), *Situated Learning: Legitimate Peripheral Participation* (New York: Cambridge University Press).

Maida, C. A. (2007), 'Introduction', in C. A. Maida (ed.), *Sustainability and Communities of Place* (New York: Berghahn), 1–17.

Maida, C. A. and S. Beck (2015), 'Introduction', in S. Beck and C. A. Maida (eds), *Public Anthropology in a Borderless World* (New York: Berghahn), 1–35.

Marcus, G. (1995), 'Ethnography in/of the World System: The Emergence of Multi-sited Ethnography', *Annual Review of Anthropology* 24: 95–117.

McCay, B. J. (2002), 'Emergence of Institutions for the Commons: Contexts, Situations, and Events', in E. Ostrom, T. Dietz, N. Dolsak, P. C.

Stern, S. Stovich and E. U. Weber (eds), *The Drama of the Commons: Committee on the Human Dimensions of Global Change,* (Washington, DC: National Academy Press), 361–402.

Morello-Frosch, R., M. Pastor, J. Sadd, C. Porras and M. Prichard (2005), 'Citizens, Science, and Data Judo: Leveraging Community-based Participatory Research to Build a Regional Collaborative for Environmental Justice in Southern California', in B. A. Israel, E. Eng, A. J. Schulz and E. A. Parker (eds), *Methods for Conducting Community-based Participatory Research in Public Health* (San Francisco: Jossey-Bass), 371–391.

Morello-Frosch, R., J. Green Brody, P. Brown, R. G. Altman, R. A. Rudel and C. Pérez (2009), 'Toxic Ignorance and Right-to-know in Biomonitoring Results Communication: A Survey of Scientists and Study Participants', *Environmental Health* 8, no. 6. doi: 10.1186/1476-069X-8-6.

National Academies of Sciences, Engineering, and Medicine (2017), *Measures of Community Resilience for Local Decision Makers: Proceedings of a Workshop* (Washington, DC: National Academies Press) doi: 10.17226/21911.

National Science Foundation (1995), 'Cultural Anthropology, Global Change and the Environment: Anthropology's Role in the NSF Initiative on Human Dimensions of Global Change', Report of a Workshop on Human Dimensions of Global Change, Washington, DC, 27–28 June.

Oliver-Smith, A. and S. M. Hoffman (1999), *The Angry Earth: Disaster in Anthropological Research* (New York: Routledge).

Ostrom, E. (2008), 'The Challenge of Common-pool Resources', *Environment: Science and Policy for Sustainable Development* 50, no. 4: 8–21.

Ottinger, G. (2010), 'Buckets of Resistance: Standards and the Effectiveness of Citizen Science', *Science, Technology & Human Values* 35, no. 2: 244–270.

Pastor, M. (2001), *Building Social Capital to Protect Natural Capital: The Quest for Environmental Justice,* Political Economy Research Institute, Working Papers Series Number 11 (Amherst, MA: University of Massachusetts).

Pastor, M. (2002), *Environmental Justice: Reflections from the United States,* Political Economy Research Institute, International Natural Assets Conference Paper Series 1 (Amherst, MA: University of Massachusetts).

Peterson, G. (2000), 'Political Ecology and Ecological Resilience: An Integration of Human and Ecological Dynamics', *Ecological Economics* 35, no. 3: 323–336.

Rappaport, R. A. (1994), 'Disorders of Our Own', in S. Forman (ed.), *Diagnosing America: Anthropology and Public Engagement* (Ann Arbor: University of Michigan Press), 235–293.

Redclift, M. (1987), *Sustainable Development: Exploring the Contradictions* (London: Routledge).

Reid, H. and B. Taylor (2010), *Recovering the Commons: Democracy, Place and Social Justice* (Champaign: University of Illinois Press).

Smith-Nonini, S. (2006), 'Conceiving the Health Commons: Operationalizing a "Right" to Health', *Social Analysis* 50, no. 3: 233–245.

Wenger, E. (2000), 'Communities of Practice and Social Learning Systems', *Organization* 7, no. 2: 225–246.

Wenger, E. (2010a), 'Communities of Practice and Social Learning Systems: The Career of a Concept', in C. Blackmore (ed.), *Social Learning Systems and Communities of Practice* (London: Springer), 179–198.

Wenger, E. (2010b), 'Conceptual Tools for CoPs as Social Learning Systems: Boundaries Identity, Trajectories and Participation', in C. Blackmore (ed.), *Social Learning Systems and Communities of Practice* (London: Springer), 125–143.

Wolf, E. R. (2001), *Pathways of Power: Building an Anthropology of the Modern World* (Berkeley: University of California Press).

World Commission on Environment and Development (1987), *Our Common Future (The Brundtland Report)* (Oxford: Oxford University Press).

Worthington, R., M. Rask and B. Jaeger (2011), 'Deliberative Global Governance: Next Steps in an Emerging Practice', in M. Rask, R. Worthington and M. Lammi (eds), *Citizen Participation in Global Environmental Governance* (New York: Routledge).

Part 1

Sustaining the Countryside

Cultivating Sustainability Literacy and Public Engagement in Intag, Ecuador

Linda D'Amico

During more than two and a half decades of engaged scholarship in northern Ecuador, I have documented ways multi-ethnic racial actors have confronted and helped shape strategies for development.[1] In the early 1990s, global and national policies facilitated extractive development and economic restructuring, which contributed to monetary changes, including the dollarisation of the Ecuadorian economy in the year 2000. At the same time, the final decade of the twentieth century marked a global era when scientists called attention to the importance of biodiversity and rainforest conservation. Ecologists and conservation organisations prioritised the preservation of Intag cloud forests for their endemic biocultural diversities and vast hydrology resources. Intag's culture and landscape became ground zero for debates about political ecology: many local citizens formed alliances with advocates of sustainable development and biodiversity conservation, while others backed projects for industrial copper extraction and a more centralised approach to governance. During 1995–2012 the rural population reorganised and halted two transnational corporations from gaining a foothold in the region, opting for sustainable alternatives (CMI 2007). Elected to office in 2007 with support of a broad coalition, Rafael Correa first instituted a moratorium on industrial mining and focused on integrative development. In 2008 the Constitution of Monticristi recognised rights of its pluri-national peoples and of Nature. Since 2009, the Correa administration pushed through a Mining Law and restricted civil liberties, while at the same time increased funding for social assistance programmes for the poor.

In this chapter, I discuss sustainability literacy as it first evolved in opposition and as an alternative rhetoric to mining. I document processes Inteña(o)s employed to increase their civic participation. They created a social movement built upon innovative synergies that linked communities of practice across cultures. Not only were individual women and men empowered and able to collaborate in new ways, collectively they began to make structural changes in their society. As primarily subsistence farmers managing fragile subtropical zones, Intag women and men had to 'read the landscape' in ways that guaranteed them livelihood and cultural rights, while considering future generations. To do this many of them applied specialised knowledge, skills and social cooperation to cultivate a living on the steep subtropical Andean slopes. In general, residents based their socioeconomic worldview on fundamental concepts that equated healthy forests with clean and abundant water, pure air, and held communities and hillsides intact.

'Sustainability' at first was a foreign construct; however, notions about protecting water resources were integral to local sustenance and culture, while being conversant in development rhetoric opened political and economic spaces. Active citizens have since constructed a working 'sustainability literacy', which consists of social inclusiveness in political processes, priorities of economic justice, and effective stewardship of forest ecosystems. Their actions reveal ways that an eco-dialogic (that acknowledges cross-species interactions) broadened their lexicon about rights, while creating practices for watershed conservation and biodiversity conservation. Their knowledge sets have led to new forms of social and political organisation, and nested communities of practice that are concrete and virtual, local and global. Even so, environmentalism continues in Intag to be a contested arena, where arguments for 'weak' and 'strong' sustainability play out (Whitehead 2014). The examples below illustrate how individual and collective actions have created a fluid concept of sustainability, adapted to specific contexts.

After a brief discussion of the social and ecological contexts of Intag, I focus on ways that rural citizens generated innovative institutions. First, I describe the emergence and work of the *Aso-*

ciación Agro-artesanal de Cafecultores de Río Íntag (AACRI) (Intag River's Association of Small Scale Coffee Farmers) and ways that agro-ecological knowledge promoted sustainability through possibilities for increased and sustained income. Second, I briefly describe the history of the community newspaper *Periódico Íntag* as it evolved into a vehicle for sharing information among communities of practice, while tracing and guiding the evolution of Intag's vision of sustainability. Third, I explore the history of the *Coordinadora de Mujeres de Íntag* (CMI) (the Intag Women's Coordinating Committee) and our collaboration in envisioning, designing and implementing a household survey that quantifies and qualifies some of the local population's priorities, definitions of sustainability, progress made and goals for the future.

Social and Ecological Contexts

The Intag-Manduriacos[2] (Intag) region (150,000 hectares) is located in northwest Ecuador and covers six subtropical western parishes in Cotacachi County and one parish in Otavalo County, all within Imbabura Province. Intag is situated on the steep occidental flanks of the Andes that extend from 650 metres above sea level (in the western-most subtropical region) to 4,000 metres (in the Andean region). In addition to human settlement, the slopes and valleys are covered with remnant cloud forests, abundant rivers and streams, agricultural lands and degraded lands, a marble rock pit, a lime/cement quarry and an underground gold mine. Ecologists identify Intag-Manduriacos as one of the planet's most biologically diverse areas, where two of the planet's thirty-four conservation hotspots intersect[3] (Meyers 1997; Wilson 1992). Andean cloud forest landscapes consist of micro-ecosystems with endemic species adapted to particular altitudes, gradients, location on the mountain (southern and northern exposures differ with regard to the amount of sunlight and/or soil type), and rainfall. These subtropical forests, some of the wettest places on earth, cover vertiginous slopes that are subject to frequent landslides, particularly in the rainy season from November through May. Transportation is slow along the two secondary and multiple tertiary dirt roads and footpaths that

connect hundreds of farms, approximately ninety hamlets and six
parish seats, or towns, to municipal seats in the Andean zones.

Intag families live in dispersed rural communities, in small
hamlets or on isolated farms. According to the 2010 census, the
area's population (in Cotacachi County) was approximately 12,000
people or 2,800 households. Most families' economic base included
small-scale agriculture and cattle-raising, and often depended
upon remittances from relative(s) who migrated to cities in Ecuador or as far away as Spain. The 2010 median household income
in Intag was 234 dollars per month – based on sales of mostly
agricultural products (including primarily cattle, corn, beans,
sugar, coffee and fruits). This figure is complemented by the value
of subsistence foodstuffs (cassava, beans, fruits, chickens, eggs,
milk, pigs and myriad other agricultural products), home/farm
ownership, other unremunerated services (López Oropeza 2011[4])
and the *Bono de Desarrollo Humano* (BDH) (the government's social
welfare payment to vulnerable families – $50 (U.S.)[5] in 2013). A di-
versified livelihood portfolio requires knowledge of various crops,
the seasons, the rural topography, changing climate and markets;
as well as organising/participating in work groups, labour, transportation and local culture. It most likely also includes at least one
family member working in an urban centre in Ecuador or abroad.
A 2012 survey indicates that most families (97.2 per cent) indicate
relative satisfaction with their lives and an openness to new ideas.

The Emergence of a Glocal[6] Approach to Sustainability

Conflict is the midwife of consciousness. (Paulo Freire)[7]

In the early 1990s, after a World Bank sponsored geological min-
eral study identified copper and other minerals in soils of primary
forests of the Toisán Range, Bishimetals, a junior partner of Mitsubishi Corporation was granted a mining concession and set up
initial explorations adjacent to the community of Junín. While the
minerals resources (less than 1 per cent) attracted extractive capital
and industry, the primary forests that buffer the Cotacachi-Cayapas
Ecological Reserve attracted global conservation groups. The com-

munity of Junín became 'ground zero' for a conflict between extractive and sustainable development. Continued steps towards extraction – and resistance to these has ensued: in 1998 local activists pressured Bishimetals to exit the region, and in early 2007 responding to local concerns the national government cancelled the Canadian company Ascendent's concession after paramilitaries attempted to establish a mining camp.

Most residents did not accept the extractive narrative as *fait accompli*. Faced with the prospect of mining, they began to redefine their roles as forest stewards who had rights to clean water and adequate livelihoods. External attention and funding provided residents with tangible economic alternatives, training and workshop funding, and organisational support. The influx of global conservation interests, NGO support, students, nature tourists and academic researchers also helped highlight Inteña(o)s' roles in their communities and the value of their culture. These cross-cultural collaborations evolved into local ideologies of social justice, livelihood rights and water security.

Indeed, through these processes, local organisations emerged that were linked to global ideas about cultural rights and the value of forest conservation. These combined with rural knowledge regarding sustenance and social organisation to create a new definition of sustainability. In the early 2000s, several Intag activists commented that the initial mining threat had 'awakened them to revalue their culture and biodiversity'. At meetings, workshops and other activities, Intag citizens voiced visions for the future, and they co-created innovative social and operational structures that spanned across communities and cultures (see figure 1). Not unlike Freire's theory of literacy where learning is built upon continual active and reflective processes (1970), many Inteña(o)s began to transform their understandings of themselves, their communities and the world. They improved upon agro-ecological techniques and procured skills to deliver community ecotourism services. As they did so, they gained scientific insights and relied upon their traditional ethos of social reciprocity to get things done. In Intag, the lexicon of 'sustainability' was new, but principles of collaborative protection of the commons and mutual respect were already fundamental to socioecological survival.

Sustainable Communities of Alternative Practices: Expanding Civil Society and NGOs

Located at about 1800 meters and with a multiethnic population of close to 1000, the parish seat/town of Apuela is the gateway to the Intag region and the site of many non-governmental organizations' offices. One of Intag's first non-governmental organization (NGO), Defensa Ecológica y Conservación de Intag/DECOIN was formed in January 1995, led by a local priest, a Cuban-American expatriate and others. Through DECOIN, with the support of outside funding, rural residents participated in workshops and fieldtrips to learn about biodiversity, conservation, effects of industrial mining, and productive alternatives. Since the formation of DECOIN, Intag has become home to more than a score of NGOs, which have received funding from national and international governments, organizations and foundations, and which regularly host volunteers from Germany, the United States, Spain and other countries, as well as international observers. In a 2012 survey, more than 58 percent of respondents indicated they regularly participated in organizations, local government, assemblies or workshops. Seventy-eight percent of survey respondents indicated they would like to increase their civic participation (CMI 2013).

Figure 1: By the author.

As Intag's social movement emerged, charismatic leaders expanded political openings for direct participation, and county residents experimented with decentralised notions of governance (Ortiz Crespo 2004). The municipality of Cotacachi County won global awards for participatory democracy[8] and international support poured into Intag for conservation and 'sustainable' development. Village councils in more than forty-four communities took on greater responsibilities to oversee watershed reserves that had been purchased and titled in the community's name with the coordination by grassroots environmental organisations and outside funds (see figure 2). Regionally, Inteña(o)s were also active in parish and county/municipal governance through the *Asamblea de Unidad Cantonal de Cotacachi* (AUCC) [Cotacachi Assembly for County Unity]. Intag citizens' actions for environmental protections contributed to the 2000 Ecological Ordinance (EO) of Cotacachi County, a precursor to Ecuador's 2008 Constitution of Monticristi, which was internationally acclaimed for guaranteeing the rights of nature and *Pachamama* as well as universal rights to *sumak kawsay*, or well-being.[9]

Local and Global Interests Converge: GLOCAL Prescriptions for Sustainability

I resided in Andean Ecuador for nearly nine years with my children (1989-1997). We began visiting the Intag region in 1989 and became friends with an expatriate family who made Intag their home. They had a nascent ecotourism business, stewarded primary forests and did some small-scale farming. After a poacher targeted the habitat of the Andean spectacled bear on their land to harvest its gallbladder for Asian markets in the early 1990s, my engaged-scholarship began. Since then, I have documented and been involved with ways diverse perspectives have merged and been infused with environmentalism in Intag.

The impact of expatriates living in Intag has been substantial—through leadership roles in organizations, bringing visibility to Intag's struggles and forming alliances with outside organizations. International visitors (volunteers, peace observers and other activists) often provide knowledge, collaboration and support. Eco-tourists and others show how much the world cares about Intag's biodiversity, and revenues from their stays provide income and prove that eco-tourism is a viable model. As of 2012, 20 percent of survey respondents from a representative sample of Inteñas indicated that they had interacted with foreigners, of those most lauded the experience, which included financial support for high school student transportation, eco-tourist/student homestays and educational assistance.

The convergence of discourse and actions from the inside and outside of has created interstices in the form of social, political and productive innovations, which add up to more than the sum of their parts. For example: German residents who choose green energy for their homes have the opportunity to contribute funds (on their electric bills) to promote subtropical forest conservation. Those funds are managed by GEO Lickt Blick Regenwals, and in Intag with coordination from DECOIN and other NGOS. The German contributions have facilitated, among other projects, the purchase of community forest and watershed reserves; creation of community managed tree nurseries; environmental education in the schools; and the construction of eco-cabins in Junín. One nine year old German boy was so moved by stories from Intag that he collected recyclables for a year, which he cashed in for more than five hundred dollars to provide fruit tress of an elementary school in Cuellaje Parish.

Similarly, Rainforest Concern, a registered charity in the UK works on collaborative projects for biodiversity conservation in Ecuador and around the globe. The director commented regarding donors' motives in 2010, *'You may or may not have been to paradise, but one thing for sure is that you can help to save a bit of paradise on earth.'* Rainforest Concern has funded the purchase of community forest reserves and education projects.

The Sloth Club, located in Japan, supports 'slow alternatives' in Japan and Ecuador and has offered assistance to AACRI and sisal handicraft producers of CMI. In 2009 the Club invited two Intag women to give seminars on their work in Tokyo and other Japanese cities. Moreover, the Sloth Club works with the Rainforest Information Centre in Australia and supports an *'integrated lifestyle model'* in Intag, in part by soliciting volunteers with skills in permaculture and other appropriate technologies.

These and other organizations have brought professional biologists, NGO workers, students, academics and volunteers from across the globe. Young adults who visit Intag are generally captivated by the local culture and biodiversity, and inspired by the power of civil society for the common good.

Figure 2: By the author.

Intag's Glocal Expressions of Sustainable Development:

This is imagination. This is the possibility to go beyond tomorrow without being naively idealistic. This is Utopianism as a
dialectical relationship between denouncing the present and
announcing the future. To anticipate tomorrow by dreaming
today… (Paulo Freire)[10]

Defining Glocal Sustainability through Coffee? AACRI
and How Apuela became the Coffee Capital of the Region

In March 1998, leaders from DECOIN helped form the *Asociación
Agroartesanal de Caficultures Río Íntag* (AACRI), whose mission
as stated on its website is 'to encourage agro-ecological practices
through the production of organic coffee and endemic forest species in order to create fair trade certification and access fair trade
markets'. Based in Apuela, AACRI successfully links farm families
across scales through extension agents, community workshops and
to Ministerial, bilateral, transnational NGO support and fair-trade
markets. In recent years, many farmers have increased their coffee
production through access to credit for inputs and extension con-
sults. An AACRI storage centre in Apuela provides farm services,
where coffee collection, quality control and processing take place in
preparation for distribution to local, national and export markets.

Global narratives about rainforest conservation and sustainability (including sustainable development) first became prominent in
the 1990s. In 1987, the UN Brundtland Commission had published
Our Common Future, which injected 'sustainable development' into
the global lexicon. It boldly promoted an integrated approach to
development: or 'a way of meeting the needs of the present without compromising the ability of future generations to meet their
own needs'. This ethos, complemented by the United Nations
1992 Rio Environment Summit and the 1995 Beijing Conference
on Women, redefined 'development' to change practices on the
ground. Sustainable development was envisioned as intertwining
economic security with environmental protection and social equity.
These priorities were further developed through the compilation
of the United Nations Millennial Development Goals in 2000.

AACRI put this lexicon of sustainable development into action: shade-grown coffee has meant diversified agro and non-agro forestry management (see figure 3). With approximately 400 families as members and 150 families as active producers (as of 2012), AACRI has played a regional role in disseminating precepts of sustainability, gender inclusiveness and strategies for organic crop

---

Fair Trade Coffee = Sustainability?

Apuela, Sunday July 21, 2013: Coffee farmers streamed into the AACRI warehouse with their sacks of de-pulped and dried coffee beans. I spoke with a woman as she waited to have her six sacks weighed and inspected. Her eldest son was in New York City, where he had been working for five years. His life was very hard and she missed him. She has hopes for her youngest son to study tourism after he completes high school—'*that way he may stick around,*' she said. Previously, eco-tourists had visited their farm on the AACRI coffee tour, and she had served them refreshments and earned some extra cash. However, she reiterated, '*Life is difficult here too—coffee is so much work for the little money we receive. At least we eat healthy products we produce, including beans, yucca, corn, oranges, avocadoes and other fruits.*'

July–August 2013: The coffee groves were abundant with ripe red berries. Farmers were congregating at the AACRI office in Apuela to settle accounts. The cooperative was a big lender in the region: AACRI lent to members in the form of coffee seedlings, organic fertilizer and other inputs. Farming coffee involved forest management, pruning, fertilizing and sometimes irrigation. The tending came to full crescendo when berries ripened and had to be handpicked. On large shade grown coffee farms, this meant intensive labor for over a month, and often required hiring day workers. With increased attendance in secondary school and a high out-migration rate in all but García Moreno Parish, day laborers were not easy to find at the going rate of ten dollars per day plus a cooked lunch and snack. Gathering ripe berries involved skill in plucking each ripe berry without disturbing the node that set the fruit for the next year; a lot of stamina, and; often times included intense socializing among the pickers.

Late July, 2013: Sunday, market day in Apuela was punctuated by families bringing their coffee to the AACRI warehouse, having it ceremoniously loaded and unloaded on pick-up trucks, then weighed and inspected. Farmers took their receipts from the warehouse and bee-lined across town to the accountant in the administrative office. Several women growers told me they welcomed the income to help meet necessities at home, even as they questioned whether it was worth all the effort. As one pineapple and coffee farmer told me, '*I prefer cattle—there just aren't coffee workers available and no profit with the low prices I'm paid.*'

Figure 3: By the author.

diversification. This has appealed to many local men and women who have expanded their kitchen gardens. As one of AACRI's first hired extension agents pointed out following five years of work, AACRI had challenged prevailing gender norms by opening up socioeconomic spaces for women. She noted that USAID and other funders had required membership accounting for gender and differently abled persons' participation; adding that women now had 'voice and vote' at AACRI assemblies, previously the exclusive domain of men.

AACRI has contributed to a new model for sustainability in Intag even as many coffee farmers still approach coffee production with a critical eye (see figure 4). In summer 2013 one hundred pounds of their organic high-quality shade-grown coffee sold for $200 (U.S.) compared to $150 (U.S.) for non-pedigreed coffee. Even so, some farmers complained, 'That price doesn't leave the producer any profit'. Although Río Intag Coffee offers a special niche price compared to the commodity price on the New York Mercantile Exchange, coffee production leaves most families with only a small supplemental income. They are not convinced that coffee farming will yield utopia; however, it has increased in the region, and helped to diversify family incomes and promote social rights and agro-ecology.

Periódico Intag: Codifying and Communicating Global Sustainability

In summer 2000, local activists met in Apuela to identify communication gaps in their social movement. In order to strengthen their message and broaden their reach, they started *Periódico Intag* (2000–2011), a community newspaper. The masthead '*El Primer Periódico Independente del Rincón más Bello y más Verde del Ecuador*' [the First Independent Newspaper from the most Beautiful and Greenest Corner of Ecuador] framed its mission, which documented the evolution of and helped define sustainability in Intag for over a decade. An expatriate writer and historian (originally from the United States) volunteered as editor. She collaborated with and trained local reporters at weekly interactive workshops. The editorial board included members of local civic organisations

Figure 4: AACRI farmer delivering her coffee harvest, August 2013, Apuela. Photo by the author.

and held reporters to high standards 'to communicate truthful and verifiable content' (*PI* 2000). In their first issue, they explained their objectives, which included critical approaches to development, enhanced opportunities for literacy and the importance of free speech and a free press. The newspaper played both an instrumental and generative role in the movement's definition.

Periódico Intag encouraged local literacy by offering information and opinions pertinent to local realities. Concurrently, it was a potent symbol that reaffirmed the worth of local actors, their discourse and their right to dissent. Editorials often took a critical view while discussing local education and exposing boondoggle development projects (projects that are valuable in appearance only). Investigative reporting brought debates into the public square: for example, in 2004–2006 *Periódico Intag* reported details of how the Canadian mining company Ascendant had illegally purchased homestead lands in Junín and utilised heavy-handed tactics in their attempt to initiate exploratory activities. In response the company tried (unsuccessfully) to sue the editor for a million dollars in a libel suit.

Periódico Intag promoted participatory democracy by advocating water and food security and economic justice through concentric circles of involvement. I, like scores of others from the U.S., Europe and Japan, subscribed to stay informed about events and activities. Young Germans in their gap year, U.S., Italian and Spanish students and volunteers contributed their energy and commitment for periods of up to a year, and sustained interest and support upon returning home. Beginning in 2007, the newspaper helped link political and other socio-environmental institutions via online Spanish and translated editions sent to English- and German-speaking readers. *Periódico Intag* communicated ideas and encouraged dialogue – an iterative creation of glocal activism – and concurrently documented and facilitated the development of other ventures for sustainability. However, according to its former editor, *Periódico Intag* folded in 2011 as funds for print media dried up. While the newspaper closed, it left behind a legacy of challenging outside interventions, public transparency and a staff of trained reporters who now apply those skills in community radio and other outreach activities.

Sustainability as Participation and Inclusion: Women's Rights as Human Rights

Gender equity entered the glocal discourse through new opportunities for civic participation and challenged local gender norms. Most women assisted their partners in small-scale agriculture production, while provisioning food and water security to their families. Domestic work kept them on the frontline of public and community health, and they often were the first to experience detrimental environmental impacts. In particular, their preoccupation for clean water was linked to their priority of human health and forest stewardship. Women were opening political spaces civically and advocated for economies of care that were socioecologically inclusive. In the mid-1990s, national legislation in Ecuador for the first time provided legal protection against domestic violence and highlighted the value of women's contributions to and positions in society. At the county level, the Cotacachi Women's Coordinating Committee formed to advise the municipal/county government. In Intag, women formed the *Coordinadora de Mujeres de Intag* (CMI) in 2002 to serve as an umbrella for local groups, and to advise the municipal coordinator. Both groups received financial and technical support from Spanish non-profit (food-security aimed) *XARXA de Consum Solidari* and the municipal government of Barcelona, Catalonia. CMI brought together ten grassroots women's groups in the subtropical Intag zone. They focused on food security issues linked through their 'gendered perspectives, solidarity, diligence and optimism' (CMI 2007). Collaborators from Barcelona supported community participation within municipal and parish governments. Each of CMI's ten women's groups (sisal artisans, aloe soap makers, ecotourism operators, agro-ecologists and others) asserted their presence in regional, local and household politics as they stepped into new social roles.

As an umbrella organisation, CMI's member organisations (and their members) were proactive in defining sustainability on their own terms and in using their definitions to guide the future of the Intag region. In 2007 with technical and financial support from XARXA and drawing on experience of its members, CMI's leadership completed and published a *Plan de Vida 2007–2011* (Life Plan), which gave a brief socioecological overview of the region, a history of the CMI and, importantly, outlined CMI's socioeconomic goals. I met with CMI's leadership in early 2012 and members expressed interest in learning more about women's rights and in finding ways to improve their households' economies. Through a series of informal and later formal conversations, we decided to

design and conduct a survey – as a means to reflect upon progress and gaps made since the *2007 Plan*. One leader pointed out,
'Rural women have the right to live in peace'. According to her
'peace' meant 'living at home without violence, in the community
without strife and within natural systems without degradation'.
One leader reiterated that to be heard, one has to participate:
'Democracy is the faith in something that can be done, to be free
to debate and/or express oneself, and to be represented. Concerning the economy', she added, 'we organise for mutual assistance
and harmony, food security and sovereignty, clean water, and the
democratisation of *buen vivir* [living well]'. The 2012 survey was
designed to build upon local knowledge and concerns, and was
conceptually guided by the CMI research team and upon Inteñas'
visions initiated in 2006–7.

Quiénes Somos: Cómo Estamos: CMI 2012 Survey Results

The survey highlights local values both in terms of how the questions were designed and the responses gathered. Inteñas' focus
upon questions linked to socioecological wellbeing demonstrates
their priorities. Generally, the responses (83.7 per cent) show that
understandings of sustainability and environmental care have
grown in recent years. Their participatory approach with new technologies of local governance, including discourse and development
projects, has been particularly successful in linking communities of
practice to watershed management and forest conservation.

We trained a local research team, which conducted extensive
interviews with women (oftentimes with their partners) from 592
households in six parishes, or 20.41 per cent of Intag's families.[11]
The CMI research team recorded responses to the eight-page
survey on paper. Later, a team of Winona State University (WSU)
students and a statistics class helped process the quantitative and
coded-qualitative data into graphs. I compiled and synthesised
results and we published those in a booklet (CMI 2013) distributed
among CMI members and parish and county officials.

Survey results show that mutual respect, clean and abundant
water are key cultural values linked to household, community

and forest health – consistent with CMI's particular concerns for peace and sustainability. Respondents' nuanced views reveal their regard of forests for long-term human wellbeing and biodiversity. Overall the results tend to show that environmentalism (as promoted by civic and other groups such as DECOIN, AACRI, *Periódico Intag* and CMI) has resonated and taken hold. More than two-thirds (67 per cent) of respondents indicated that their community owns its watershed reserves, from which we may infer that women and their families were directly involved in community forest management in some capacity – as is traditional with regard to community projects concerning common resource properties. Almost 60 per cent of respondents reported having participated in local and regional assemblies, which points to their involvement in local governance.

More than 97 per cent of respondents to the question 'Do you enjoy living in Intag?' report satisfaction: despite conflicts over development models and economic challenges, Intag women chose to live there (as stated by several respondents) for the 'tranquility and rich family life'. Reading the landscape for long-term sustenance corresponded to participation in their communities. Of all respondents, 98.8 per cent believed they should conserve forests. They correlated healthy forests with water security, purified air, a place for humans and animals to live, timber, firewood, ecotourism and recreation. More than 70 per cent of respondents indicated they did not approve of industrial mining as a regional development initiative for a variety of reasons – including the fact that extractive development creates social divisions in communities, adversely impacts health and degrades water quality and agricultural lands. Of the remaining respondents, 8.5 per cent were ambivalent to the question of mining, less than 5 per cent did not have an opinion, and 14.23 per cent supported mining as an opportunity to earn wages.

Conclusions

Intag women and men have evolved a *modus operandi* that is collaborative and intercultural with an emphasis on socioecological wellbeing within contexts of mutual influence (see figure 5). Since 1996, regional actors such as DECOIN, *Periódico Intag,* AACRI, CMI and others have promoted innovative narratives of sustainability, participation and social equity in Intag. In 2011 the newspaper was dissolved and the staff transformed its mission as the *Casa Palabra y Pueblo* to provide access to information through community radio, Internet, library and education facilities. AACRI and CMI maintained outreach activities that involve women and men

---

***Nota Bene*: Creating Cross-cultural Communities of Practice with Winona State University Students**

I returned to Winona, MN in the fall of 2012 from a seven-month stint of fieldwork and carried with me a suitcase filled with 592 eight-page surveys. WSU students assisted in systematizing the survey data and participated in two travel-study trips to present preliminary results and meet with CMI leaders. Through such world-mediated approaches to higher education, they were challenged to directly grasp principles of political ecology, sustainability and environmental justice. While in the cloud forest, students engaged in community projects, and one proclaimed that she had "*a whole new concept of what luxury is,*" including a deep appreciation of social relations and biodiversity. Another student remarked that Inteñas "*are my role models for sustainability.*" Upon returning to snowy Minnesota after trips in the winters of 2013 and 2014, students took the semester to organize Climate Summits involving three days of student designed projects and events to raise awareness about biodiversity and planetary health. Global Studies 460 was not a typical class. Students came from multiple disciplines within the Colleges of Liberal Arts, Science and Engineering, Education, Business and Nursing, with diverse and overlapping skills and interests. Climate Summit projects ranged from the construction of a 'green' house out of recycled soda bottles, an original choreographed dance, academic research and poster presentations, a concert to raise funds for microcredit loans at the Intag Credit Union in Apuela, photography exhibits, radio interviews, a children's project that made trees out of recycled materials, viewing films on sustainable foods with free samplings, readings of original stories and other creative work. The three-day events highlighted biodiversity conservation, environmental citizenship and sustainability. Students were challenged individually to be creative, work with team members and communicate effectively. They found such mutual accountability tough and inspiring as they stretched to think, coordinate, and be responsible in new ways. Students explored how citizens in diverse societies manage the commons for the common good. A political science and Spanish major stated succinctly '... *I learned I wasn't just going to wake up one day and live the perfect "sustainable" life, but that sustainability is largely a process that reconsiders our place in the world, and our responsibility to put effective policies into place.*' In that way, WSU students learned from and later disseminated Intag's glocal and evolving model for sustainable futures.

Figure 5: By the author.

in sustainable practices. DECOIN continued prioritising forest conservation and environmental education. Such communities of practice are nested and stem from basic household concerns about water and food security. Those priorities are linked to global conservation issues. Inteña(o)s' proactive and generative approaches to environmental rights offer creative solutions and solidarity across scales.

In spite of all these changes, as a concept alone sustainability does not resolve the social and ecological issues in Intag and problems exist within each institution, including funding challenges, transparency and leadership development. New pressures have arisen as Ecuador's current national government granted the Llurimagua mining concession to a Chilean company in 2012, while insisting that 'responsible mining' was possible and that Ecuador should not act like 'a beggar sitting on a bag of gold'. Nevertheless, the examples discussed above show that after more than a decade and a half of increased civic participation in Intag, community-based and regional environmentalism have endured with practices infused with intercultural and gendered ideologies.

Acknowledgements

I am grateful for support from the American Philosophical Society, Winona State University Dean of Liberal Arts, the Global Studies Department, WSU Foundation, Ecuadorian Fulbright Commission and the Ruth Landes Memorial Research Fund that aided the realisation of different phases of my research. In particular, colleagues and friends from various Intag-Manduriacos communities and NGOs were helpful and generous in sharing their time and knowledge, without which I could not have shaped my ideas. I appreciate Carl Maida and Sam Beck's efforts in organising the IUAES panel on communities of practice in Manchester 2012, in addition to an anonymous reviewer's comments and Mary Ellen Fieweger's comments on an early draft. I am thankful for Ezra Vázquez D'Amico's assistance in editing this chapter, and as always, I am grateful to Ezra and Peonia for their inspiration and encouragement.

LINDA D'AMICO is a cultural anthropologist who specialises in Kichwa cosmology and gender in the Otavalo highlands, as well as political ecology and environmentalism in the subtropical cloud forests in Northwest Ecuador.

Notes

1. My engaged work began in the early 1990s and I was a founding member of DECOIN. I have assisted in grant writing on various projects and volunteered as a journalist and supporter for the community newspaper. I have attended scores of meetings and assemblies, and engaged U.S. and Ecuadorian university students in civic outreach and intercultural exchange projects.
2. Intag-Manduriacos is the western-most part of the subtropical zone of Cotacachi County. Manduriacos is located in the lowest altitudes of García Moreno Parish and is differentiated by its relatively recent human colonisation, tropical climate and a 'wild west' type atmosphere. The AgroIndustrial gold mine is located near the village of El Corazón, where illegal logging of primary forests in not uncommon, and a large hydroelectric dam on the Guayllabamba River is being built near the village of Cielo Verde.
3. According to biologist Norman Meyers (1997), much of the world's biodiversity is located in small areas of the planet. As much as 20 per cent of the plant species and a still higher proportion of animal species are confined to 0.5 per cent of Earth's land surface. These species are endemic to their areas, so if the local habitats are eliminated, these species will suffer extinction. The Intag region is threatened with habitat destruction.
4. The *bono* or social welfare payments of $35 per month subsidised households in need and was increased to $50 per month in mid-2012 prior to the 2012 presidential elections when Correa won a decisive victory. However, for provincial, county and parish elections on 17 February 2013 Correa *lost* in all ten of Ecuador's largest cities (the office of mayor) and half of the provinces. Cotacachi County elected a candidate from the alternative *Buen Vivir* Party, and in Intag, the Parish Presidents and Boards had mixed results with both *Buen Vivir* and *Alianza País* members elected.
5. Ecuador adopted the United States dollar as its currency in 2000, during a severe financial crisis.

6. Glocal is the connectivity and co-presence of local and global people, ideas and institutions.
7. Shor and Freire (1987: 176).
8. During his three terms as mayor, Tituaña's administration won international awards, including the International Prize Dubai, UAE, for 'Best Practices' in 2000; the InterAmerican forum via the 'Dreamer Prize' in 2001; and UNESCO's 'Cities for Peace Prize' in 2002.
9. The 2008 Constitution of Monticristi was ushered in by the Correa era of the 'Citizen Revolution' and hailed internationally for guaranteeing respect for the rights of nature, or the *Pachamama* (a multicultural nod to the Kichwa Mother of the Cosmos), universal rights to *sumak kawsay* (another nod to Kichwa ideology referring in this case to an integrated well-being). However, in 2012 many citizens were wary of what they termed the administration's 'double discourse': the contradictions were clear in the supposition that industrial mining was the path to *sumak kawsay*/well-being as political authority was re-centralised.
10. Shor and Freire (1987: 187).
11. The survey was conducted in the six subtropical parishes of Cotacachi County: Apuela, Plaza Gutiérrez, Peñaherrera, Cuellaje and García Moreno. We did not include the Selva Alegre parish in Otavalo County.

References

Anderson, B. (1991), *Imagined Communities* (New York: Verso).
Brundtland Commission (1987), *Our Common Future* (United Nations).
Coordinadora de Mujeres de Intag (CMI) (2007), *Plan de Vida de las Mujeres de la Zona de Intag: 2007–2011* (Otavalo: Publisher).
Coordinadora de Mujeres de Intag (CMI) (2013), *Quiénes Somos, Cómo estamos: Coordinadora de Mujeres de Intag 2012 Encuesta* (Otavalo: Gruppo).
López Oropeza, M. (2011), 'Entre la Identidad y la Ruptura Territorial: La Contrucción Socio-histórica y Socio-económica en Intag' (Masters thesis, FLACSO, Ecuador).
Meyers, N. (1997), 'The Rich Diversity of Biodiversity Issues', in *Biodiversity II: Understanding and Protecting Our Biological Resources*, (ed.) M. Reaka-Kydla, D. Wilson and E. O. Wilson (Washington, DC: Joseph Henry Press), 125–138.
Periódico INTAG, December 2000. No. 1.

Ortiz Crespo, S. (2004), *Cotacachi: Una Apuesta por la Democracia Partici-pativa* (Quito: FLACSO).

Shor, I. and P. Freire (1987), *A Pedagogy for Liberation: Dialogues on Trans-forming Education* (South Hadley, MA: Bergin and Garvey Publishers).

Whitehead, M. (2014), 'Sustainability', in *Critical Environmental Politics*, (ed.) C. Death (New York: Routledge), 257–266.

Wilson, E. O. (1992), *The Diversity of Life* (New York: Norton).

Spaces for Transdisciplinary Dialogues on the Relationship between Local Communities and Their Environment

The Case of a Rural Community in the Calchaquí Valley (Salta, Argentina)

Marta Crivos, María Rosa Martínez,
Laura Teves and Carolina Remorini

Introduction

Our research team in applied ethnography has a long history of intervention in rural and urban populations of Argentina to deal with problems that affect communities. In every case, we interacted with and supported professionals from different fields of knowledge in order to diagnose and try to solve problems that affect these populations, understanding these from a local perspective. We paid particular attention to the strategies that address problems emerging from the daily subsistence activities of domestic groups. The advantage of having a broad ethnographic record has allowed us to observe the deep transformations this region experienced over the last decades. These transformations are mainly connected to changes in the type of endeavours traditionally linked to the *fincas*[1] and to the implementation of public policies on health, education, housing and tourism and the way allowances or resources were delivered to individuals.

Regarding public health policies, 'primary health attention' is one of the most extended strategies in rural areas of the country, including Molinos Department. This strategy especially focuses on health promotion and prevention of infectious diseases, growth and nutritional status control and pregnancy monitoring. Infectious diseases are thought to play a major role in the population's nutritional status and widely influence their quality of life. Interventions that prevent infectious diseases and undernourishment are based on health education and detection and control of risk factors, mainly individuals' hygiene and food habits, house construction materials and sanitary conditions, such as access to drinking water and sewage disposal. We took into account the importance of parasite infection as an indicator of human and environmental health, and its implications for the diagnosis and prevention of environmental disturbances associated with it.[2]

Changes in Lifestyle in the Calchaquí Valleys

The Calchaquí Valleys are part of the southern region of the Andes in the northwest of Argentina. This region has been inhabited for over 2,500 years, initially by aboriginal people, called *Diaguita* or *Calchaquí*, who spoke the *Kakan* language. Some other groups, who spoke *Quechua* came here as a result of the Inca expansion and settled in the region in the fifteenth century. This resulted in a degree of cultural homogeneity and social practices that characterise the entire Andean region. The present population constitutes a mixture of indigenous and Hispanic elements.

According to the official census (2009) there are 2,494 people living in Molinos Department of whom 1,000 live in Molinos town proper. The town of Molinos is a rural setting located 2,020 metres above sea level and 200 kilometres from the city of Salta, founded in the middle of the seventeenth century. This town's type of settlement and access to land has its origins in the Spanish *encomienda*[3] and continues today in the *fincas* as a way of organising space, production and regional social articulation (Garreta and Solá 1993). The present economy is based on vast farm production, cattle breeding and domestic farming for self-consumption. Although some people still perform those activities, young people are mainly engaged in other tasks such as commerce, wage labour jobs – both inside and outside of Molinos, or even state-administrative jobs. They are involved in professional or technical practices at hospitals or in schools to a lesser extent. Today, tourism is an important source of income, which, in turn, increased textile activity and encouraged the transformation of old buildings into multi-service hotels. Wine growing reached its peak in the last few years and several *fincas*, whose wine production was traditionally handcrafted, were recently acquired by foreign and national industrial groups (Martínez and Crivos 2010).

Several new economic projects have been put forward with the support of regional and national organisations as well as of national and foreign non-governmental organisations, among them *Comunidades Unidas de Molinos* (CUM)[4]. This organisation comprised of people from communities nearby the town brings together the members of a group of families that cooperate in the implementation of projects that are directed towards the promotion and development of indigenous people. There are other institutions connected to the activities of the *fincas* that promote training and work-orientation workshops for their residents. Some of the most important projects are the *Pro-Huerta* and the *Pequeña Agricultura Familiar* programmes[5] from the National Institute of Agricultural Technology, *INTA* (Cieza 2010), and the National Ministry of Social Development. As regards the NGOs, the Foundation 'Nature for the Future', financed by Mitsubishi Corporation and supported by the government of Salta, launched a project known as *El Patrimonio tiene Oficio* [Our heritage has a trade] to 'promote [local] sustainable development and to protect the cultural and natural heritage of the Calchaquí Valleys' in Salta. For the last twenty years, the association of craftsmen and producers, *San Pedro Nolasco de los Molinos and Coquena*, has been in charge of part of the production and sale of wool and textile handicraft (Teves 2011). Similarly, other projects aim at improving the infrastructures of health institutions and the supply of medicines.

As head of Molinos Department, the town of Molinos is home to the administrative offices of the provincial government. The current features of this town are completely different from those we observed during the 1970s when we first started our research (Crivos 2004). Since that time, access roads to the town and drinking water and electricity services were developed in the last four decades. In the 1990s, different modes of communication were added – television and the Internet are in use in the community. Solar panels supply electric energy to areas far from the centre of the town. The residents of Molinos consider these advances as improvements to their quality of life even though some *fincas* still do not have access to all of these services (Martínez and Crivos 2010).

The pastures of an old *finca* that twenty years ago were located at the margins of the small town of Molinos are now home to a group of homogeneous houses constructed with governmental funds. During this period, Molinos Township tripled its population, owing its growth to the socio-political transformations in the region in the last decade.

Educational and sanitary institutions have increased in number and in the quality of service. For example, twenty years ago, there was only one regular school; today, that same institution offers primary and secondary education, and there also is a kindergarten. In 2012, a new tertiary education institution was established. Since Molinos offers access to public secondary education, many young people from the surrounding communities move to town to access this resource. To house these students while they attend school, shelters were built with the help of ecclesiastical organisations. As a consequence, a higher number of young people are either staying in the area or delay their migration to cities (Martínez and Crivos 2010).

As regards health services, Molinos has one provincial hospital located inside the town and six sanitary posts in the *fincas*, located several kilometres apart from one another. Although an increasing number of people visit the hospital or one of the sanitary posts, some illnesses are still being treated in the domestic realm or with the advice of *médicos campesinos* or traditional healers because biomedicine is not considered capable of diagnosing and treating them (Remorini et al. 2012).

Molinos' hospital only deals with births and more easily treatable pathologies. More complex pathologies are treated in health centres located in nearby cities. Each *fincas* sanitary post has a full-time nurse or sanitary agent and is visited by hospital physicians once each week. Access to these facilities is limited, sometimes due to long distances, the absence of adequate transportation, and to economic problems that make transportation even more difficult. This situation not only contributes to the persistence and relevance of local traditional medical practices, especially among the inhabitants of the *fincas*, but also accounts for the pragmatic and opportunistic use of official medical practice.

Our Strategy

Our strategy grows out of our extensive historical trajectory, interdisciplinary methods and university extension resources to address parasitic infections and their impact on the quality of life and sanitary conditions of rural populations in the northeastern region of Argentina.[6] Based on our experiences, we assert that it is necessary to generate and foster spaces that promote the interaction among all actors involved in decision-making processes, in an egalitarian political environment to create strategies collaboratively for handling the sanitary conditions of parasitic infections. The participation of a broad spectrum of actors – residents, members of governmental and non-governmental organisations, and scientific and technical investigators – must be involved in the discussions to produce alternatives for the reduction of parasitic infections.

Our methodology consists in the combination and alternative use of diverse interview (semi-structured, open-ended) and observation techniques, including participant observation by following the routines of the members from different generations within domestic units and their social interactions. Our surveys centre on the activities that involve the use of environmental resources as the actors engaged them in every instance of their execution, and their connections. We especially focus on the results that arise from the transformations of those activities and their consequences on the environment, and the population's health and quality of life.

To support the spaces for participation and discussions, we hosted workshops and focus groups in Molinos and its nearby communities. These work groups, or 'communities of practice' were made up of different social actors directly or indirectly linked to the problems of human and environmental health. These were local inhabitants, teachers, sanitary agents, doctors, biochemists and scientific researchers from the university in the field of biology and anthropology, and governmental and non-governmental organisations.

Between 2012 and 2013, we held three meetings in the local hospital with Molinos Department's health staff and several local government agents in attendance. Three other meetings were held in Molinos' primary school and four other meetings in the secondary school; teachers and students from each institution attended all of them. A workshop was hosted in the Higher Education Programme and another one took place in the Interpretation Centre and Museum Indalecio Gómez, both of which were attended by teachers of the Programme.

In 2012, inhabitants, priests, police officers and town and hospital authorities attended a workshop that was held in the parish hall of Molinos church. Likewise, CUM organised another workshop in Tomuco that was focused on adult women, young people and children. In 2013, the schools of Colomé and El Churkal hosted workshops in which sanitary agents, teachers, parents and students participated. In Amaicha, one workshop was held in the sanitary post, and Tacuil also hosted another workshop in its Primary School.

In all these meetings the exchange of information and experiences from different perspectives was encouraged to identify common concerns and to generate strategies to solve them. People and groups involved in acknowledging health problems and their resolution were able to interact. They got to know and express different perceptions and interpretations and present, analyse and negotiate their own expectations in relation to those of others in the region. Surveys were also conducted to generate exchanges and activate the recollection of information about the uses and knowledge related to natural environmental resources involved in daily routines and their health impact. In accordance with the needs of local institutions, several activities were carried out to meet the greatest concerns in the community. This entailed training health personnel and gathering information about the health and nutritional conditions of children.

About the Experience:
Actors, Perspectives and Emerging Problems

In the first stage of this research project several meetings were held in the hospital and schools to build awareness of the socio-environmental factors of parasitic infection. In these institutional contexts, we were able to optimise the involvement and commitment of the different social actors. We were also able to confirm and increase the value of local knowledge and practices, articulating them with scientific knowledge and demonstrating a multiplying effect that had a wide impact in the region.

The programmes and projects in educational and health institutions that were implemented incorporated a wide range of strategies and perspectives and the participation of local actors. Simultaneously, university researchers and their project designs were modified to interact more fruitfully with the local population and within the framework of university extension projects. These projects now foster the active participation of local residents by promoting persistent questioning of the experts and their adequacy in addressing the problem at hand, its resolution and possible benefits.

The workshops provided the space and context for generating awareness of parasitic infection, providing information about its negative effects on human and environmental health. The notification about the meetings held and their goals was spread through the media, face-to-face contacts and written communication. Attendance of the activities in the town was not consistent. However, in El Churkal and Colomé *fincas*, many people from different sectors of the population attended the meetings held in primary schools. In the town's hospital, the director decided to make the activity compulsory for all personnel. In the schools, the activities were carried out with students from different grades during class hours; however, the meetings for parents and teachers held after school hours were not as well attended as expected.

This kind and level of participation is not new for the residents of Molinos and its institutional authorities. The latter claim that there is little participation in training or informative activities by the town people, unless there is some type of benefit for the attendees and/or organisers. This clearly explains why many health-promotion and illness-prevention activities organised by the hospital are minimally attended. Hospital personnel stated that this situation is due to the 'lack of interest' on the residents' part, although this remark usually points to women who are considered the sole individuals in charge of family health and well-being, and the absence of men's participation in what are considered domestic activities. This is reinforced by public policies that target women with messages and benefits from social programmes. The level of participation and participation by gender is strengthened by health policies. According to government policies, the procurement of 'benefits' (higher coverage, free-of-charge medicine, milk and food for pregnant women and children) or cash allowances would require some form of 'compensation' by the poorest families. In the past, compensation meant voluntary work and compulsory health controls, while today only the latter is present. This relationship produces benefits, obligations and debts, which, if they are not settled, entail institutional penalties. A sanitary agent said the following about this:

> We need to encourage mothers to devote more time and attention to their children or to feeding them, because mothers might have some other things to buy first. I think this Plan[7] has to move in that direction and give mothers an incentive: to make them accomplish something or do something in exchange for something else. But I haven't seen this in practice ... I usually tell some people that, at least, they should buy the child a fruit.

This opinion represents a common perspective about deprived families dependent on state institutions. They are said not to 'profit from the opportunities', are 'careless' or 'irresponsible' or even 'lack education' or the necessary 'values' to assume their family health care obligations responsibly. In this regard, 'values' in particular are issues transmitted through religious institutions, such as catechesis, religious ceremonies, food kitchens and nurseries.

At school, similar perceptions exist about the children who come from those 'deprived' families. Both institutions support messages and initiatives from governmental and international organisations (such as the Ministry of Health or UNICEF) that propose universal actions and conceptions related to health and human development. Not being critically evaluated or questioned regarding adequacy to local contexts, these universal notions become a fundamental part of projects and develop into the standards used to evaluate the results to be achieved.

From a governmental or non-governmental organization institutional point of view, people being served are seen as having deficits or are perceived as deprived, while the role of institutions are understood as facilitating people's education, and improving or correcting their lifestyles. The imposition of disqualifying families and individuals justifies the intervention of institutional agents to promote changes in their habits, behaviours and inappropriate or 'risky' attitudes. This context prevents people's values, interests, perspectives and strategies from being surfaced or entering into a discussion in a safe common place. Instead it produces confrontation, rejection or resistance, critical obstacles for institutional practices that are ignored. Within this framework, the local residents, the alleged beneficiaries, have little room for the spontaneous, genuine expression of their demands, interests, perspectives or problems. This is an obstacle in the active involvement of beneficiaries in institutional projects, making them appear inflexible, resistant and uncooperative, as indicated by the following:

> In many families, the main cause is – as they [The Sanitary Agents] know since they have contact with them – primary malnutrition. That is, 'I don't have anything to give my child to eat ...' so, these people use the parasites as an excuse ... They come here with their own diagnoses ... and they directly ask S. [The Biochemist] 'aren't you going to do some tests? Because he is not eating! I give him food every day, but nothing happens and he does not gain any weight, I'm sure the child has a parasite infection'. They ask for them [tests]. (Physician)

> Something that is also cultural is children's eating habits [...] because of their parents' habits, children eat [...] food with lots of sugar, such as sodas [...] meat [...] or fried foods, like French fries ... [...] all foods, which are not [...] in a way, healthy for the child's growth. (Sanitary Agent)

[…] we give those families education in their own houses. Sometimes we have undernourished children and we have to talk about supplementary nourishment, and there's when the mom says 'he is not hungry and he doesn't eat' so … I've already talked to her […]. We try to explain everything to her, then we talk about the importance of breast-feeding […] nowadays, mothers are not really like they were in the past, it seems that now they have more alarm signals, for example, if they notice the kid has diarrhoea, they bring the child here [to the hospital]. (Sanitary Agent)

People 'get' things (messages, goods and services), and according to those who offer those things, people should give something back or do something in order to 'show' they are giving those things their deserved value. These types of relationships are compatible with a vertical social and domestic organisation, in which elders assume responsibilities and are models, sometimes the only ones, who make decisions (the mayor, or the 'patron in the *finca*'). The historical roots of this model of organisation are expressed in social, economic and political institutions and in several activities, which clearly represent the lifestyles of people in the region. The vertical, hierarchical relationships that characterise local models of social organisation do not allow for an adequate balance in this give-and-take situation.

In view of this situation, instead of considering the reasons for this imbalance – which would entail listening and paying attention to other voices and assuming one's own critically – new ways of interacting with the local population are generated so as to attract their attention and to guarantee the success of institutional projects. In accordance with national educational policies, the importance of local traditions and public actions oriented towards human and environmental health is favoured in the schools through the implementation of workshops dealing with topics such as history and pre-history of the region, and environment and pollution, among others, as indicated by the following comment:

For example, […] water cycles were taught in the first grade […] the problems of the sun and how it affects our skin were dealt with in the second grade […] while in the third grade, trees and their benefits were taught [...] in the fourth grade, students learnt where the town was before and what had happened, why had the town been changed [...] in the fifth grade, students learnt how to purify water with natural methods [...]. (Primary School Headmaster)

Generally, the purpose of these workshops is to sensitise and involve the school population in topics that are considered of critical importance and that are supposedly unknown to them. Surveys with primary and secondary school students about their knowledge of the region's natural resources indicated that they recognised domestic activities, such as nutrition and treatment. However, when asked to reflect upon environmental problems and possible solutions, students had limited knowledge about pollution, garbage handling, risks associated with consumption, illnesses connected to environmental factors, and natural catastrophes. Although these aspects of the human–environment relationship are considered problematic by the school, as evidenced by workshops provided on these topics, environmental concerns are clearly not recognised by the students as being relevant to their daily lives.

The hospital has recently started to offer, as a therapeutic practice, dance and gym sessions to encourage the expression and interaction of people in that new space. The idea to carry out this type of activity was triggered by the concern for the social factors that encouraged certain chronic pathologies, namely hypertension, diabetes, being overweight and other issues derived from problems such as alcoholism, which have an impact on the mental health of the residents – abuse, family violence, rape and suicides – and that are recognised by physical indicators among those seeking care at the hospital. At first, when the health professional is confronted with health problems that involve psychosocial components in their origin and treatment, he calls on a psychologist to assist him. If this alternative fails as well, the professional tries to understand the 'lack of response' to the proposal:

We called the psychologist and we were at his disposal, because [...] as human beings and as an institution, we thought it was important to offer that support [...] I thought we were exaggerating [...] because, I don't know [...] it seemed that nobody else cared [...]. (Hospital physician)

Final Reflections

Molinos is a clear example of how the introduction of varied governmentally enforced projects can generate social and cultural incentives for rural populations to undergo major lifestyle changes, chiefly through new productive activities and public policies that try to nurture them. Although these new activities indeed produce transformations in the social and natural environments, there is very little space left for local residents' reflections about their consequences and future projections and, thus, for the proposal of strategies for the support of community life. Instead, community life, itself, is questioned when the goal is to find a path to institutional or personal satisfaction that uses and optimises available resources.

The town and its surrounding area form a friendly experimental field for these different types of activities. Within this context, we observed that local institutions are centred on their own practices, which sometimes are not enough to meet the demands they themselves create. The aim of raising 'communities of practice' – defined as a group of people connected by participating or being involved in a common activity or practice, recurrent and sustained over time (Vásquez Bronfman 2011) – becomes blurred by institutional activities that guarantee no other commitment from their beneficiaries than the one that arises from the mandatory nature of the school and the specific needs of the hospital.

In light of this situation, residents of Molinos observe, are interested in, or reject these proposals according to their own interests or priorities, thus making a pragmatic selection – either voluntarily or not depending on the institutional context – of offers or components. People are constantly deciding upon and combining alternatives, in a synergistic manner, in terms of how these proposals actually affect their daily lives. Our ethnographic research on subsistence activities at the domestic level allowed us to better understand these decisions and residents' reasons by exploring their individual paths. At the same time, our research allowed us to evaluate convergences and divergences regarding the impact of different ventures on local development, considering those individuals' paths and experiences.

We were also able to observe how institutional-centring is closely connected to individual-centring. Considering the institutional offer, that of schools and hospitals, proposals focus on those individuals who are considered deprived of health, education and certain prescribed values as these institutional define them. In general, individuals visualise their problems and eventual solutions without considering, to the fullest extent, the social context in which their problems emerge. Articulating the interests of different sectors of community life, this eluded dimension that poses problems and solutions within the social network that creates them and solves them is activated during the scheduled meetings.

In this regard, the spaces created by these meetings promoted a certain interaction among individual and institutional interests that went beyond their dividing limits. The presence of those spaces allowed us to redefine problems that were, at first, considered personal and unique and then to project them on a community scale. The consideration and analysis of problems, as well as the search for alternative solutions, produced interesting comparisons and correlations among the professional and scientific viewpoints and those arising from people's experiences derived from their longstanding settlement in the region. In spite of the divergences in the knowledge and experiences of different actors involved, knowledge about human and environmental health was enriched and expanded. An emerging community of practice, in which community and social knowledge constitute each other, was generated through the exchanges taking place in the meetings. Beyond the success or failure of these events in terms of quality and variety of participating individuals and groups, we acknowledge the possibility of making these forms of knowledges operational through a community of practice. In this way, knowledge acquisition is accelerated through incorporating the new forms of knowledge in both institutional and individual daily practices.

As we have shown, most of the initiatives currently accepted by government institutions (health and education mainly) are grounded in ideas and objectives defined outside of the local context. They are associated with established goals of public policies enacted nationally, even when professionals make an effort in to adapt them to the local situation. However, the opportunities to introduce changes or innovations according to people's daily experiences and the forms of social learning through interactions between health staff and local population are limited. In that sense, there is a little room for horizontal exchange and mutual learning as is typical of other situations in the domestic sphere. On the contrary, vertical relationships and ways of authority prevail in these institutional contexts.

New challenges derived from transformations in the economic activities, educational goals, health and nutritional transitions, are seen as problems that could be treated as isolated from each other, and included in the programmatic schedule of each institution. Common goals, articulation mechanisms and mutual collaboration sustained over time are not as frequent as a community of practice would require. However, drawing on the results obtained until now, we are able to recognise some features that partially fit with the idea of an 'emerging community of practice'. As Vazquez Bronfman (2011) pointed out, to shape a community of practice, the keyword is to cultivate, rather than to create, as the term 'cultivate' implies to help and support the development of something already existing (even in embryonic form) rather than to deliberately create a community of practice. Based on this idea, it is necessary to start by recognising existing communities in specific contexts. Moreover, to do this, we must first identify the activities or issues that bring together people. Considering this, one of the recurring problems of projects that seek participatory ways of knowledge management is the great difficulty of sharing this knowledge, in order to redefine problems, re-think them, and to then assess alternative solutions, taking into consideration the multiple viewpoints and interests within a local community. However, it is within this process that people who participate in the community of practice learn from each other and are able to collaborate. In this sense, our work offers an experience of knowledge management about parasitic infections, one that exhibits the challenges and opportunities underlying the proposal of intersectoral encounters as a strategy for sharing knowledge and practices of very different origins. This is an essential condition for the emergence of communities of practice to address issues of human and environmental health affecting the residents of the Calchaqui Valley.

Marta Crivos is Professor of Theoretical Orientations in Anthropology, Facultad de Ciencias Naturales, Universidad Nacional de La Plata. She is a researcher at Consejo Nacional de Investigaciones Científicas y Técnicas, Laboratory of Research in Applied Ethnography. Her research focuses on interactions between human communities and their natural environment.

María Rosa Martínez is Professor of South American Ethnography, Facultad de Ciencias Naturales, Universidad Nacional de La Plata. She is currently at the Consejo Nacional de Investigaciones Científicas y Técnicas, Laboratory of Research in Applied Ethnography. Her research focuses on the role of intergenerational relationships in environmental-issues management in rural populations.

Laura Teves is Professor of Theoretical Orientations in Anthropology. She is at the Laboratory of Research in Applied Ethnography and her research focuses on network analysis in ethnography and the role of personal networks in the articulation of micro/macro social processes.

Carolina Remorini is Professor of South American Ethnography, Facultad de Ciencias Naturales y Museo, Universidad Nacional de La Plata. She is a researcher at Consejo Nacional de Investigaciones Científicas y Técnicas, Laboratory of Research in Applied Ethnography. Her research focuses on the cross-cultural study of child development.

Notes

1. *Finca* is the name used in Salta to refer to rural agricultural property (Dávalos 1937: 36).
2. Extension project (2012–2013): 'Construcción intersectorial de estrategias para el mejoramiento de la calidad de vida con énfasis en las parasitosis, el estado nutricional y los factores socio-ambientales, en Molinos, Valles Calchaquíes septentrionales, provincia de Salta'. Facultad de Ciencias Naturales y Museo de la Universidad Nacional de La Plata.
3. *Encomienda* is the Spanish word for 'commission'. It refers to the feudal system used by Spain in the New World. In this system, the Native Americans would work on the land and pay tribute to the Spanish conquerors in return for spiritual and terrestrial care.
4. http://lacum.blogspot.com/
5. These national programmes aim at improving food safety and sovereignty and at favouring the participation and organisation of vulnerable sectors of society.
6. Extension project (2003–2004 and 2006–2007): 'Parasitosis y enfermedad parasitaria en poblaciones periurbanas y rurales en el área de la Reserva Privada UNLP Valle del Arroyo Cuña Pirú, provincia de Misiones: estrategias para su diagnóstico, tratamiento y prevención'. (2006–2007): Construcción intersectorial de estrategias para el manejo y control de las parasitosis. Experiencia en la Escuela Nº 172, Municipio de Aristóbulo del Valle, Misiones. Facultad de Ciencias Naturales y Museo de la Universidad Nacional de La Plata.
7. *Asignación Universal por Hijo* [Universal Child Allowance].

References

Cieza, G. L. (2010), 'Procesos organizativos y acceso a la tierra en el Valle Calchaquí. El Caso "El Churcal", departamento de Molinos, Salta', *Tesis de Maestría. Procesos Locales de Innovación y Desarrollo Rural -PLIDER-. Facultad de Ciencias Agropecuarias y Forestales*. Universidad Nacional de La Plata, http://sedici.unlp.edu.ar/bitstream/handle/10915/18177/Portada.%20CIEZA.%20PLIDER.pdf?sequence=3 (accessed 10 July 2014).
Crivos, M. (2004), 'Contribución al estudio antropo-lógico de la medicina tradicional de los Valles Calchaquíes (Salta, Argentina)', *Tesis de Postgrado. Universidad Nacional de La Plata*. PrEBi. Proyecto de Enlace

de Bibliotecas. SeDiCI. Servicio de Difusión de la Creación Intelectual, http://sedici.unlp.edu.ar/handle/10915/4285 (accessed 20 May 2014).

Dávalos, J. C. (1937), *Los valles de Cachi y Molinos* (Buenos Aires: La Facultad).

Garreta, M. J. and M. F. Solá (1993), 'Fincas rurales en el norte del Valle Calchaquí. Procesos de conformación, cambios y relaciones sociales', *Cuadernos del Instituto Nacional de Antropología y Pensamiento Latinoamericano* nº 14: 41–58, 1992–93.

Martínez, M. R. and M. Crivos (2010), 'About the Hospital and Other Medical Alternatives in Molinos Everyday Life', Complete work published in *Proceedings XVI International Oral History Conference*. CD.

Remorini, C., M. Crivos, M.R. Martinez, A. Aguilar, A Jacob, and M.L. Palermo (2012), 'Aporte al estudio interdisciplinario y transcultural del "Susto": Una comparación entre comunidades rurales de Argentina y México', *Revista Dimensión Antropológica* (CONACULTA_ INAH, México) Año 19, vol. 54: 89–126.

Teves, L. (2011), 'El Estudio Etnográfico de la Actividad Textil como aporte a la Caracterización del Modo de Vida en el Pueblo de Molinos y zona de influencia (Provincia de Salta)', *Tesis de Postgrado. Servicio de Difusión de la Creación Intelectual (SEDiCI), UNLP*, http://sedici.unlp.edu.ar/handle/10915/5239 (accessed 4 April 2014).

Vázquez-Bronfman, S. (2011). 'Comunidades de práctica,' *Educar*, 47(1), 57–68.

Affective Solidarities?

Participating in and Witnessing Fair Trade and Women's Empowerment in Transnational Communities of Practice

Debarati Sen

> When we were young it was the age of unions; now it is the age of NGOs, they are the ones who can bring real reform to these plantations with their new ideas and projects. See how they have involved all these young people from the West to improve our workers' lives. (Mr Pradhan, manager, *Sonakheti* tea plantation)

These celebratory comments about how effectively nongovernmental organisations (NGOs) involve volunteers and visitors from Western countries in plantation reform came from the manager of *Sonakheti*, a fair trade certified tea plantation in Darjeeling district. Mr Pradhan's observations reflect the increase in 'voluntourism', a combination of aid work and tourism. Voluntourists practice sustainable tourism, corporate social responsibility and ethical consumption (Vrasti 2013: 9). As a feminist researcher interested in women's political lives within fair trade certified plantations I was naturally interested in the effects of fair trade-related voluntourism on women's everyday political and work lives. But my interest was heightened even more when plantation authorities urged me to observe the activities of these volunteers rather than the operations of traditional labour unions that had recently negotiated an across-the-board wage increase for plantation workers.

As I spent time in Darjeeling's fair trade certified plantations I realised that the popularity of market-based sustainability and social justice initiatives like fair trade had engendered new possibilities for consumer-citizens in the global North to demonstrate their affective solidarity with producers in the global South by visiting certified production sites to participate in and witness the effects of fair trade on worker's livelihoods. Their acts of participating in, witnessing, recollecting and documenting the effects of fair trade in turn produced new kinds of knowledge about plantations while affecting the plantation public sphere. Ethnographically documenting these emerging acts of voluntourism is important to understand the reach, dynamics and effects of emergent 'communities of practice' in the playing field of sustainable development. While existing research, most notably Brown's work (2013), examines U.S.-based actors in these new communities of practice, it is important that we document the new self-appointed voluntourists who operate transnationally to shape fair trade practice and discourse in the developing world. While feminist scholars have examined similar dynamics between Western and non-Western actors within transnational campaigns for women's human rights (Chowdhury 2011), in this chapter I use similar feminist frames to attend to the politics of voluntary 'small acts' (Brown 2013) as they unfold in Darjeeling, India.

The potential these voluntary acts of solidarity and related transnational praxis hold for increasing the bargaining power of producer-citizens (plantation workers) vis-à-vis the state becomes salient in India since the state regulates wages and other plantation benefits via the plantation labour act. Fair trade as an empowering venture must address the issue of bargaining power of producers since wages and benefits are baseline determinants of quality of life for plantation workers. As I witnessed, fair trade-engendered solidarity practices are erasing the complex history of workers' struggle against the state and established systems of power through collective bargaining. Fair trade enthusiasts operate on a limited understanding of the political lives of women plantation workers. I argue in this chapter that, in Darjeeling's tea plantations, fair trade as transnational praxis has inadvertently pushed justice seeking and delivery to a non-state sphere that is not accountable to the workers in terms of citizenship rights, often articulated through labour organising affiliated with political parties. Further, this privatisation of justice indirectly undermines the possibility of using fair trade to strengthen collective bargaining institutions and inadvertently decreases the state's accountability to workers. My chapter contributes to the new line of enquiry in sustainability research that centres on making meaning around sustainability practice and creation of new forms of value (Brown 2013; Sen 2014; West 2012) within communities of practice.

In the rest of this chapter I provide ethnographic evidence of the growing disconnection between these new kinds of solidarity-based transnational praxis and their effects on plantation associational life, concluding with some theoretical reflections on these affective solidarity practices and their effects. These findings are based on my ethnographic research in Darjeeling district, West Bengal, India, between 2004 and 2011. I conducted participant observation and semi-structured interviews with forty-seven fair trade enthusiasts who visited two tea plantations, *Sonakheti* and *Phulbari*, where I conducted most of my research for this chapter. These fair trade enthusiasts fell into three broad groupings: six tea buyers, thirty-one student visitors and ten student NGO volunteers.

Practicing and Witnessing Fair Trade

My analysis of the forty-seven interviews revealed certain key phrases fair trade enthusiasts used to describe their purpose for visiting fair trade certified plantations. The most frequently cited reasons reflected their affective states: 'to connect with workers'; 'to help in fair trade projects'; and sometimes 'to learn about workers' lives', 'understand them', or 'show our support for workers'. Most enthusiasts were European or North Americans who came from diverse backgrounds. The students, who worked as interns in local NGOs, were between eighteen and thirty years old and had some involvement with fair trade related activities or alternative sustainability initiatives in Western countries. The independent tea buyers and NGO volunteers were slightly older, ranging from their late twenties to fifty years of age. Most were consumers of fair trade products in their home countries. A few were tourists travelling on their own who decided to spend a week or two on a sustainable farm. Some had searched online for places where they could participate in fair trade initiatives. They were interested in organic agriculture in the global South and came to experience it on plantations.

Voluntourists' first point of entry into fair trade related work was the plantation management. Upon their arrival they were assigned to a 'host', usually a plantation worker placed fairly high in the plantation hierarchy, who participated in a plantation 'homestay' programme. These living arrangements spatially limited fair trade enthusiasts by slotting them within the plantation hierarchy, which closed off certain forms of spontaneous interaction with workers. They were exposed only to a certain class of plantation workers, usually better-off ones, and were inundated with well-rehearsed fair trade propaganda. If visitors wanted to interview workers, their hosts picked the interviewees and also served as interpreters. Those enthusiasts who walked about the plantation on their own expressed surprise at how closely the owner kept tabs on where each visitor went on such excursions. This monitoring was explained as a safety measure.

The only way enthusiasts could learn about fair trade or participate in actual 'fair trade' processes was through participating in Joint Body-managed 'capacity building' projects.[1] As new worker-management associations, the Joint Bodies are outside the purview of state monitoring and lack any institutionalised transparent means of operation. All plantation workers in Darjeeling are members of local labour unions that are connected to regional political parties and at times broker deals with the state-controlled tea authorities. It is important to understand that local labour unions are also instrumental in mobilising support for Nepali subnationalism within India.[2]

The two plantations I researched held more frequent Joint Body meetings when the concentration of fair trade enthusiasts was high. Volunteers and visitors were invited to attend Joint Body meetings, which were represented as proxy unions and as sites of critical dialogue and discussion between workers and management. In contrast, the trade unions were portrayed as organisations of violent outsiders who disturbed the peace in plantation communities by politicising simple workers trying to maintain their traditional ways of life. A junior manager, whom fair trade enthusiasts assumed was an average worker, usually convened these Joint Body meetings. The worker-representatives, mostly women, were treated respectfully in front of the visitors.

In a typical meeting the manager would begin with a long list of projects being planned or undertaken with the fair trade premium funds. The manager questioned the workers, who usually responded by describing the ways they benefitted from these projects. Workers seldom brought up any grievances about the projects or the general condition of the plantation in these meetings. Even though workers' complaints about the Joint Body were widespread, they never brought these up in front of fair trade enthusiasts, who were equated with management. There was absolute silence on the issues of wages, overtime work, casualisation of workers, water shortages and inadequate medical facilities that workers would otherwise discuss.

Fair trade enthusiasts were kept busy engaging in meetings and myriad projects during their short visits. During my interviews with them I probed to see how they understood the everyday reality of Darjeeling's plantations and the agency they gave fair trade in shaping it. As an interlocutor and interviewer, I came to view the picture taking shape in the visitors' minds. They would eventually transmit their views of the plantation community and production locales to sites of consumption (in the West) through narrating their eyewitness accounts of fair trade in their home communities and occasional online forums.

I asked Denis, a student volunteer, what he found out about the plantation and the effects of fair trade on women workers from his visit. He replied:

> Thanks to Phulrani, I could attend a Joint Body meeting. I know that the children could now access the newly stocked library because of fair trade. She told me about organic agriculture. I had heard that plantations are really harsh on their workers, but it seems that is not true for the fair trade-certified ones. There seems to be a lot of projects going on. I even helped the local children to pick plastic on Sunday.

Knowing that Denis had mentioned wanting to connect with average workers and learn about their struggles, I probed further. I asked what else he knew about Phulrani's life besides her involvement with the Joint Body. At this Denis looked completely puzzled and we ended our conversation there for the day.

As I reflected on my interactions with fair trade enthusiasts like Denis I realised how certain institutional arrangements framed their orientation to and experience of plantation life. Coupled with this dynamic, their interest in learning about plantation life post-fair trade was a barrier since they had already summed up pre-fair trade plantation life as a case of one-sided worker exploitation. While they were not mistaken about worker exploitation in the postcolonial plantation system in India, they assigned a remarkable amount of agency to fair trade for rectifying such exploitation, which foreclosed possibilities of seeing women plantation workers as having active political lives beyond fair trade and of recognising where the structural issues in the plantation came from.

Therefore Denis and his like never found out that Phulrani had also been a very active member of the labour union since 1985 and was planning to resign her Joint Body membership very soon because she had been refused a loan for her husband's medical treatment. Phulrani told me she was tired of the Joint Body and its projects. I asked why she, a long-time member, wanted to leave the Joint Body. I asked, 'Don't you like taking visitors around?' Phulrani replied sarcastically, 'They are nice people, they are our guests, but they are only interested in fair trade and not in us. They want to know more about what the Joint Body is doing than what we are doing. That is why I do not want to tell them anything about myself. Badmouthing the Joint Body is out of the question; I will lose my job then'. Thus, the stories workers shared with fair trade enthusiasts were always incomplete.

Denis's and Phulrani's descriptions of their encounter point to a disconnect typical of exchanges between fair trade enthusiasts and plantation workers. Workers like Phulrani did not value the Joint Body – hence her comment that fair trade enthusiasts are 'not interested in us'. Workers considered it their duty to tell fair trade enthusiasts about the fair trade projects because those were what a lot of visitors wanted to participate in. Meanwhile, fair trade enthusiasts participated in fair trade-related projects in a misguided attempt 'to connect' with producers. As I mentioned earlier, the most common purpose that fair trade enthusiasts identified for their visits was the desire to connect with local initiatives. The process of connection, as we see here, is fraught with irony since the interactions follow a defined pattern, always within a certain frame.

Ellie told me that she approached the Joint Body at Phulbari plantation to introduce her and Andy to 'indigenous organic cultivation'. I asked how they found out that the organic methods were indigenous. Andy explained that he had long conversations with the plantation managers, who told him about local shamanic traditions and their effects on the practice of organic and biodynamic agriculture. Andy said, 'I am so glad that fair trade certification is also reviving these local shamanic traditions'. When I asked what they learned, Ellie said, 'We met the local shaman, and he told us that fair trade and organics had improved the air which surrounded the plantation, and it improved the average worker's health'. I knew that the local shaman had given them his stock narrative about fair trade improving workers' health. He had told me the same thing when I first met him. The same shaman, in other contexts not involving visitors, constantly complained about the acute water shortage on the plantation that was producing various kinds of ailments. He complained, 'We might breathe fresh air, but cannot control what we eat and drink'. He implied that average workers could not access good nutrition because of all the chemical-laced conventionally grown food that formed their staple diet. He often joked that 'the tea plant is better cared for than we are'. The form of storytelling about their lives that workers engaged in was limited by their scripted roles when interacting with voluntourists.

Unlike students and volunteers, the tea buyers perhaps had the most deprecatory views about the workers whom they were ultimately aiming to support. I was able to meet and interview seven independent tea buyers who came to the two plantations. Overall, their stated purpose for visiting was to understand how workers lived and worked in fair trade certified organic plantations in Darjeeling. Tea buyers were always housed in the plantation guesthouse instead of homestays, which is how they maximised their interactions with the plantation owner to negotiate good buying deals. Among fair trade enthusiasts I interacted with, the tea buyers spent the least amount of time with average workers.

A fair trade tea buyer proudly commented to me, 'At least fair trade is doing something good for these illiterate workers, or they would create so much union trouble'. Later, while researching another independent buyer online, I found an interview about the status of a fair trade certified plantation this buyer had visited in Darjeeling in which she proclaimed that 'plantation workers never go on strike, while strikes by the local militant Gurkha population are rife at other plantations'.[3] She seemed to be unaware that all plantations in Darjeeling have unions and all plantation workers receive similar benefits through a uniform wage structure mandated by the federal government. But missing in this tea buyer's analysis is the fact that union activity for workers' rights has taken many critical turns in Darjeeling over the last two or three decades because of situated historical and political developments related to ethnic subnationalism and pressures of new market-based interventions. Most alarming is her subtle celebration of the plantation owner's ability to quell agitating Gurkhas/Indian Nepalis through fair trade, perpetuating the age-old colonial and orientalist representational trope of Nepalis as a martial race with a streak of useless rebelliousness. Although the tea buyers were enthusiastic about connecting with workers, their image of plantation workers in Darjeeling contrasted with their desire to understand workers' actual lives in fair trade certified plantations.

Similarly, many American volunteers who returned from Darjeeling would contact me in the U.S. to tell me about presentations they made at their universities or churches about the benefits of fair trade in Darjeeling. Through site visits and narratives, these enthusiasts cultivated a sense of themselves as activist consumers participating in real change. However, the effects of their visits and the publicity they gave to plantations can only be understood by examining how the management and workers felt about the changes brought about by fair trade in the years since 1990.

The significance and effects of the witnessing practices created by these peculiar solidarity initiatives can be best understood by locating these practices as a continuation of the longer history of sidelining unions prevalent in Darjeeling's plantations since the 1980s. Such practices began with the weakening of labour-focused leftist unions. Through long-term research I discovered that fair trade's entry into plantation life in the early to mid-1990s coincided with a period of union busting peculiar to Darjeeling district. It became apparent that fair trade inadvertently provided a necessary cover for the gradual creation of a privatised political field within plantations. The building of fair trade-related institutions within plantations, like the Joint Body, only furthered this process. The Joint Body gradually became the face of plantation public life and a poor proxy for elected collective organising bodies. It constantly deflected fair trade enthusiasts' attention from labour unions as agents of structural change within plantations and valorised the Joint Body as a point of introduction to learn about the region and plantation life. Outside visitors could rarely independently engage with workers and learn about their home-grown efforts to improve their livelihoods and their struggles for justice.

Conclusion

The world-renowned Darjeeling tea industry is an important revenue earner for the Indian state. Over the past few decades prevailing collusion between plantation owners and the local tea bureaucracy has succeeded in keeping wages and benefits for workers stagnant. Regional political mobilisation for many years has also been influenced by the collusions between plantations and the state in terms of decisions to put the wage issue on the local political agenda (Sen 2012). In such a situation it is imperative that we ask what fair trade enthusiasts are able to volunteer for and change amidst these regional modalities of state intervention in plantation life. The celebration of NGO-isation within plantations is the most recent incarnation of plantation profiteering where fair trade-related resources (people and money) are being deployed to detract from productive conversations about the effectiveness and presence of unions in plantations.

Whereas movements like fair trade aim to create global accountability structures to stop exploitation and promote empowerment for producers, some of its self-selected advocates through their voluntourism and transnational solidarity projects actually end up localising accountability in a way that undermines workers' collective bargaining rights and their citizenship rights vis-à-vis the state at the regional and national levels. In Darjeeling's plantation workers' struggles for economic and social justice have in large part been voiced through labour unions. In recent years it has been labour union activism and important shifts in regional politics of subnationalism – not any fair trade project – that has brought about plantation wage increases.

These 'small acts' (Brown 2013) of solidarity that unfold in postcolonial space and time are central to the fair trade movement in many ways: fair trade secures a market and makes the movement real for its consumer participants. Fair trade volunteers identify and work towards meeting the 'needs' of the disenfranchised and documenting their successes. Ironically, the solidarity projects enabled by fair trade enthusiasts produce partial truths about associational life in postcolonial fair trade certified places. These half-truths circulating in virtual and real space in turn sustain relationships of material and discursive dominance of the North over the South. Sadly, the exercise in de-fetishisation that the fair trade movement promises to its supporters and beneficiaries is fraught with contradictions that often render postcolonial plantation workers as 'people without history'. In transnational communities of practice fair trade practices 'illustrate forms of neo-colonialism and have potential to reinforce a dependent, subordinate position of developing nations vis-à-vis advanced capitalism societies' (Brondo 2013: 155–156).

The way that power works in transnational communities of practice within the fair trade movement prevents fair trade enthusiasts from asking different kinds of questions that could revitalise existing collective bargaining institutions instead of creating new institutions like Joint Bodies. The creation of new standards for witnessing, experiencing and measuring fair trade's success systematically make labour unions and workers' citizenship rights vis-à-vis unions and the state progressively less relevant. The practices of fair trade enthusiasts and their effects on plantation politics in Darjeeling remind us of Jacqui Alexander and Chandra Mohanty's (2013: 971) caution about the rhetoric of social inclusion in neoliberal times in which ideas about social justice, empowerment and social transformation take queer forms such that radical ideas

> can in fact become a commodity to be consumed ... no longer seen as ... connected to emancipatory knowledge. ... Neoliberal governmentalities discursively construct a public domain denuded of power and histories of oppression, where market rationalities redefine democracy and collective responsibility is collapsed into individual characteristics ... Such normative understandings of the public domain, where only the personal and the individual are recognizable and the political is no longer a contested domain.

In Darjeeling we witness the effects of solidarity-based neoliberal governmentalities enabling union busting while promoting social justice for poor workers. Fair trade-enabled voluntourism also helps us understand how neoliberal governmentalities are furthered not only by formalised biopolitics but by 'cultivating emotional and communicative competencies required from adaptable workers and transgressive entrepreneurs' (Vrasti 2013: 118).

DEBARATI SEN conducts feminist ethnographic research in the Indian Himalayas on women organic tea producers' subjective engagements with and mobilisations around sustainable development. She has published in refereed journals like *Feminist Studies, Environment and Society, Society and Natural Resources, Critique of Anthropology*. Her book on *Everyday Sustainability: Gender Justice and Fair Trade Tea in Darjeeling* is published by SUNY press.

Notes

1. The Joint Body is a new kind of worker-management collective body required for fair trade certification. Its key charge is to disburse fair

trade premium money that plantations receive for operating capacity-building projects. The Joint Body is supposed to have union representatives, but during my research I found Joint Bodies are largely under management control. A key difference between Joint Bodies and traditional labour unions is that members to the Joint Body were handpicked by plantation managers, whereas unions consist of elected representatives, and every worker is a union-member.

2. Darjeeling's plantation workers are descendants of Nepali plantation workers who were brought to India in the mid-1800s when the British established tea plantations in this region. Nepali people are a minority within the Indian nation-state, and since the 1980s Nepalis living in Darjeeling have mobilised to seek their own state within the Indian nation. I refer to these movements as Nepali subnationalism. Plantation labour unions have always been part of the citizenship struggles waged by Indian Nepalis, who are ostracised and seen as outsiders. The subnationalist movement's key goals have been advocating for acceptance of Nepalis as rightful citizens of India through territorial demands. More recently the movement advocated for reform of plantation labourers' wages, forcing the Indian Tea Board to agree to a wage rate increase.

3. To protect the identity of my informants, I have abstained from citing the websites where they wrote their accounts using their real names. For informants who have made their comments or activities available to the general public, I have used their real names instead of pseudonyms to document their acts of participating in and 'witnessing fair trade' – a central theoretical and empirical claim of this chapter.

References

Alexander, J. M. and C. Mohanty (eds.) (2013), *Feminist Genealogies, Colonial Legacies and Democratic Futures* (London: Routledge).

Brondo, K. V. (2013), *Land Grab: Green Neoliberalism, Gender and Garifuna Resistance in Honduras* (Tucson: University of Arizona Press).

Brown, K. (2013), *Buying into Fair Trade: Culture, Morality and Consumption* (New York: New York University Press).

Chowdhury, E. H. (2011), *Transnationalism Reversed: Women Organizing against Gendered Violence in Bangladesh* (Albany: SUNY Press).

Sen, D. (2012), 'Illusive Justice: Subnationalism and Gendered Labor Politics in Darjeeling Plantations', in *New South Asian Feminisms: Paradoxes and Possibilities*, (ed.) S. Roy (London: Zed Books), 131–150.

Sen, D. (2014), 'Fair Trade vs. Swaccha Vyāpār: Women's Activism and Transnational Justice Regimes in Darjeeling, India', *Feminist Studies* 40, no. 2: 444–472.

Vrasti, W. (2013), *Volunteer Tourism in the Global South: Giving Back in Neoliberal Times* (London: Routledge).

West, P. (2012), *From Modern Production to Imagined Primitive: The Social World of Coffee from Papua New Guinea* (Durham: Duke University Press).

Part 2

Sustainable Urbanism

Communities of Practice at the *Cidade do Saber*
Plural Citizenship and Social Inclusion in Brazil

Carla Guerrón Montero

When a devastating flood hit Salvador, the capital of the state of Bahia in 1995, Mariela and her family were forced to leave their modest home in a low-income neighbourhood and live in the streets; for a few months, they lived literally, under a bridge. They received assistance and moved to a temporary camp far from the city's centre; soon upon its construction, the camp was stigmatized as dangerous even though it was composed mostly of working-class families who had been affected by the flood. The camp was not well connected to the city centre and many lost their jobs in the transition. Mariela and her neighbours organized to acquire the resources they lacked in their homes. They started by setting up a children's nursery. Under the guidance of Mariela, who became president of the Mother's Association, they also created a community school and a literacy program for adults, both with volunteer teachers. "We were so proud of how we were able to dribble hunger, poverty, and have a nursery and a community school" (interview M. T., June 26, 2008). Later they built a library and an organic garden. After six years of washing clothes and organizing raffles to obtain funds, the Association received financial support from the *Banco do Brasil* to set up an assistance project focused on delivering vocational training for young adolescents. The aim of this project was to provide alternatives to drug trafficking and sex work for the neighbourhood's youth. The project was successful and for years, about 260 young men and women per year trained to become *baianas de acarajé* (1), seamstresses, bakers and waiters and waitresses. In less than ten years, the assumed dangerous temporary camp became a thriving neighbourhood. Risking her own physical and mental health, Mariela remained the recognised leader of the project until 2007 (interview M. T., June 26, 2008). Mariela's journey and her achievements illustrate one salient characteristic in Brazil. The country not only has some of the world's most pronounced social and economic inequalities but also some of the most innovative mechanisms to achieve social inclusion. Mariela's project exemplifies an organic community of practice at play in the state of Bahia. Communities of practice are organisational forms promoting learning through information sharing; they refer to groups of individuals who learn together and assist each other in internalizing and interpreting knowledge (Kapucu 2012). This chapter discusses another, much larger and farther-reaching, community of practice in the same state, in the city of Camaçari: the *Cidade do Saber* (CDS). Mariela's story is entangled with this community of practice, as she was recruited in 2007 to join the CDS and to become its outreach coordinator. Mariela recounted to me:

When I first came to the CDS I was very afraid, but it has been a very good experience for me. People from Camaçari come and see the facilities and think that they don't fit. My job is to make them realize that they do fit, just like it happened to me when I first came here. I wondered: 'Why did they offer *me* a job here?' Now I am the happiest I have been. I have a good job with a decent salary and I am part of a project that is bringing social inclusion to my state (interview M. T., June 26, 2008).

Mariela's enthusiasm reflects the pronounced value of communities of practice. However, while there is substantial literature addressing the positive outcomes of communities of practice (Lave and Wenger 1991; Wenger 2000, 2005, 2010; Edmonds-Caddy and Sosulski 2012; Kapucu 2012), there is less discussion about its limitations (but see Haneda 2006, Kanno 1999, Toohey 1996). To contribute to filling this gap, this chapter addresses both the accomplishments and limitations of communities of practice formed organically at the CDS, the largest educational project of social inclusion, local participation, and citizenship in the state of Bahia. Although the CDS is not framed as such, I interpret this project as an example of communities of practice where faculty, staff, administrators, and students are potentially producing a new way to understand what it means to be a modern Brazilian citizen.

This chapter is based on ethnographic and library research conducted for nine months in 2008 and 2009, as the first social scientist invited to study the CDS. Data sources include field notes based on participant observation in the Centre's day-to-day activities and every course offered; 80 audio-taped interviews with students, instructors, administrators, staff, interns and public officials; and participation in activities and events carried out outside regular class hours. I complemented this information with library research at the Public Libraries of Salvador and Camaçari, and at the Centre for Latin American Research and Documentation (CEDLA) in The Netherlands in summer 2010. Additionally, I regularly communicate with my CDS collaborators.

Defining Communities of Practice

Learning and knowledge are interconnected. Learning is a social process occurring within the context of engaged networks and relationships; knowledge is a situated product of the activity, context and culture in which it is developed, a 'co-production of the mind and the world' (Seely Brown et al. 1988: 1–2). The concept 'communities of practice', first proposed by Lave and Wenger in 1991, has been applied across a number of fields to facilitate connectedness among groups. Communities of practice – organisational forms promoting learning through information sharing – refer to groups of individuals who learn together and assist each other in internalising and interpreting knowledge (Kapucu 2012). They imply a greater engagement for sustainability by local and global actors, lasting professional and community relations and a framework where 'experts' are equal partners with those who are in the position of learners.

Lave and Wenger (1991) developed the concept of communities of practice, defining them as social constructs that are self-organising and that 'share the capacity to create and use organisational knowledge through informal learning and mutual engagement' (Wenger 2000: 3). The concept has been applied to several disciplines and subjects such as language and gender research (Eckert and Mc-Connell-Ginet 1992), second language acquisition (Toohey 1996), critical anthropology (Lave 1988, 1991, 1996), organisational knowledge management (Hemmasi and Csanda 2009), online communities (Schwen and Hara 2003), intergovernmental networks (Agranoff 2008) and cultural psychology (Seely Brown et al. 1988).

Key elements of communities of practice are the concepts of situated learning, knowing and belonging. Likewise, the individual and the context are understood as co-constitutive within such communities (Lave and Wenger 1991). As Haneda (2006: 807) states, 'individuals do not simply receive, internalize, and construct knowledge in their minds but enact it as persons-in-the world participating in the practices of a sociocultural community'.

These communities provide organisations with a way to capture tacit or implicit knowledge by connecting people with similar interests, allowing them to encapsulate and share information (Hemmasi and Csanda 2009). Wenger et al. (2002) assert that most such communities are formed on a voluntary, informal basis and that this organic approach is key to their success. However, proven cases demonstrate that communities of practice can also be formed intentionally.

Communities of Practice and Marginality: The City of Knowledge

Brazil's educational system is central in maintaining the country's striking inequalities (Ireland 2008; Rosemberg 2000; Rosemberg and Puntch 2003). Education was shaped by the colonialists' affinity towards classical and elitist training (Haussman and Haar

1978: 33). The Church and the elite believed that mass education was neither possible nor desirable; literacy for the poor was assumed to generate 'social anarchy' as late as the 1950s (Ireland 2008). These beliefs produced a system that combines Herbartian idealism and formalism, which assumes that the method applied to education is 'scientifically' approved, and therefore infallible (Da Silva and Davis 1996). Consequently, the student is to blame for inadequate learning (Ireland 2008).

Despite advances over the last seventy years,[1] Brazil's quality education is intimately related to wealth distribution, one of the most unequal and concentrated in the world. Geographically, most Brazilians without access to education or who are illiterate are in the northeast (22.4% in 2004); ethnically, indigenous peoples and peoples of African descent have the highest rates of illiteracy (Ireland 2008). Traditional public K-12 schools have a narrow standard curriculum and generally lack athletic and arts/humanities facilities. Higher education has been largely exclusive, with few non-whites admitted until recently when affirmative-action quota policies were instituted.

The *Cidade do Saber* (*Instituto Professor Raimundo Pinheiro* – City of Knowledge) or CDS reacts to this traditional educational system. It is the largest educational project of social inclusion, local participation and citizenship in Bahia, and one of the largest in Brazil. Not without political controversy, the CDS was inaugurated in March 2007, during the presidency of Luiz Inácio 'Lula' Da Silva (2003–2011) from the *Partido dos Trabalhadores* (Workers' Party). While Da Silva's government avoided direct provision of literacy, it introduced a new discourse giving priority to poverty relief emergency programmes and adult literacy. The regime also focused on fostering inclusive education for historically marginalised populations, including Afro-descendants, members of *quilombolas* or maroon communities, and rural populations (Ireland 2008: 725).

The CDS offers free access to education, cultural events, sports and leisure activities to economically disadvantaged residents of Camaçari. Luiz Caetano, former mayor and current federal senator,[2] and Prof. Raymundo Pinheiro, a teacher and politician assassinated in 2003, envisioned the CDS. Mostly funded by the Town Hall (*Prefeitura*) of the Municipality of Camaçari,[3] it is administered by the Institute Professor Raimundo Pinheiro, a non-government entity legally established as a social agency by the Municipality. Its mission is to 'promote and democratize access to cultural, sporting and educational goods, granting excellence in the construction of citizenship' (Soares-Palmeira et al. 2006: 11). To date, it has served approximately 90,000 children, youth and adults, and it is recognised as a model of inclusive education in Brazil, receiving six prestigious awards between 2007 and 2015.

Camaçari has approximately 242,984 inhabitants and is located about 42 km from Salvador, Bahia's capital (IBGE 2017). Camaçari's population grew in the 1970s, when it received internal immigrants working for the newly established industries (Gileá de Souza 2006). While non-residents generally portray it as a cultural backwater, the municipality is an economic powerhouse as it has the first planned industrial complex in the nation. In fact, Camaçari is one of the richest municipalities in northeastern Brazil, with a GDP of $15,891,624 billion (U.S.). Economic activities revolve around the petrochemical industry, the most important source of income since 1978 (Roos 2003). Since 2000, Camaçari has also attracted the tourism and automotive industries, as well as Poloplast, a conglomerate made up of twenty small companies. In spite of this economic growth, its social development has not kept pace: it occupies the second place in the state for its economic development index (IDE) but the tenth place for its social development index (IDS), with a poverty index of 21.3 per cent in 2000 (Gileá de Souza 2006: 107–108).

The CDS is based on the concept of 'plural citizenship'. Whereas legal scholars define the term as the opposite of 'national citizenship' (Marques and Albernaz 2010), for the CDS it means that wider access to education, culture and sports shortens social distances and generates sustainable human development.[4] As Soares-Palmeira et al. state, 'the conscientious exercise of citizenship is the best way to transform human rights from intent into reality' (2006: 14). Although not fully articulated in the development plan of the institution, the notion of plural citizenship recognises the existence of sub-citizens, the emergence of new collective identities in Brazil, and the social and legal issues that surpass the nation-state (such as international human rights). The administration takes pride in offering high-quality education. The Centre's general director, Ana Lúcia Alves da Silveira, noted, 'Our students are people who otherwise would have not studied at a school like this. This is their only opportunity, and we cannot make any mistake' (A.L.S., 10 February 2008). A critical characteristic of the CDS, which distinguishes it from other projects, is that it fosters the pursuit of knowledge to produce well-rounded, educated individuals. Its goal is *not* to insert them into the Bahian workforce. In other words, the Centre is not a vocational school, but an epicentre of knowledge to counter the limited social capital (Bourdieu 1997) of Camaçari's population and to recognise its community cultural wealth (Yosso 2005) by advancing social inclusion.

The CDS is divided into three coordinating units: Culture and Art, COART; Sports and Leisure, CODEL, and Pedagogy. It offers more than fifty musical, artistic, language and athletic activities, from ballet and capoeira to violin and water gymnastics. One of its most evident attractions is its infrastructure. In addition to thirty-two rooms for instruction, it has a library, the state's second-largest professional theatre with 568 seats, a semi-Olympic swimming pool, four auditoriums and a gymnasium. It offers symphony concerts, symposia, theatrical and music presentations, and cultural fairs at little or no cost.

Constructing the Pillars: Sustainability in the Making

At the CDS, communities of practice formed organically around the institution's foundational concepts. I focus on the communities formed specifically by administrators and instructors. I make a clear distinction between the administrators and instructors of the Centre, while recognising that there are individual administrators who share the more radical views about social inclusion education espoused by many instructors. Administrators and instructors agree that their work is to translate sustainability concepts to a wider audience to generate sustainable human development and environmental and ecological sustainability locally, regionally, nationally and globally.

However, precisely because the CDS is not a vocational school but one whose purpose is to foster the 'conscientious exercise of citizenship', there are tensions and conflicting views within these communities about the best way to run the Centre and its guiding theoretical principles. Some revolve around the extent to which the theoretical pillars of the school – social inclusion, citizenship and critical thinking – are defined and applied daily. Since instructors and administrators understand these concepts differently, their implementation produces divergences. Some examples follow.

Social inclusion, fundamental for the development of this project, is the most difficult concept to define and implement. At its most basic, the CDS defines social inclusion as the tangible possibility of integrating any Camaçarian – regardless of colour, gender, nationality, literacy level or motor and mental abilities – without making distinctions. However, actual experiences demonstrate the difficulty of making this statement a reality. For example, at a planning meeting on 16 June 2008, several instructors noted that the social and racial differences that permeate Bahia were not left behind at the Centre's classrooms.

The official definition of citizenship used by the CDS is 'the rights and obligations of a person, based on respect for differences and the ethical relationships of people with themselves, others, and the world' (L.M., personal communication). This definition is expanded and, at times, contradicted, in practice. For example, Isabella Neves, who runs a recycling workshop, defines citizenship as protection of the environment. For her, environmental and sustainability literacy (Moseley 2000; Jordan et al. 2009) should be fundamental cornerstones of instruction; thus, students should understand the value of recycled materials in their lives. 'If you respect the environment, you are already a citizen of Brazil and the world' (I.N., 29 March 2008). For many instructors, an unofficial understanding of citizenship revolves around daily coaching on hygiene. These lessons are not administrative mandates, but most instructors carry them out. For instance, and although not related directly to her course, the karate teacher reserves a space in each class to discuss the importance of cleanliness, dressing properly and behaving appropriately. A more comprehensive understanding of citizenship, one that incorporates engaged civic participation (such as running for office or voting during elections), is not addressed directly at the CDS. However, in line with Freire's ([1971] 1993) notion of *conscientização* (consciousness raising), the Centre has become a vehicle used by students, faculty and staff to express their rights as Brazilian citizens by becoming grassroots organisers. In this regard, the CDS has fostered a form of democratisation of public life, or what Holston (2009) calls 'insurgent citizenship'. An example worth mentioning is the case of Arnoldo. Arnoldo was a young Camaçarian taxi driver unconcerned with social or political issues. While working the night shift in Camaçari, he was robbed, shot and badly injured. Resulting from this assault, he lost mobility of his legs and was confined to a wheelchair. After mourning his misfortunes for a period of time, Arnoldo decided to start anew by taking swimming lessons at the CDS. Soon after, he became so interested in and dexterous at the sport that he initiated a rigorous professional training schedule. Within a few years, he was representing Brazil at Paralympics games in South America. His story inspired several individuals in similar situations in the area, and with the legal and institutional support of the CDS, Arnoldo formed the Association of People on Wheelchairs of Camaçari (*Associação de Cadeirantes de Camaçari*). This association assists people on wheelchairs at the CDS and within the municipality, and works closely with other organisations in the state that aid individuals with special needs and attitudes.

The concept of critical thinking is based on Paulo Freire's (1993, 1994) popular education framework, which was crucial for alternative literacy programmes throughout Latin America (McLaren 1999; Seda Santana 2000). The CDS believes that its activities – with their emphasis on creativity and motivation – stimulate critical thinking and self-knowledge. Rosa Bauman, plastic arts instructor, noted, 'If a person comes to the CDS to find out about its programmes and then stays, that is knowledge that should be recognised and supported because Camaçarians do not have the culture to make culture' (R.B., 10 May 2008).

Lave and Wenger (1991) propose that three crucial character-istics of communities of practice are mutual engagement, joint activity involving a collective negotiation process and shared repertoire. All are present in the communities formed among in-structors and administrators. However, control of resources and knowledge are intrinsic components of communities. While ne-gotiation between the administration and instructors occurs daily, unequal relations of power exist.

Of the three coordinating units of the CDS, CODEL is the most successful in incorporating the Centre's theoretical concepts into classes and presenting a unified front to the administration, thereby forming a coherent community of practice. Because of its many sections and the nature of its activities, COART has more difficulty embracing an amalgamated pedagogical approach. Instructors navigate between structured and less structured ap-proaches (Stein and Rankin 1998), partly because many have had experience with social mobilisation and political consciousness. Thus, it is not uncommon that a course on recycling is taught as a course on ecological consciousness raising, or that a theatre course utilises Augusto Boal's pedagogy known as 'theatre of the oppressed' (Boal 2006). To the question 'Whose knowledge counts, and whose knowledge is discounted?' many CDS instructors an-swer that their students' empirical knowledge must be recognised. Therefore, they disagree with rigid curricula and view learning as part of the social fabric and a natural and inescapable aspect of life (Wenger 1998).

Although the term is not used directly, generating culturally relevant curricula is a key objective among COART's instructors. Susana Teixeira, arts instructor, provided a good example of the difficulties of reaching this objective. She was requested to teach six hours of theory followed by practical activities, but knowing the class population she chose to spread out the six hours of the-ory and combine them with hands-on activities, producing a very successful model for her workshops. However, after reporting on her approach, she was told to maintain the structure originally proposed. Susana and her colleagues believe that instructors must be flexible to meet their students' needs. This perspective conflicts with the views of the pedagogy unit, which expects each unit's curriculum and philosophy to be normative.

One uncontested outcome of the presence and expansion of the CDS is that it has provided a sense of place and identity to a city of migrants (Parente 2006; 2007). As Gileá de Souza (2006) states, "It is common in the municipality for residents to affirm that there is no cultural identity [in Camaçari] or that there are no symbols that differentiate the municipality from others. However, one can observe that the place has its own identity and that there is an identity among the populations that make this place" (2006: 132). In a very short time, the CDS has become a hallmark of the Municipality, a symbol of the possibilities of creating a collective identity—some sense of homogeneity in a town composed of a heterogeneous population, a population of migrants with no particular connection to the town and without any particular reason for having a sense of pride about their place of residence. In a survey carried out by the Journal Camaçari Notícias in 2009, the CDS was selected as the uppermost pride of Camaçari with 36 percent of the votes, followed by the Municipality's 42 km of beaches (29.91%) and the industrial complex (24.78%). According da Silveira, the CDS is to Camaçari what the Eifel Tower is to Paris. "We are the largest centre of social inclusion, plural citizenship and knowledge. In Brazil, there is nothing like it" (Camaçari Notícias, Tuesday May 17, 2009).

Conclusions

The CDS was conceived and funded by the local government in Camaçari, resulting in a top-down approach to social inclusion. However, almost since its formation, it has become a laboratory of community-based transformational sustainability practices. Thus, studying the CDS contributes to understanding how a framework for social justice in education is constructed, and demonstrates the complexities of creating an agenda that incorporates individual success and collective solidarities (Walker 2003).

My research points to promising outcomes regarding individual success. The CDS expands opportunities to children and adults otherwise marginalised within Brazil's educational system. For example, ballet students (mostly girls) benefit from a partnership between the CDS and the prestigious ballet school EBATECA (*Escola do Ballet do Teatro Castro Alves*). Founded in 1962, EBATECA follows the method of the Royal Academy of Classic Ballet of London. A number of former CDS ballet students have initiated professional careers, and four girls and one boy were granted Bolshoi fellowships to train at the first Bolshoi School outside of Russia, in southern Brazil.

In a music appreciation class, adults of all ages and professions study Beethoven's and Mozart's lives, along with the staff, notes, harmony and rhythm. For most, this is the first time they have heard about classical composers or the art of music. This approach cultivates growth in artistic expressions, contrasting with what Gomes (2011) calls the cultural alienation produced by Camaçari's limited opportunities.[5]

Another example comes from the courses run by Olivia Meireles, an artist with twenty years of experience using recycled materials to create art. Her courses incorporate discussions of global warming, carbon emissions and basic recycling concepts, while also teaching her students the techniques for making paper, transforming it into papier-mâché and using it to make objects of art. She wants to go beyond nominal environmental literacy to reach operational environmental literacy, which involves the capacity to perceive and take positions on environmental issues (Moseley 2000: 24).

Undoubtedly, the strength of the Centre – in addition to its stupendous infrastructure and considerable economic resources – is its faculty. The administration has sought out qualified and dedicated instructors, who have achieved tangible outcomes in their students' lives.[6] Instructors are patient and provide information that is suitable to the students' cultural knowledge, while also being rigorous, disciplined and demanding. This mirrors Nussbaum's (2000) capabilities pedagogy, which acknowledges that working-class experiences are important knowledge resources, a model based on Freire's pedagogy (Levinson et al. 2007), and connected to Lave and Wenger's (1991) situated learning paradigm. The larger question of collective solidarities remains to be answered. For example, Olivia notes that, although the CDS' efforts are laudable, its work to generate broader understandings of environmental issues is insufficient. She adds, 'We need to develop our ecological conscience. We need to recognise the enormous debt that the industrial sector has toward the municipality. These workshops are only the beginning of what we should be doing' (S.T., 29 March 2008).

The problems with constructing collective solidarity are also present in the Centre's curriculum. While most instructors agree with the value of offering ballet or ballroom dance classes, some believe the curriculum should be Afro-centred, given the composition of Camaçari's population. Aside from *capoeira*, no other course connects directly with Brazil's rich African heritage. The music section focuses on teaching classical instruments such as guitar, piano and violin. As a result, the Centre resists the production of what Prudente (2003) calls a '*quilombo utópico*', an educational alternative to the uniculturalism of the official curriculum through teaching African drum percussion. Conversely, it could be argued that by offering Camaçarians the opportunity to sample a classical high-culture education, the CDS *is* challenging the uniculturalism of the official curriculum.

In an operation of this magnitude, not surprisingly tensions coexist. There are conflicting views about what should be the core goal of the Centre and whether it is realistic to expect to accomplish more than one goal simultaneously and competently. For some, producing Brazilian citizens implies instilling students with a sense of order and progress, in line with the definition of Brazilian collective identities (Schneider 1991; Freyre and Horton 1986). For others, the CDS should be a laboratory for the production of committed social citizens, willing and able to hold local, regional and national governments accountable. The tension between offering students a taste of high-culture education and contributing to the formation of a more literate and well-versed underclass without any substantial social transformation is a constant at the Centre.

The communities of practice formed by administration and staff at the Centre understand their mission differently. The administration believes that matters related to family or children's therapy, hunger, unemployment, access to transportation or disability issues cannot and should not be addressed by the CDS. The CDS should exclusively be concerned with social inclusion: fair and equal treatment of students and excellence in the courses offered. Consequently, if a student has been abused, its role *is not* to provide psychological or social assistance, but to incorporate and welcome the student into the school and not discriminate against behaviours that might be the direct result of the abuse. For many instructors, however, this view is somewhat myopic and non-holistic. Instructors experience the outcome of having to teach children who walk for two hours to arrive at the Centre, who have not had breakfast or lunch, or who have family or behavioural problems. In planning meetings, private conversations and interviews, many instructors repeatedly highlighted the need to offer psychological and even financial assistance to the most pressing cases of abuse or neglect. Many also called for psychological assistance for themselves as they felt burned out and ill-equipped in their jobs. Additionally, the Centre's pillars do not include a fundamental discussion of embracing diversity. In fact, the concept of social inclusion used at the Centre obscures the recognition of privilege and oppression in Brazilian society. Smith (2016) asserts that in Bahia the black body is simultaneously idealized as the representation of the state and cast as dangerous and in need of control. Black citizens in Brazil are denied both their social rights and the right to life, thus becoming nationals and non-citizens in a disjunctive democracy (2016:82). While individual instructors and administrators recognise that they are working with historically oppressed populations, there is no systematic effort to incorporate these conversations in the curriculum.

Ultimately, this project challenges the hierarchical Brazilian educational system from within. However, a few questions remain unanswered. How can we measure the outcomes of the CDS? How do its programmes prepare their students to take advantage of economic opportunities, thus improving their quality of life? How will a project not focused on providing new workforce skills produce well-rounded citizens with social skills that may enhance their opportunities? Contradictions develop as a result of the tension between the need to follow a mandate for critical thinking and the consequences of accomplishing the mandate for the future creation of Brazilian notions of citizenship *and* nationhood.

CARLA GUERRÓN MONTERO is Associate Professor of Anthropology at the University of Delaware. She has a joint appointment with the Latin American Studies Program, and is affiliated faculty of the Departments of Women's Studies and Africana Studies. A cultural and applied anthropologist, her research has centred on phenomena of globalisation, and more specifically, tourism, in Latin America and the Caribbean.

Notes

1. Illiteracy rates for those over fifteen years of age have declined from 56% in 1940 to about 7% in 2012 (UNESCO 2012).
2. Workers' Party, 1985 to 1988; 2005 to 2008; 2009 to 2012; 2015–present.
3. The Municipality of Camaçari includes three districts: Camaçari, Abrantes and Monte Gordo.
4. In the national rank of the Human Development Index in Municipalities, Camacari has a IDH-M of 0,73 occupying position No. 2078 among 5.565 in 2017 (Atlas do Desenvolvimento Humano no Brasl 2017).
5. Today, the CDS has its own Popular Symphonic Orchestra.
6. With few exceptions, instructors at the CDS are not full-time employees. They are hired to teach one or more courses on a temporary basis.

References

Agranoff, R. (2008), 'Enhancing Performance through Public Sector Networks: Mobilizing Human Capital in Communities of Practice', *Performance & Management Review* 31, no. 3: 320–347.

Atlas de Desenvolvimento Humano no Brasil. 'Atlas De Desenvolvimento Humano no Brasil'. Atlas de Desenvolvimento no Brasil., last modified 2020, accessed February 25, 2017, http://www.atlasbrasil .org.br/2013/en/perfil_m/3234/.

Boal, A. (2006), *The Aesthetics of the Oppressed*, trans. A. Jackson (London: Routledge).

Bourdieu, P. (1997), *Outline of a Theory of Practice* (Cambridge: Cambridge University Press).

Camaçari Notícias (2009), 'Camaçari Notícias', *Camaçari Notícias*, Tuesday May 17, 2009.

Da Silva, N. and C. Davis (1996), 'Failing Is Prohibited', in *Brazilian Issues on Education, Gender, and Race*, (ed.) S. de Sa Barreto and D. M. L. Zibas (São Paulo: Fundação Carlos Chagas), 131–168.

Eckert, P. and S. McConnell-Ginet (1992), 'Think Practically and Look Locally: Language and Gender as Community-based Practice', *Annual Review of Anthropology* 21: 461–490.

Edmonds-Cady, C. and M. R. Sosulski (2012), 'Applications of Situated Learning to Foster Communities of Practice', *Journal of Social Work Education* 48, no. 1: 45–64.

Freire, P. ([1971] 1993), *Pedagogy of the Oppressed* (New York: Continuum).

Freire, P. (1994), *Pedagogy of Hope: Reliving Pedagogy of the Oppressed* (New York: Continuum).

Freyre, Gilberto and Rod W. Horton (1986), *Order and Progress: Brazil from Monarchy to Republic* (Berkeley: University of California Press).

Gileá de Souza, J. (2006), 'Camaçari, as Duas Faces Da Moeda: Crescimento Econômico y Desenvolvimento Social', Mestrado do Análise Regional, Departamento de Ciênciais Sociais Aplicadas, Universidade de Salvador.

Gomes, R. (2011), Reporte Núcleo de Música, COART, Cidade do Saber, Camaçari, Bahia.

Haneda, M. (2006), 'Classrooms as Communities of Practice: A Reevaluation', *TESOL Quarterly* 40, no. 4: 807–817.

Haussman, F. and J. Haar (1978), *Notes from Education in Brazil* (Hamden, CT: Archon Books).

Hemmasi, M. and C. M. Csanda (2009), 'The Effectiveness of Communities of Practice: An Empirical Study', *Journal of Managerial Issues* 21, no. 2: 262–279.

Holston, J. (2009), *Insurgent Citizenship: Disjunctions of Democracy and Modernity in Brazil* (Princeton, NJ: Princeton University Press).

Instituto Brasileiro de Geografia e Estatística (IBGE 2017), 'Cidades', Instituto Brasileiro de Geografia e Estatística. Instituto Brasileiro de Geografia e Estatística, accessed February 25, 2017 http://www.cidades.ibge.gov.br/xtras/perfil.php?lang=&codmun=290570.

Ireland, T. D. (2008), 'Literacy in Brazil: From Rights to Reality', *International Review of Education* 54, no. 5/6: 713–732.

Jordan, Rebecca, Frederick Singer, John Vaughan, and Alan Berkowitz (2009), 'What should Every Citizen Know about Ecology?' *Frontiers in Ecology and the Environment* 7 (8): 495–500.

Kanno, Y. (1999), 'The Use of the Community-of-practice Perspective in Language Minority Research' *TESOL Quarterly* 33: 126–131.

Kapucu, N. (2012), 'Classrooms as Communities of Practice: Designing and Facilitating Learning in a Networked Environment', *Journal of Public Affairs Education* 18, no. 3: 585–610.

Lave, J. (1988), *Cognition in Practice* (Cambridge: Cambridge University Press).

Lave, J. (1991), 'Situating Learning in Communities of Practice', in *Perspectives on Socially Shared Cognition*, (ed.) L. B. Resnick, J. M. Levine and S. Teasley (Washington, DC: American Psychological Association), 63–82.

Lave, J. (1996), "Teaching, as Learning, in Practice." *Mind, Culture, and Activity* 3: 149–164.

Lave, J. and E. Wenger (1991), *Situated Learning: Legitimate Peripheral Participation* (Cambridge: Cambridge University Press).

Levinson, B. A., D. E. Foley and D. C. Holland (eds.) (2007), *The Cultural Production of the Educated Person* (Albany: SUNY Press).

Marques, C. Salgueiro da Purificação and R. O. Albernaz (2010), 'O Pluralismo Jurídico e a Cidadania Plural', Fortaleza, CE, Anais do XIX Encontro Nacional do CONPEDI, Junho 9–12.

McLaren, Peter (1999), 'A Pedagogy of Possibility: Reflecting upon Paulo Freire's Politics of Education: Memory of Paulo Freire', *Educational Researcher* 28 (2): 49–54, 56.

Moseley, C. (2000), 'Teaching for Environmental Literacy', *The Clearing House* 74, no. 1: 23–24.

Nussbaum, M. C. (2000), *Women and Human Development: The Capabilities Approach* (New York: Cambridge University Press).

Parente, Sandra (2007), *Camaçari: Historias Que Não Contei* (Salvador, Bahia: Fast Design).

——— (2006), *Camaçari: Sua Historia, Sua Gente* (Salvador, Bahia: Fast Design).

Prudente, C. L. (2003), 'A Pedagogia Afro da Associação Meninos do Morumbi: Entre a Carnavalização e a Cultura Oficial', Doutorado, Universidade de São Paulo, USP.

Roos, W. (2003), *Shaping Brazil's Petrochemical Industry: The Importance of Foreign Firm Origin in Tripartite Joint Ventures*. CEDLA Latin American Series, vol. 60 (West Lafayette, IN: Purdue University Press).

Rosemberg, Fúlvia (2000), 'Ambiguities in Compensatory Policies: A Case Study from Brazil', in *Distant Alliances: Promoting Education for Girls and Women in Latin America*, (ed.) Regina Cortina and Nelly Stromquist (New York: Routledge Falmer), 261–294.

Rosemberg, F. and A. Puntch (2003), 'Multilateral Organizations and Early Child Care and Education Policies for Developing Countries', *Gender and Society* 27, no. 2: 250–266.

Schneider, R. M. (1991), *Order and Progress: A Political History of Brazil* (Boulder: Westview Press).

Schwen, T. and N. Hara (2003), 'Communities of Practice: A Metaphor for Online Design', *The Information Society* 91, no. 3: 257–270.

Seda Santana, I. (2000), 'Literacy Research in Latin America', in *Handbook of Reading Research*, (eds.) M. Kamil, P. Mosenthal, P. D. Pearson and R. Barr (Mahwah, NJ: Erlbaum), vol. 3, 41–52.

Seely Brown, J., A. Collins and P. Duguid (1988), *Situated Cognition and the Culture of Learning* (Cambridge: BBN Systems and Technologies Corporation/Institute for Research on Learning).

Soares-Palmeira, M., M. L. Coutinho Lima, M. F. Silva Santos, D. Bittencourt, M. Oliveira Nery and V. Vasconcelos (2006), *Institutional Development Plan for the CDS, 2006–2012* (Camaçari, Bahia: CDS).

Smith, Christen A. (2016), *Afroparadise: Blackness, Violence, and Performance*. First ed. (Champagne, IL: University of Illinois Press).

Stein, F. and L. Rankin (1998), 'Developing a Community of Practice', *The Journal of Museum Education* 23, no. 2: 19–21.

Toohey, K. (1996), 'Learning English as a Second Language in Kindergarten: A Community of Practice Perspective', *Canadian Modern Language Review* 52: 549–576.

United Nations Educational, Scientific and Cultural Organization (UNESCO) (2012), *Adult and Youth Literacy, 1990–2015: Analysis of Data for 41 Selected Countries* (Montreal, Canada: UNESCO Institute for Statistics).

Walker, M. (2003), 'Framing Social Justice in Education: What does the "Capabilities" Approach Offer?' *British Journal of Educational Studies* 51, no. 2: 168–187.

Wenger, E. (1998), *Communities of Practice* (Cambridge: Cambridge University Press).

Wenger, E. (2000), 'Communities of Practice and Social Learning Systems', *Organization* 7, no. 2: 225–246.

——— (2010), 'Communities of Practice and Social Learning Systems: The Career of a Concept', in *Social Learning Systems and Communities of Practice*, (ed.) Chris Blackmore (London: The Open University/Springer-Verlag), 179–198.

———— (2005), *Communities of Practice: Learning, Meaning, and Identity* (Cambridge: Cambridge University Press).

Wenger, E., R. P. McDermott and W. Snyder (2002), *Cultivating Communities of Practice: A Guide to Managing Knowledge* (Boston: Harvard Business Review Press).

Yosso, T. (2005), 'Whose Culture Has Capital? A Critical Race Theory Discussion of Community Cultural Wealth', *Race, Ethnicity and Education* 8, no. 1: 69–91.

The Role of Communities of Practice in Urban Rights Activism in Istanbul, Turkey

Danielle V. Schoon and Funda Oral

This chapter examines the 'community of practice' (CoP) model as an effective method of cultivating urban sustainability and public engagement, particularly the role of such communities in advocating for the 'commons', or the shared resources of a city. Although the term 'commons' often refers to natural resources like land, air and water, in urban contexts the concept has also been used to advocate for green space, affordable housing and public transportation. The commons is also the cultural resources of a society; debates over the origins and ownership of culture can be just as contentious (Comaroff and Comaroff 2009). Here we present a particular case from Istanbul, Turkey, in which a CoP was formed to advocate for the spatial preservation of a particular neighbourhood, known as Sulukule, and the cultural heritage of its *Roman* ('Gypsy') residents.[1]

Sulukule was a *Roman* neighbourhood located in old Istanbul that, despite efforts by activists, was demolished by the municipality in 2009. Almost half of the dislocated Sulukule community now lives in a nearby neighbourhood called Karagümrük. Schoon conducted 14 months of fieldwork there in 2011–2012 with some of the dislocated *Romanlar* and the activists who continue to work with them after the demolition. The research was participatory and included collaboration with Oral, one of the founders of the Sulukule Children's Art Atelier, which was open from 2010 to 2015. Oral is an activist and community leader with a degree in business administration, and she was the director of the atelier.

Her co-founder, Zeynep Gonca Girgin Tohumcu, is a *Roman* musician and Associate Professor of Music at the Istanbul Technical University (İTÜ) Turkish Music State Conservatory and she taught music classes at the atelier. During her fieldwork, Schoon volunteered as an English language instructor at the atelier and also observed the weekly music and dance lessons.

This chapter explains how collaborations like ours were able to flourish at the atelier and play a transformative role in the dislocated community. We demonstrate how Sulukule, no longer a neighbourhood community or even a place existing in real space, emerged from the demolition as a community of practice. Shaped by and for the dislocated *Roman* youth, the atelier also welcomed people from outside the neighbourhood to contribute expertise in law, architecture, urban planning, education, child psychology, business, art, music and dance, in order to enhance the ability of the CoP to bring about change and educate the public. As the atelier was not registered as a civil society organisation or association, it was able to retain both autonomy and flexibility.

The atelier also contributed to a larger social movement against 'urban renewal' (*kentsel yenileme*) in Istanbul. For urban-rights activists, Sulukule came to represent a lifestyle that is threatened by neo-liberal governance. Activists proposed that Sulukule's heritage should be recognised as part of Istanbul's commons, so the children at the atelier were frequently called upon to represent Sulukule to the larger Turkish society by publically performing music and dance. The atelier teachers hoped that the prejudice that is the basis for structural inequalities affecting Istanbul's urban underclass might be challenged through this kind of public education. Furthermore, the networks that were formed among the dislocated youth with local and international activists, artists and academics contributed to the growing 'right to the city' movement in Turkey that culminated in the Gezi Park protests of summer 2013.[2]

Urban Renewal in Istanbul and the Case of Sulukule

Istanbul's current urban landscape began to take shape in the 1980s. The major cultural, economic and political changes brought into being after the 1980 military coup included economic liberalisation, which removed barriers to foreign investment and privatisation, and a new system of urban governance (Keyder 1999). Bedrettin Dalan, Istanbul's first mayor after the coup, headed the project of turning Istanbul into a 'global city' via a series of redevelopment projects, with the support of the military and then Prime Minister Turgut Özal. Although these were largely stalled for much of the 1990s, the rise to power of Recep Tayyip Erdoğan (formerly the mayor of Istanbul) and the AK Party[3] in 2002 led to a number of reforms that included urban development projects (Angell et al. 2014: 650). Istanbul was once again on the path to becoming a 'global city'. The Turkish state has been directly involved in 'urban renewal' and Erdoğan himself has advocated for specific development projects (ibid.: 650–651). Widespread disapproval of such interventions culminated in the Gezi Park protests, which drew worldwide attention to the tensions that exist in Turkey over the ongoing processes of free-market liberalisation and democratisation. These processes are occurring in tandem – efforts to address human rights and question the role of the state are happening in the context of major government-led reforms. While urban development projects have dislocated thousands of minorities to the outskirts of the city, the expansion of civil society and social media in the early 2000s created new opportunities for various human rights issues to be addressed in the public sphere. The most salient example of these processes interacting in both complementary and contradictory ways took place in Sulukule, whose demolition was one of the AK Party's first large-scale 'urban renewal' projects.

Sulukule was a local name for the area because of the presence of a historic 'water tower'; it was comprised of the Neslişah and Hatice Sultan neighbourhoods. It was the oldest continuously settled *Roman* neighbourhood in Europe (Somersan and Kırca-Schroeder 2007: 721). From at least the 1950s until they were shut down by the municipality in the early 1990s, entertainment houses (*eğlence evleri*) run by *Roman* families in Sulukule provided nightlife entertainment to locals and tourists and sustained the local economy. Some of Istanbul's most famous *Roman* musicians and dancers come from Sulukule (or say that they do, since this signals a lineage of professional musicianship).

Sulukule was subjected to multiple redevelopment projects in the twentieth century, beginning with those led by Prime Minister Adnan Menderes from 1956 to 1960 and extending into urban restructuring policies under Prime Minister Özal in the 1980s. In 1958, Sulukule residents were moved up towards the neighbourhood of Edirnekapı to make way for two new boulevards; two other small-scale demolitions occurred in 1966 and 1982. As the dislocated residents often say, they kept getting moved up the hill (*'yukarı tarafa taşındık'*). After the entertainment houses were shut down, the neighbourhood experienced a swift decline and gained a reputation for prostitution and drugs.

In October 2006, Sulukule was declared an urban renewal area and the Sulukule Renewal Project was approved in 2007. Activists referred to this as 'government-led gentrification'; the area had both touristic and commercial value because of its central location. The plan encompassed a total of 645 dwellings and 45 shops. The municipality justified the demolition to the public with reference to Sulukule's association with criminal activities. TOKİ (Turkey's Mass Housing Administration) and a private Turkish architectural firm (*AARTI Planlama*) were responsible for implementing a new housing project in the area.

Such projects are happening in multiple neighbourhoods of the Historic Peninsula and all over Istanbul. Poor tenants are displaced when higher-income groups move in, often supported by discourses of conservation as new tenants have the resources to restore or preserve the historic houses in what are becoming fashionable neighbourhoods. Law number 5366, popularly known as the 'Urban Transformation Law', enacted in 2005, gives expropriation powers to municipality mayors and allows them to implement renewal projects without permission from local residents or property owners (Kuyucu and Ünsal 2010).

A coalition of Turkish civil society organisations, academics, journalists, artists and activists, known as the Sulukule Platform was formed in 2006 in order to combat the demolition of Sulukule. They organised benefit concerts and street rallies, circulated petitions against the demolition, and gave press conferences in Turkey and abroad. Their aim was to convince the city to rehabilitate the neighbourhood rather than to demolish it, emphasising the historical importance of the area and the cultural heritage of the *Romanlar*. They proposed that the area's conservation should be a participatory process that involved the local *Roman* residents, appealing to UNESCO's concept of 'intangible heritage'. Scholars like Adrian Marsh contributed research into the presence of the neighbourhood in late Ottoman documents and formed links with advocacy organisations like the Open Society Foundations and the European Roma Rights Centre (ERRC) (see Demirovski and Marsh 2012). Foreign and Turkish journalists, like Hacer Foggo, reported on the demolition and disseminated information to the public. Members of the Istanbul Chamber of Architects contributed valuable information regarding the rights of Sulukule's tenants and the legal limitations of the municipality's policies. They also litigated three separate cases against the municipality, along with the Istanbul Chamber of City Planners, the Sulukule Roma Association, and the ERRC. STOP (*Sınır Tanımayan Otonom Plancılar* or Autonomous Planners Without Borders) drafted an alternative plan for Sulukule that would provide a higher-quality living environment and employment opportunities for the current *Roman* residents. Despite these efforts, the municipality went forward with plans to demolish the historic houses and replace them with 'neo-Ottoman' condominiums built by *TOKİ*. The last remaining house within the urban renewal zone was demolished on 12 November 2009.[4]

Residents who could prove ownership were offered apartment units in a state housing development built by *TOKİ* in Taşoluk, located forty kilometres outside the city. While some tried to resettle there, employment was almost impossible to find and the bus ride into the city centre took almost two hours. Most of the dislocated residents returned to the city centre to live in Karagümrük, just up the hill from their old neighbourhood, or other areas such as Fener and Balat. Some of them maintain a loose community based on their affiliation with Sulukule and their shared experience of dislocation.

Sulukule as the Commons

Sulukule Platform activists deployed a narrative of shared urban heritage, or the commons (*müşterekler*), in their fight to save Sulukule. The concept has its origins in the legal term, 'common land', but has since been expanded to include all of the shared resources of a city. It was elaborated by David Harvey as part of his discussion on the 'right to the city',[5] which rests on the ideas of accessibility, interaction and public participation in the use and production of urban space. As Harvey writes:

> The right to the city is far more than the individual liberty to access urban resources: it is a right to change ourselves by changing the city. It is, moreover, a common rather than an individual right since this transformation inevitably depends upon the exercise of a collective power to reshape the processes of urbanization. The freedom to make and remake our cities and ourselves is, I want to argue, one of the most precious yet most neglected of our human rights (2008: 1).

The commons is thus posed in opposition to an emphasis on the individual. The vision of Istanbul's future embodied in the concept of the commons is one of collective stewardship, against the value of private property or land speculation. 'Right to the city' activists call on Turkey's government to stop selling the collective resources of the city to outside and corporate interests. For them, Sulukule came to represent an urban lifestyle under threat – a small neighbourhood community with a locally sustainable informal economy and social networks replaced by overpriced condominiums that do not take the needs of local residents into account.

Alongside issues of land ownership and housing rights, the Sulukule Platform activists emphasised the cultural resources of Sulukule; the area had been on UNESCO's World Heritage list since 1985. Activists highlighted the contributions of the *Romanlar* to Istanbul's cultural identity and suggested that Sulukule's demolition would be a collective loss. The barrier they encountered was that Turkey's *Romanlar* are rarely considered central to Istanbul identity; in fact, the public at large perceives them as outsiders, despite their centuries-long presence. The demolition of Sulukule was relatively easy for the municipality to justify to the public because the neighbourhood was perceived as dangerous and inaccessible.

Activists attempted to combat this perception by organising a large-scale event that invited Istanbul residents to enter Sulukule and see for themselves that it was not dangerous. In 2007, forty days before the demolition, they organised a '40 Days, 40 Nights' event in Sulukule with presentations, panel discussions and concerts to increase awareness about the culture and history of the neighbourhood. They held pop-up meetings as well as exhibitions and workshops for locals to inform them about their rights and the possible results of the demolitions. Several international figures got involved, including the lead singer of Manu Chao and the music group Gogol Bordello, which showed up to play a concert. As a result, the demolition was postponed for a short time, but ultimately was not prevented. In part, this was because the municipality presented its own narrative of heritage conservation in Sulukule, proposing that they would integrate the area into the city and at the same time prevent the decay of historical buildings by evicting residents who are unable to invest in their maintenance.

Harvey admits, 'Questions of the commons are contradictory and therefore always contested' (2011: 103). By way of example, he asks a rhetorical question: Is the biodiversity of the Amazon forest a global 'commons'? If so, is the expulsion of its indigenous populations justified in order to preserve biodiversity? He goes on, 'Behind these contestations lie conflicting social interests. At the end of it all, the analyst is often left with a simple decision: whose side are you on, and which and whose interests do you seek to protect?' (ibid.). Regarding the 'right to the city', the vision of solidarity and urban community encompassed by the concept of the commons is attractive to urban rights activists, but does not always resonate with poor, marginalised residents who make temporary, strategic alliances but do not necessarily have affinities with larger movements (see Schoon 2018). The Sulukule Platform was criticised by some for not representing the competing demands of the entire community. Who should own the city, its history and culture, is an ongoing debate. The competing claims to urban heritage between the municipality and the Sulukule Platform activists underscore contending visions of the future of Istanbul as a 'global city'.

The Sulukule Children's Atelier

After the demolition, the Sulukule Platform changed shape and direction as its cause shifted; some of its members founded the Sulukule Volunteers Association and implemented small projects in the dislocated community. One such project focused on providing afterschool assistance to children, another on providing money-earning opportunities for women like screen-pressing textiles. Oral had intervened on behalf of the children of the neighbourhood from the beginning of the urban renewal project to ensure they enrolled or remained in school despite their dislocation. She quickly realised that the children were very interested in playing music, both the music of their parents as well as popular forms like Hip Hop, and that music could be used as a tool for education and solidarity. By giving the children a place to practice music, Oral hoped to perpetuate the cultural heritage of the Sulukule *Romanlar* and help the children heal from the trauma of dislocation. For several years, they met for classes in local coffee shops or wherever they could find space. With funding from the Istanbul European Capital of Culture Agency to rent a small house next to the demolition site, the Sulukule Children's Art Atelier (*Sulukule Çocuk Sanat Atölyesi*) was officially opened in 2010 in collaboration with the İTÜ music conservatory.

Directed by Oral, the atelier was dedicated to preserving the musical heritage of Sulukule by providing music and dance lessons to the dislocated children in Karagümrük. Local musicians and conservatory teachers set up a programme of musical training for children between ages seven and eighteen years old, and two hundred children applied to the programme. Most of them were *Romanlar* from Sulukule but some were the children of *Roman* families in other neighbourhoods or non-*Roman* children who lived nearby. One of the atelier's aims was to increase the self-confidence of the children to express their cultural heritage, demand their civil rights and communicate openly with non-*Roman* society. Oral felt that, after the neighbourhood was demolished and the community dislocated, it was important to keep the children together in an environment where they could be creative and learn how to collaborate. At the end of 2012, there were about eighty children attending the atelier participating in lessons and workshops each week in classical, Turkish and *Roman* music. Over time, the atelier also became a kind of informal community centre where older children ran Hip Hop workshops and supplementary lessons were given to support the public school programme.

In a few short years, the atelier became a place owned, in a sense, by the children. Some of them had keys to the building so they could practice music and dance, or meet with their friends. The atelier also created a performance group of twenty children that was often invited to play at public festivals and concerts. They appeared in magazines, newspapers and television and radio programmes. A Hip Hop group, *Tahribad-ı İsyan* (Revolt's Destruction), also found support and flourished at the atelier. The advocacy and promotion of the group by Oral garnered international attention and resulted in various projects, including music videos, local concerts and art installations (see Schoon 2014). The group used the atelier for practice and, in return, they offered Hip Hop lessons for the younger kids.

The atelier was a meeting place not only for its students but also for their parents and other community members who often came to Oral with requests for personal, economic or legal advice and support. Local and international scholars, journalists, artists and activists also came and went from the atelier over the years, investigating the demolition or proposing a collaborative project. These collaborations functioned to educate the Turkish public about sustainable urban development and the pitfalls of state-led gentrification. Via online communication, they also reached other communities as far away as London and New York. Volunteers wrote grants in various languages and appealed to their social networks for donations. The atelier participated in the U.S. Department of State International Visitor Leadership Program for Promoting Social Change through the Arts and also received the Roma Integration Award from the European Commission in 2014.

The atelier closed at the end of August 2015 because the children grew up. Several of them went on to study at the music conservatory at Marmara University. The members of *Tahribad-ı İsyan* continue to offer Hip Hop lessons at another location in Istanbul, and these days their students are often Syrian refugee children. They also just successfully launched their first album, *Suç mu?* The ongoing success of the Hip Hop group is a testament to the ability of the Sulukule Platform activists to persist in keeping Sulukule on the map, long after its demolition. The atelier at first attempted to salvage something lost by the demolition of Sulukule, but in fact created something new.

The Atelier as a 'Community of Practice'

Although the Sulukule Platform was unable to save the physical neighbourhood, out of its demolition a new community was formed, one based on mutual practice rather than ethnicity or place. The encounter between Sulukule's residents and Istanbul's 'right to the city' activists enabled the creation of a 'community of practice' (CoP), as defined by Jean Lave and Etienne Wenger (1991) and further developed by other scholars (Brown and Duguid 1991; Wenger 1998; Wenger et al. 2002; Wenger-Trayner and Wenger-Trayner 2015). Although these scholars largely applied the CoP model to education or management in the workplace, the applicability of the concept to transformational sustainability research and practice is demonstrated by the case of the Sulukule atelier.[6] It utilised informal, situated learning and apprenticeship to facilitate knowledge sharing and social identity (Lave and Wenger 1991), as well as horizontal organisation and mutual engagement in order to empower the community (Wenger 1998).

Lave and Wenger propose that communities of practice involve the intentional and voluntary participation of learners, not only in what is being learned but also in the process of becoming a full member of the CoP. In other words, learning in this context involves a social process (1991: 29). This process works through 'situated learning' (learning that is integral to and inseparable from generative social practice) and 'legitimate peripheral participation', which suggests that there are multiple and changing ways of being engaged in the community (ibid.: 32–37). The *Roman* community that lived in the Sulukule neighbourhood had shared space, economic interdependence, culture and social networks. This was intentional, of course, but also relatively organic in its formation. On the other hand, the CoP that emerged out of the demolition was deliberately created through the work of the atelier. Newcomers from other neighbourhoods and groups were integrated through the practice of learning and teaching music and dance. Teachers and students engaged in apprenticeship based loosely on the way children had learned music and dance from their parents in Sulukule. However, at the atelier it was acknowledged that the relationship of learning between teacher and student was mutual; a new community was being formed through practice; and individuals were being constituted through this engagement. As Lave and Wenger explain, situated learning involves 'the whole person' engaging in activities 'in and with the world' so that the 'agent, activity, and the world mutually constitute each other' (1991: 33).

At its core, the atelier was a social learning space that opened up new opportunities for dislocated Sulukule youth to learn and grow through social engagement. As stated in the atelier's mission statement, it was intended to help Sulukule's *Romanlar* network with people from many different parts of the city and, indeed, the world. Music and dance provided a particularly effective means of mediating such interactions, engaging public interest in issues of urban sustainability and communicating to a wider audience.

Conclusion

We conclude by emphasising three points about the Sulukule atelier and communities of practice. First, although Lave and Wenger's approach has been criticised for not accounting for conflict (see Cox 2005: 531), we propose that CoPs are in fact well suited to deal with conflicting agendas because they are fluid and flexible. Participants are not required to agree on everything, boundaries do not have to be well defined, and participants do not even have to be co-present. They must only share understandings about what they are doing and its impacts on their lives and community (Lave and Wenger 1991: 98). The Sulukule Platform activists experienced some conflict at the intersection of 'right to the city' and Romani rights agendas; however, they could all agree on the benefits of mutual learning and civic engagement. Although what constitutes Istanbul's commons is an ongoing debate, communities of practice can enable action instead of allowing disagreement to result in stagnation.[7] Oral believes that everyone's quality of life improves when citizens have the opportunity to collaborate and exchange knowledge, and this was at the core of the atelier's mission. This leads to our second point: the atelier can serve as a model for children's art education, particularly in contexts of vulnerability. The atelier offered children tools of knowledge and practice without jeopardising their creativity. Rather than simply passing on knowledge from teacher to student, the music and dance classes facilitated mutual engagement and created the opportunity for the transformation of participants and their world.

Finally, for anthropologists and other social scientists, CoPs provide an avenue for integrating research and practice and encouraging researchers to acknowledge their role in producing knowledge. Participatory research allows scholars to contribute to the community of study and to make practical use of the research. For example, in 2011, Oral and Tohumcu edited and self-published a collection of research and oral narratives about Sulukule. It combines activists' narratives about the demolition process and the stories of individual children at the atelier with Tohumcu's research on Istanbul's *Romanlar* and their role in shaping the city's musical environment. It has been used as an educational and informative tool that intends to impact urbanisation policies. The broad network of scholars, artists and activists created by the atelier was able to disseminate knowledge in terms that were broadly understood by local and global publics, ensuring greater engagement.

Communities of practice bring together diverse perspectives and create connections that transcend local boundaries. They engender public engagement and recruit both local and global actors. The challenges presented by rapid urbanisation in places like Istanbul require interdisciplinary action and collaboration. CoPs like the Sulukule Children's Art Atelier can encourage researchers, activists, policymakers and the broader public to engage in collaborative and creative transformational practice and urban sustainability.

Acknowledgements

We would like to thank Brian Silverstein, Salih Can Açıksöz, Anne Betteridge, Zehra Aslı Iğsız and Carol Silverman. This research was made possible by the financial support of the Fulbright-Hays Doctoral Dissertation Research Abroad Fellowship and the Institute of Turkish Studies (ITS) Summer Research Grant and Dissertation Writing Grant. Earlier versions of this paper were presented at the annual meeting of the Gypsy Lore Society in 2012 and the annual meeting of the American Anthropological Association in 2016. Special thanks to Zeynep Gonca Girgin Tohumcu, who contributed to the original paper. This research would not have been possible without the generous contributions of people in the field, particularly the members of the Sulukule Platform: they have our deepest appreciation. Many thanks to Sam Beck and Carl Maida for inviting us to contribute to the book and for their helpful feedback. Any remaining errors are our own.

Notes

1. We use the Turkish, *Roman* (singular, or adjective) and *Romanlar* (plural), to refer to Roma in Turkey, as that is the term they use to refer to themselves. We use Roma or Romani to refer to those living in Europe, or when they appear in quotes.
2. In summer 2013, a relatively small protest movement to protect a public park in Istanbul escalated into a massive national movement against the oppressive tactics of the government to limit free speech and the right to assemble.
3. The Justice and Development Party (*Adalet ve Kalkınma Partisi,* abbreviated AKP in Turkish) is a conservative party that has governed Turkey since 2002.
4. This house was owned by Gülsüm Bitirmiş; she became an important local figure in the struggle against demolition, as she had lived in Su-

lukule for over fifty years and, with the help of Sulukule Platform activists and the media, attempted to resist the demolition of her home. The demolition of this last house in Sulukule was a symbolic blow to all that the activists had been working for. A few streets that had been part of the Sulukule neighbourhood but were not included in the urban renewal zone still remain.

5. The 'right to the city' was first posed by Henri Lefebvre in *Le Droit à la Ville* in 1968. The concept has been central to the right-to-the-city movement in Istanbul.

6. Andrew Cox proposes that 'the ambiguities of the terms community and practice are a source of the concept's reusability allowing it to be reappropriated for different purposes, academic and practical', but that this can also be a source of misunderstanding or confusion (2005: 527).

7. Erbatur Çavuşoğlu and Murat Cemal Yalçıntan released 'An Alternative to Revitalise Sulukule as a Neighborhood' in 2009 and explained some of the advantages and disadvantages for the Sulukule Platform of being an open structure without a leader.

References

Angell, E., T. Hammond and D. van Dobben Schoon (2014), 'Assembling Istanbul: Buildings and Bodies in a World City: Introduction', *City: Analysis of Urban Trends, Culture, Theory, Policy, Action* 18, no. 6: 644–654.

Brown, J. S. and P. Duguid (1991), 'Organizational Learning and Communities-of-practice: Toward a Unified View of Working, Learning, and Innovation', *Organization Science* 2, no. 1: 40–57.

Çavuşoğlu, E. and M. C. Yalçıntan (2009), 'An Alternative to Revitalise Sulukule as A Neighborhood', Paper presented at the IAPS Symposium at Istanbul Technical University. October 12–16, 2009.

Comaroff, J. L. and J. Comaroff (2009), *Ethnicity, Inc.* (Chicago: University of Chicago Press).

Cox, A. M. (2005), 'What are Communities of Practice? A Comparative Review of Four Seminal Works', *Journal of Information Science* 31, no. 6: 527–540.

Demirovski, M. and A. Marsh (2012), 'To Start Roma Integration, Stop Roma Evictions', *Open Society Foundations*, 7 October, https://www.opensocietyfoundations.org/voices/start-roma-integration-stop-roma-evictions (accessed 27 June 2017).

Harvey, D. (2008), 'The Right to the City', *New Left Review* 53.
Harvey, D. (2011), 'The Future of the Commons', *Radical History Review* 109.
Keyder, Ç. (ed.) (1999), *Istanbul Between the Global and the Local* (Lanham: Rowman & Littlefield).
Kuyucu, T. and Ö. Ünsal (2010), 'Urban Transformation as State-led Property Transfer: An Analysis of Two Cases of Urban Renewal in Istanbul', *Urban Studies* 47, no. 7: 1479–1499.
Lave, J. and E. Wenger (1991), *Situated Learning: Legitimate Peripheral Participation* (Cambridge: University of Cambridge Press).
Schoon, D. V. (2014), '"Sulukule Is the Gun and We Are Its Bullets": Urban Renewal and Romani Identity in Istanbul', *CITY: Analysis of Urban Trends, Culture, Theory, Policy, Action* 18, no. 6: 720–731.
Schoon, D. V. (2018), 'Between Global Solidarity and National Belonging: The Politics of Inclusion for *Romanlar* in Turkey', in S. Beck and A. Ivasiuc (eds), *Renewing Research and Romani Activism* (Oxford: Berghahn Books), in press.
Somersan, S. and S. Kırca-Schroeder (2007), 'Resisting Eviction: Sulukule Roma in Search of Right to Space and Place', *Anthropology of East Europe Review* 25, no. 2: 96–107.
Wenger, E. (1998), *Communities of Practice: Learning, Meaning, and Identity* (Cambridge: Cambridge University Press).
Wenger, E., R. McDermott and W. M. Snyder (2002), *Cultivating Communities of Practice* (Cambridge: Harvard Business Press).
Wenger-Trayner, E. and B. Wenger-Trayner (2015), 'Introduction to Communities of Practice: A Brief Overview of the Concept and Its Uses', http://wenger-trayner.com/introduction-to-communities-of-practice/ (accessed 27 June 2017).

Cultivating Civic Ecology
A Photovoice Study with Urban Gardeners in Lisbon, Portugal

Krista Harper and Ana Isabel Afonso

Introduction: Urban Gardens as 'Communities of Practice' in Building Civic Ecology

Urban gardens are a form of self-provisioning, leisure and activist practice that is cropping up in cities around the world (Mougeot 2010). There are several key frames for efforts to promote urban gardening: ecological sustainability, economic rights, healthy food and social cohesion (FAO 2010). Urban gardens are an important arena for civic ecology, defined as 'local environmental steward-ship actions taken to enhance the green infrastructure and community well-being of urban and other human-dominated systems' (Krasny and Tidball 2012: 268).

Since the 1990s, we have seen scholarly debate on the societal dynamics of community gardens, starting in geography and urban planning and branching out. Levkoe and others see urban gardens as a form of grassroots community building and food justice activism (Krasny and Tidball 2012; Levkoe 2006). Susser and Tonnelat (2013) see urban gardens as one way residents are asserting 'the right to the city' or reclaiming an 'urban commons'.

Clearly, urban gardening inspires high hopes as a form of civic engagement for environmental sustainability. Its critics, however, warn us of the potential for hierarchies of race and class to play out in food movements such as urban agriculture (DeLind 2011;

Guthman 2008), or the potential for urban gardens to be co-opted as a form of neoliberal governance, replacing public investment in city services with voluntarism (Pudup 2008; Rosol 2012). We agree that one must cultivate a critical awareness of power relationships in urban gardens. At the same time, urban gardeners' struggle for access to land can lead to community-based interventions in the food system and the urban fabric (DeLind 2002; Sokolovsky 2010; Tidball and Krasny 2007). These shared struggles potentially foster transversal alliances across divisions of class, ethnicity, age, disability as well as other forms of difference (Young 2000). These alliances require ongoing work, not only to build relationships but also to recognise and appreciate difference within the community formed by collective action.

How do such alliances happen in the realm of civic ecology, where efforts to enhance green space and community well-being intersect? Bendt et al. (2012) studied public-access community gardens in Berlin as sites of social environmental learning, drawing from Lave and Wenger's concept of communities of practice (Lave and Wenger 1991). Communities of practice are 'a system of relationships between people, activities, and the world' (ibid.: 98) in which participants can learn alongside one another. Communities of practice depend on three social dimensions: mutual engagement, a feeling of joint enterprise and a shared repertoire of symbols, rituals and stories (Wenger 1998). Bendt et al. (2012) found all three of these elements appearing in different forms in Berlin's community gardens. Gardeners learned from one another – not only about horticulture but also about urban politics, self-management of shared spaces and social entrepreneurship.

We discuss communities of practice operating within an urban gardening organisation in Lisbon, drawing from our participatory action research (PAR) partnership between academic researchers and the members of that organisation. We present the history and contemporary terrain of Lisbon's urban gardens and then discuss the cultural values that gardeners attach to access to land for cultivating food together in the city. What visions of civic ecology emerge from the community of practice of urban gardeners working to establish a permanent space for their activities? We reflexively examine how our own Photovoice research process facilitated discussion of key values within the organisation, closely examining their discussion of the themes of 'clandestinidade and institutional conflicts' and 'sustainability'.

Case Study: Urban Gardening on the Edge of Lisbon, Portugal

Since 2011, we followed the development of a gardening project under way in Alta de Lisboa, a neighbourhood that until the 1950s was part of the zona saloia, a belt of farmlands encircling the city of Lisbon. Alta de Lisboa's history is characteristic of many outer neighbourhoods that grew rapidly in the postwar years. As Portugal industrialised and urbanised, Alta de Lisboa became the site of shantytowns, where migrants from rural Portugal and former African colonies lived. Local residents planted informal gardens on vacant municipal lands to supplement wages, in a practice that is common throughout the city (Luiz and Jorge 2012). This use of land was not illegal, but access to land was precarious in that the city could remove gardens at will. Many urban gardeners interviewed used the term horta clandestina for garden spaces in this precarious institutional context.

In the 1990s, the Câmara Municipal of Lisbon entered into a public–private partnership with the Sociedade de Gestão de Alta de Lisboa (SGAL) to redevelop the area. The vast real estate development replaced the shantytowns with a housing project of new public housing units for residents of the old shantytowns alongside market-rate condominiums for middle-class residents. Residents complain, however, that the neighbourhood lacks vitality and cohesion across class and ethnic groups, counter to the planners' stated goals of creating a 'social mix' (Cordeiro and Figueiredo 2012). Many residents' hortas clandestinas were removed to create the new 'Parque Oeste', a formal green space built on creekside land.

Against this backdrop, a neighbourhood-level NGO called Associação para a Valorização Ambiental da Alta de Lisboa (AVAAL) is trying to foster what it calls ecologia cívica (civic ecology) through community and school gardens among other programmes. AVAAL came together in response to the destruction of gardens as part of the urban renewal process. It was founded in 2009 by two residents representing Alta de Lisboa's 'social mix': Jorge Cancela, a Portuguese landscape architect, and António Monteiro, a retired resident who is an elder member of the Cape Verdean community. Together they gathered a diverse group of neighbours around the common goal of gaining a permanent space for a community garden, at a time when the Lisbon municipality had not yet launched its programme of *parques hortícolas*. AVAAL's proposed *Parque Agrícola da Alta de Lisboa* (PAAL) aims to create a secure, recognised plot of land for residents to cultivate. Cancela and Monteiro identified a vacant public lot behind a sports centre and next to the highway overpass. They consulted dozens of prospective gardeners, and Cancela integrated those perspectives into a plan for the park, using a participatory design process. AVAAL brought a petition and these architectural plans to the City Council.

After long negotiations and a grant from a private foundation, AVAAL built the first part of the *Parque Agrícola* in 2013 – the *Horta Acessível*, which is the first handicapped accessible garden space in Portugal. The *Horta Acessível*, highly visible at the entrance of the park, provided a concrete symbol of AVAAL's vision of urban agriculture as an inclusive and egalitarian space for all. With the ongoing financial crisis, however, 'public–private' partners put off releasing funds to complete the rest of *Parque Agrícola*. AVAAL's leaders have held their coalition together through several years of delays. The larger part of the *Parque Agrícola* finally opened in April 2015, after six years of community organising and long negotiations with the municipality and private developers to get financial support for construction.

AVAAL interested us not only because it is one of the largest organisations concerned with urban gardens but also because it represents a diverse range of residents and gardeners. There are older gardeners from rural Portugal and Africa and young urban professionals who are interested in sustainable cities, as well as gardeners with disabilities who grow food in AVAAL's *Horta Acessível*. AVAAL's leadership envisions a role for all the different members as they come together: older gardeners from rural Portugal and Lusophone Africa may share traditional ecological knowledge with younger gardeners who grew up in the city and are new to gardening. The organisation is a microcosm of the people and projects that make up urban gardening in Lisbon today. All share a common interest in sharing and using the spaces left behind by the big developers of the city, but they bring different motivations and attach different meanings to the urban gardening community of practice.

Photovoice: Negotiating Shared Understandings of Civic Ecology in Urban Gardening

We used Photovoice to learn how a diverse group of AVAAL members saw their activist work towards creating an urban agricultural park and fostering 'civic ecology' in the neighbourhood. We have used traditional ethnographic interviews and participant observation to get to know urban gardeners, working with AVAAL and other organisations since 2011. Photovoice offers a different way to elicit participants' perspectives and to use images to generate discussions. Wang, Burris and Ping (1996) developed Photovoice as a method that combines participant-generated photography, discussions and photo exhibitions to study community concerns from multiple perspectives. We used Photovoice to do participatory action research – an approach to doing research *alongside* participants that aims for negotiation, dialogue and reciprocity in setting the research agenda, collecting and analysing data, and communicating and applying results from the research (Gubrium and Harper 2013).

We recruited eleven active AVAAL members (five men and six women) to participate. The group ranged in age from their twenties to seventies and was varied in terms of education, socioeconomic status, disability and, to a lesser extent, ethnicity. At the first meeting, we explained the Photovoice process and community-based research ethics. We asked which themes the photographers would like to document and explore through photography. After an animated discussion, the photographers covered a large poster board with possible themes. We encouraged them to narrow this list to five key themes by voting and negotiating among themselves. The resulting themes were 'institutional conflicts and *clandestinidade*', 'inclusive agriculture', 'construction of community', 'happiness and agriculture as therapy' and 'sustainability'. At the end of the first workshop, we provided participants with digital cameras on loan and asked them to contribute up to five photos for the next workshop. Six weeks later, the Photovoice group reconvened and discussed the photo collection, which the group viewed as a slideshow at AVAAL's headquarters. Each photographer offered brief framing comments, and we facilitated a general discussion of each photo. We later held a photo exhibition at AVAAL's headquarters as a way of stimulating interest in gardening among neighbourhood residents. AVAAL also used the images produced by gardeners in the redesign of their website.

We used Photovoice to gain insights on how participants perceived the practice of urban gardening and their own efforts to secure a legally recognised space for gardens. For the participants, however, the Photovoice discussions provided an opportunity to reflect together on their organisation's goals and values. Here we focus on two themes related to civic ecology: 'clandestinidade and institutional conflicts' and 'sustainability'.

Clandestinidade and Institutional Conflicts

In the first workshop, photographers discussed several themes related to clandestinidade and institutional conflict and, in the end, combined these into a single category. This showed us that AVAAL members supported clandestine gardeners' use of public land even as they were working to create a legally recognised space for gardening. They saw themselves as allies or even advocates attempting to address the precarity of hortas clandestinas. Looking at images, people often brought up related stories that cannot be seen in the images themselves, or that are in the background of the image. One photographer, a retiree, contributed an image related to the theme of 'clandestinidade and institutional conflicts' (see figure 1).

Although we could see nice lettuces growing in a small plot edged with a strip of rusty corrugated metal, during the discussion the photographer spoke at length about the vulnerability of clandestine gardens:

Figure 1: *'Horta clandestina'* ('Clandestine garden'). Photo by José Mora.

> People come there and start to grow a little garden, but sometimes it happens that they go there and suddenly there's nothing. For instance, when the time comes for harvesting potatoes, thieves make off with the potatoes and leave nothing but the leaves for the gardener. He goes underneath and nothing – no potatoes.

This photographer felt that gardeners would be better protected against theft and vandalism if more space for gardens were legalised by the city – like the proposed Parque Agrícola. Another retiree agreed, saying that the problem was 'You have nowhere to complain'. Earlier, he had shown pictures of public parks that were in disrepair and spoken about the city's responsibility to maintain green spaces. These seemingly inconspicuous pictures opened up tacit knowledge about the concerns of gardeners working informal plots and discussion of what institutions ought to be accountable for in providing access to green space.

In another slide on this theme, a younger photographer presented a picture of a vacant lot slated for redevelopment in Amadora (another peripheral neighbourhood in the Lisbon Metropolitan Area). In the picture (see figure 2), informal garden plots extend down a hill behind a large billboard that reads: *Melhoria da qualidade de vida* (Improving Quality of Life). The photographer wondered whether the gardens in the photo would be destroyed by the construction project, and added:

> I think that the ones who make decisions should pay more attention to what people really want. When they make those political decisions like 'Now we are going to build here an urban park with nice grass and swings', they should listen to the residents in the community. To the people who will use that space.

In the discussion that followed, participants strongly contrasted residents' perspectives against the developer's top-down view of what constitutes quality of life in terms of the management of public space. While for the residents quality may mean having space to grow kitchen gardens, for developers it may mean destroying residents' spontaneous use of the land and building in its place a

Figure 2: *'Melhoria da qualidade de vida'* ('Improving Quality of Life'). Photo by Cristina Ferreira.

formal and tidy urban park, ignoring how residents actually use their free time.

Another photographer, a younger professional woman, used the camera to express more abstract ideas through a concrete image of an urban interstice next to the proposed site for the urban garden (see figure 3):

> This is next to the *Parque Agrícola* – it's the North-South highway overpass, the boundary of the park. On the one hand, there is almost nothing happening … it is a desert because it is gloomy, except that the middle zone, which picks up water that falls between the two lanes of the North-South, and there some weeds can grow. So that's a little bit like us, because we also need to adapt, we need a little light and a little water and goodwill, to have the *Parque Agrícola.*

For the photographer, this image provided a visual metaphor for the patience and flexibility required to complete the *Parque Agrícola*, after three years of AVAAL petitioning the city and urban development corporation. Speaking of AVAAL, Jorge stated: 'We are

Figure 3: *'Adaptamos e resistimos'* ('We adapt and resist'). Photo by Elisabete Serra.

not guerrilla gardeners. We *want* to be legal'. AVAAL has organised transversal politics by demanding recognition and resources from the City of Lisbon, linking working-class gardeners' desire for secure usufruct rights (*Clandestinidade*) to middle-class gardeners' vision of gardens as a cure for social and ecological anomie (Institutional conflicts).

Sustainability

As anthropologists studying urban environmental mobilisations, we were especially interested in learning how AVAAL's most active members viewed concepts related to ecological sustainability. At the first Photovoice workshop, participants listed many themes on the board related to the environment and sustainability, including 'social permaculture', 'local production', 'green agriculture' and more. None of these themes received a majority of votes. We encouraged participants to think of ways of grouping the themes that had attracted votes, like civic ecology and sustainability. In hindsight, we may have pushed them to develop the theme of sustainability because participants good-naturedly joked, 'OK, we'll do it for your sake ...' when we suggested it.

In the end, the theme of sustainability was less generative, in a Freirian sense, than other themes. We learned that although AVAAL members often characterise practices as sustainable in meetings and informal conversations, they found it difficult to represent sustainability visually within the urban neighbourhood. As every ethnographer knows, failures and mistakes are also data because they make visible the gaps and tacit knowledge. Only a few, mostly younger, participants took photos related to it, and overall 'sustainability' photos seemed to generate less interest than others. For example, one young woman showed a picture she had taken in a small village outside of Lisbon as a symbol of a more sustainable way of life. This image did not speak to the group's common experience and so the discussion moved on quickly. Reflecting upon the ways that people did and did not connect with the theme, it might be that sustainability is a secondary motivation for many members of the group, even though it is a stated goal of the association.

One picture representing sustainability did generate discussion and enthusiasm: a photo from the school garden programme in which an older gardener was teaching a group of children (see figure 4). The photographer explained how the picture related to sustainability:

> This is civic ecology because what Sr. António is doing is passing on the learning and knowledge that he has, in this case it's planting basil, but it's also teaching the children that they have to handle things carefully and take care to grow it. And the detail here is the care, because they had to make little holes for various seeds to grow. So I chose this because it is the passage of learning.

Her discussion of the image linked sustainability to traditional ecological knowledge of older rural Portuguese and immigrant gardeners who learned to grow food before chemical fertilisers and pesticides were widely available – organic farmers *avant la lettre.*

Figure 4: Planting seeds in school gardening program. Photo by Cristina Morais.

Another photo of a garden was categorised as *clandestinidade* but generated a different sense of sustainability in this exchange between two older gardeners and Afonso:

> Senhor J: I do not know if it's the crisis but people ... have economic problems. So they go looking to have a little bit of land, some space to grow stuff.
>
> Senhor A: And there are plenty who no longer buy [food].
>
> Senhor J: I don't buy! Because with the reforms, the people there in the gardens are going around on 200-odd euros a month. With water, electricity and gas, they have to get a supplement. At the same [time] they can feel good about themselves, it serves as gardening therapy, it serves as a leisure activity, while also ...
>
> Afonso: It gives some domestic sustenance ...
>
> Senhor J: Some sustainability. Exactly.

We learned that when AVAAL members use the term sustainability, they do so in an expansive, flexible way that encompasses meanings of households' economic subsistence and the social reproduction of traditional ecological knowledge.

Sustainability discourses are used in a variety of political settings from the local to the global to make claims about future pathways for action (Krause and Sharma 2012; O'Connor 1994; Peet and Watts 1996). AVAAL's activists linked the term sustainability to the food security and wellbeing of low-income people in the city who are enduring the ongoing effects of Portugal's economic crisis. Participants also linked sustainability to the passing down of horticultural skills and heritage through practical learning, thus valorising older gardeners' knowledge as a form of ecological stewardship for future generations. These themes appeared far more often than abstract ecological concepts more prevalent in the global environmental movement, such as biodiversity, climate change or peak oil. Activists recast gardening itself as contributing to a 'plural political ecology of knowledge' (Escobar 1996: 65). The connection to global environmental issues is emergent rather than defining for their work.

Concluding Thoughts

Photovoice discussions provided a space to develop and gain insights on AVAAL members' shared repertoire of ideas related to urban gardens. AVAAL's most active members placed a high priority on lobbying the city for permanent access to public land for gardening – reframing residents' longstanding activities in *hortas clandestinas* as itself a legitimate form of civic ecology. They conceptualised the term sustainability flexibly, placing ideas related to social reproduction, heritage and household subsistence alongside ecological concerns.

AVAAL's members have since moved on from planning and collectively hashing out rules for the community garden to managing a new common green space. Because the process of gaining access to land and funds for the garden took a long time, AVAAL's small group of a dozen core members have had time to develop trust and mutual understanding of varied visions of urban gardening that were expressed in the Photovoice discussions. With the garden complete, there are now 100 members working in the garden and taking part in meetings. The expanded membership do not know each other well, which can lead to disagreements about the purpose and proper form of urban gardening. At meetings to discuss the regulations of the *Parque Agrícola*, we witnessed the broader membership engaging in debates over rules related to genetically modified seeds, the kinds of containers and small structures that should be permitted, and how to structure the annual fees fairly. Cancela had this on his mind when we interviewed him:

> Sustainability for me means 'for a long time', and that's the challenge – what structures of socialisation will appear? How will people organise themselves when problems occur – how will people discuss problems, how will they solve them? ... All the people here will share a common space – but maybe not yet common values ... That's just the diversity of life. But people will have to have a common way of organising themselves.

In the coming years, we will see whether AVAAL will be able to expand its core of activists and to engage the wider membership in the collective project of building transversal alliances for civic ecology. We may see more conflict within the group as it scales up, digs in and starts growing food instead of just talking about it. The sustainability of AVAAL's *Parque Agrícola* will depend in part on how effectively the organisation can scale up their community of practice by working alongside one another, developing a sense of joint enterprise and forging a shared repertoire (Wenger 1998). Photovoice offered us a window onto the way a diverse group of citizens negotiate the meanings of urban space and their own efforts to transform it through gardening.

KRISTA HARPER is Professor of Anthropology and Public Policy and Administration at the University of Massachusetts Amherst. An ethnographer who has worked in Portugal, Hungary and the United States, she is co-author of Participatory Visual and Digital Methods and co-editor of Participatory Visual and Digital Research in Action.

ANA ISABEL AFONSO is Professor Auxiliar in the Department of Anthropology of the Universidade Nova de Lisboa and researcher at CICS.NOVA (Interdisciplinary Centre for the Social Sciences), Portugal. A specialist in applied and environmental anthropology, she has published extensively on wind energy debates and rural landscapes. She is author of *Sendim* and co-editor of *Working Images* (with Sarah Pink and Laszló Kürti).

References

Bendt, P., S. Barthel and J. Colding (2012), 'Civic Greening and Environmental Learning in Public-access Community Gardens in Berlin', *Landscape and Urban Planning* 109, no. 1: 18–30.
Cordeiro, G. and T. Figueiredo (2012), 'Intersecções de um bairro online: Reflexões partilhadas em torno do blogue Viver Lisboa', in *A cidade entre bairros*, (eds.) M. M. F. Mendes, C. Ferreira, T. Sá and L. Crespo (Lisbon: Caleidoscópio), 9–20.
DeLind, L. B. (2002), 'Place, Work, and Civic Agriculture: Common Fields for Cultivation', *Agriculture and Human Values* 19, no. 3: 217–24.

DeLind, L. B. (2011). 'Are Local Food and the Local Food Movement Taking Us Where We Want to Go? Or Are We Hitching Our Wagons to the Wrong Stars?', *Agriculture and Human Values* 28, no. 2: 273–83.

Escobar, A. (1996), 'Constructing Nature: Elements for a Poststructural Political Ecology', in *Liberation Ecologies*, (eds.) R. Peet and M. Watts (New York: Routledge), 46–68.

Food and Agriculture Organization of the United Nations (FAO) (2010), *Growing Greener Cities* (Rome: FAO).

Gubrium, A. and K. Harper (2013), *Participatory Visual and Digital Methods* (Walnut Creek, CA: Left Coast Press).

Guthman, J. (2008), 'Bringing Good Food to Others: Investigating the Subjects of Alternative Food Practice', *Cultural Geographies* 15, no. 4: 431–447.

Krasny, M. E. K. G. Tidball (2012), 'Civic Ecology: A Pathway for Earth Stewardship in Cities', *Frontiers in Ecology and the Environment* 10, no. 5: 267–273. http://doi.org/10.1890/110230.

Krause, E. L. and A. Sharma (2012), 'Sustainability "Wars" in a New England Town', *Futures* 44: 631–41.

Lave, J. and E. Wenger (1991), *Situated Learning: Legitimate Peripheral Participation* (New York: Cambridge University Press).

Levkoe, C. Z. (2006), 'Learning Democracy through Food Justice Movements', *Agriculture and Human Values* 23, no. 1: 89–98.

Luiz, J. T. and S. Jorge (2012), 'Hortas Urbanas Cultivadas por Populacões Caboverdianas na Área Metropolitana de Lisboa: Entre a Producão de Alimentos e as Sociabilidades no Espaco Urbano não Legal' [Urban Gardens Cultivated by Cape Verdean Population in the Lisbon Metropolitan Area: Between Food Production And Sociability in Illegal Urban Space], *Miradas en Movimiento* January: 142–58.

Mougeot, L. (ed.) (2010), *Agropolis: The Social, Political and Environmental Dimensions of Urban Agriculture* (New York: Routledge).

O'Connor, M. (ed.) (1994), *Is Capitalism Sustainable?* (New York: Guilford).

Peet, R. and M. Watts (1996), *Liberation Ecologies: Environment, Development, Social Movements* (New York: Routledge).

Pudup, M. B. (2008), 'It Takes a Garden: Cultivating Citizen-subjects in Organized Garden Projects', *Geoforum* 39, no. 3: 1228–40.

Rosol, M. (2012), 'Community Volunteering as Neoliberal Strategy? Green Space Production in Berlin', *Antipode* 44, no. 1: 239–57.

Sokolovsky, J. (2010), 'Civic Ecology, Urban Elders, and New York City's Community Garden Movement', *Urban Life: Readings in the Anthropology of the City*, (eds.) G. Gmelch, R.V. Kkemper, W.P Zenner (Long Grove, IL: Waveland Press), 243–55.

Susser, I. and S. Tonnelat (2013), 'Transformative Cities: The Three Urban Commons', *Focaal* no. 66: 105–21.

Tidball, K. and M. Krasny (2007), 'From Risk to Resilience: What Role for Community Greening and Civic Ecology in Cities?', in *Social Learning Towards a More Sustainable World*, (ed.) A. Wals (Wageningen, Netherlands: Academic Publishers), 149–164.

Wang, C., M. A. Burris and X. Y. Ping (1996), 'Chinese Village Women as Visual Anthropologists: A Participatory Approach to Reaching Policymakers', *Social Science and Medicine* 42, no. 10: 1391–400.

Wenger, E. (1998), 'Communities of Practice: Learning as a Social System', *Systems Thinker*, http://www.co-i-l.com/coil/knowledge-garden/cop/lss.shtml.

Young, I. M. (2000), *Inclusion and Democracy* (Oxford: Oxford University Press).

Knowledge Production and Emancipatory Social Movements from the Heart of Globalised Hipsterdom, Williamsburg, Brooklyn

Sam Beck

University–Community Engagement

Universities remain centres of liberal learning; however, by following business models (Strathern 2000) and responding to market pressures of a globalised neoliberal economy, academic knowledge is commoditised and becomes a high priced, scarce or luxury good (Basch et al. 1999). A change is taking place in how and where students acquire their knowledge and its relationship to personal and professional practice and how to live a life of hope (Freire 1996). Universities have refocused their mission to prepare students for careers, with the liberal arts providing the skills development part of the curriculum. While academics and their students are increasingly pressed to 'engage' the world, administrators are stripping the undergraduate liberal arts orientation to its utilitarian function in favour of science, technology and medicine. Simultaneously a techno-mechanical approach to learning is giving rise to distance learning, what McKenna referred to as 'predatory pedagogy' (2013, see McLaren 1995). Didactic presentations of knowledge that must be memorised remain central to 'teaching' with its focus on transferring knowledge from experts to students in large classes, also known as 'banking' (Freire 1970). Such monologist and techno-mechanical pedagogy assumes an unequal power arrangement that silences and pacifies students while imposing the instructor's language.

An alternative pedagogy is the potentially more egalitarian dialogic, a social interaction focused on 'transformative learning' (Cranton 2006; Mezirow 1991), a praxis that has an inherent potential for 'transformative action' (McLaren 1996: xi). This kind of learning is not merely the mimesis of apprenticeship (Coy 1989; Sennett 2008: 179–93) or a studio model. Beyond providing a dialogue-rich environment, dialogic is relational and hence an endlessly engaged process of social interaction that supports self-reflection and self-direction to build confidence and change the way a learner perceives and thinks (see figures 1 and 2). This perspective leads to a deeper form of learning (praxis); the dialectical arrangement of action-reflection that points to theorising and intentionally informed action (Freire 1973, 1996) and importantly hope (Gadotti 1996). Under these conditions, learning is a continuous process enhancing the ability for further action and change. When tied to experience and reflection, it is powerful indeed (Lave and Wenger 1991).

Figure 1: Marty Needelman of Brooklyn Legal Services Corporation A. Photo by the author.

Figure 2: Juan Ramos, Assistant Executive Director of Save Our Streets (SOS). Photo by the author.

Schön demonstrated that 'reflection-in-action links the art of practice ... to the scientist's art of research' (1983: 69). In a later work (1990), he indicated that practice sites are places for knowledge production, not only where knowledge is applied. This occurs through a process of reflective practice (Schön 1983). Internships focused on developing critical thinking skills are applications to in-context, in-process, work-related problem solving. Community service learning engages students in citizenship participation and instils the idea of 'service' (Butin 2010). Each demonstrates the linkage between theory and practice, makes abstract subject matter relevant as real-world experiences and delivers practice-based exposure (see figure 3).

Such experiences extend the notion of college learning by recognising the value added by non-classroom experiences and identifying learning as a social activity (Dewey 1916). Here we face a conundrum that refocuses what 'learning' and 'teaching' is all about and who it is that is involved with students besides the academic (see Goldstein et al. 2014 as an example). The case of Cornell's Urban Semester Program in New York City exemplifies Dewey's notion about how truths 'tested by experience and by consequential action in public' (Bender 1997: 44) found resonance in a university setting. This approach to teaching and learning involves undergraduate students in internships, community service

Figure 3: Father Jim O'Shea and Efrain Hernandez of Reconnect Industries. Photo by the author.

and participatory research in non-profit social justice organisations in Williamsburg, Brooklyn.

Williamsburg

The media now describe Williamsburg as if no one else lives there
except the new class of artists, hipsters and young urban professionals. It is portrayed as the heartland of innovation brought
to New York City by the "'creative class' of people who came to
live in Williamsburg (Florida 2002). The Latino population living
there is either ignored, discussed as the victim of gentrification
and displacement, or living under slum conditions. However,
Latino Williamsburg always included creative types, represented
by neighbourhood artists. The mythic image of contemporary
Williamsburg as that of a frontier that needed to be cultivated and
civilised, essentially 'colonised', by an in-migrating creative class
to make it a place of value (Moses 2005) is propagated by government agencies and real-estate developers.

After the Second World War, New York City maintained a
strong manufacturing base, with a well-organised white ethnic
working class. Williamsburg, then a working-class community
with a large manufacturing area along the East River, underwent
a significant transformation. As more prosperous white ethnics
left for new post-war housing in the suburbs and the better parts
of New York City, the Hasidim, Puerto Ricans and Dominicans
arrived, and African Americans moved into Bedford Stuyvesant.
They all came for copious well-paying factory jobs; in 1961 there
were nearly 100,000 manufacturing jobs in the area.

White ethnic working-class neighbourhoods transitioned into
mixed Latino and black neighbourhoods. Williamsburg attracted
the Hasidim who initially settled in the older Jewish section and,
as their population numbers increased, spread out. Together with
changing demographics, the demolition of Williamsburg's built
environment began in 1948 with the construction of the Brooklyn
Queens Expressway (BQE), planned under the direction of Robert Moses as early as 1937 (Caro 1974). When the BQE opened to
traffic in 1952, the highway cut through the Broadway business

district and densely populated neighbourhoods of working-class Orthodox Jews, Italians, Poles and Russians eliminating many homes as it cut Williamsburg in half. Between 1950 and 1960, the census tracts next to the BQE lost almost 9 per cent of their population. Hasidic Jews who survived the Holocaust found this area attractive and Puerto Ricans who left their island homeland to settle interspersed among the Hasidim. The Hasidim sought to recreate Eastern European *shtetl* life in Williamsburg (see figure 4). Their necessity to live close to the *Rebbe*, the charismatic spiritual leader of the community, raised real-estate prices because the area where the Hasidim settled was relatively circumscribed and competition

Figure 4: Two members of the Hasidic community on Shabbat. Photo by the author.

for housing near the religious leader was intense (Kranzler 1961, 1995; Mintz 1992: 27–42; Rubin 1997).

Williamsburg's built environment changed drastically, with the abandonment of manufacturing in the 1960s and 1970s, leaving wide swaths of abandoned loft and industrial buildings along the East River. The housing situation worsened considerably with rapid and widespread deindustrialisation and the loss of jobs. Landlords who kept their buildings, while collecting rent, withdrew as much capital as they could without investing in their upkeep, leaving buildings in disrepair, even cutting off heat and electricity. Some landlords torched their buildings to collect insurance very much like in the Bronx (Finucane 2007; Mahler 2005). In the 1970s New York City nearly went bankrupt resulting in the withdrawal of municipal services (Tabb 1982). As a result, Latinos tended to live in cold, leaky and dark apartments making life in Williamsburg wretched and a daily struggle. A compelling documentary by Diego Echeverria recorded the darker side of those times (1984).

Gentrification and Its Discontents

Those from the earlier Jewish community, a smaller group of newcomer professionals and more affluent neighbourhood people purchased three- and four-story buildings as real-estate prices dropped. Paradoxically, as the growing Hasidic area was being renovated, driving up real-estate prices, other parts of Williamsburg experienced economic deterioration causing real-estate prices to decline.

In the 1980s unoccupied loft and industrial buildings in the Northside became attractive squats for artists who were being priced out of Manhattan. They settled in the part of Williamsburg the Polish, other East Europeans and Italians called home. For well over a century, Irish, German and Austrian capitalists flourished here with their businesses, homes and churches. Williamsburg was known for its many German breweries like Schaefer, Rheingold and Pils among other breweries that disappeared by the 1970s.

By the 1990s a young 'hip' population moved into North Williamsburg, away from both the Hasidic and the Latino communities, the latter perceived as particularly dangerous due to its reputation for drug dealing, crime and shootings that spilled out into other sections (Anasi 2012). Young people moved in because they could find larger apartments that, when shared, made them more affordable than Manhattan. Hip retail shops, cafes, restaurants and galleries replaced the ethnic community's retail sector, altering street life, supported by the young and hip, which thrived in the neighbourhood. Creative people moved in, with various art forms flourishing, giving rise to the 'hipster' designation, echoing what had happened in SOHO decades earlier (Zukin 1989).

Another attractive feature in the neighbourhood is the L train that connects Williamsburg with Greenwich Village and the 'hip' East Village, and made for an easy commute between Williamsburg and Manhattan. The Williamsburg Bridge empties into the equally hip Lower East Side. Other subway lines similarly tied Williamsburg to Manhattan and became important corridors of gentrification. The re-zoning of the area in 2005 brought about the construction of luxury housing along the waterfront with prices competing with those of Manhattan. This generated the growth of a more stable population of young families and international investors. The rise of real-estate prices and the dramatic escalation in rents caused the displacement of Latinos. Artists, hipsters, young urban professionals and gentrifying retailers displaced the apartment-renting working poor and middle class. As gentrification increased and as the Hasidic community grew, pressure for affordable housing for the Latino population increased because landlords understood that the price of housing they rented to Latino families could be doubled and tripled when renting to the new groups looking for housing. Pressure increased on Latinos, severely impacting on the size and density of their population on the Southside (*Los Sures*).

It was not only the hipsters moving into Williamsburg that threatened the coherence of the Latino community. The Hasidim, a population whose adherence to pro-natal customs expressed in Jewish scriptures and the aspiration to recover its lost Holocaust populations, brought about swift population growth. According to one Jewish leader, the Hasidim are doubling in population size every ten years and with such a rate in growth they are rapidly outstripping their ability to house the new families that are being formed. While the Hasidim decided not to move into Northside Williamsburg, the Southside was open for settlement. Hasidic developers grabbed up as much property as they could, selling or renting out housing on the Northside to non-Hasidic populations; they also sold and rented housing to Hasidim on the Southside and into neighbouring Wallabout and Bedford Stuyvesant, subsidising many of those who make up the dense community of ultra-Orthodox Jews. They were encouraged to do so by the Hasidic leadership to make it possible to keep Hasidim in the neighbourhood and create enough density to keep out anyone else. Anything South and West of Broadway rapidly became Hasidic housing and for the most part pushed the earlier Latino community out. The Transfiguration Roman Catholic Church, one of the Latino community's centres, became an island in the middle of the Hasidic community. The Church, once an important centre for Williamsburg Puerto Ricans as they migrated from the mainland, became central to immigrants from the Dominican Republic who replaced them.

Los Sures

Los Sures was that part of Williamsburg that became home for Puerto Ricans as they arrived from Puerto Rico. A few Puerto Ricans came earlier, in the 1930s settling in the waterfront area of Brooklyn near and in Williamsburg. Puerto Ricans also settled into an area that is now included as part of Bedford-Stuyvesant. This is where Our Lady of Montserrat Roman Catholic Church was created in 1965 to serve the Spanish-speaking population in the area. It was carved out of the ground floor of an apartment building whose upper floors served as classrooms and residences for the clergy. It quickly became a Puerto Rican church. The other Roman Catholic Churches in the area, Transfiguration, Saint Peter and Paul, Most Holy Trinity, Saint Mary's and All Saints, in the past, served white ethnic Catholics, remnant Irish, Germans and Italians; replaced by the new Spanish speakers.

Puerto Ricans are citizens of the United States, a status that differentiates them from other Latinos that came to Williamsburg as immigrants. While they worked in many parts of New York City, many held jobs in the Greenpoint-Williamsburg area, a centre of employment for manufacturing. The Brooklyn Navy Yard alone employed thousands in the 1930s, and during the Second World War, when shipbuilding was at its heights, it employed as many as 70,000 people. The area also was a centre for garment manufacturing, employing thousands of local women. Puerto Ricans arrived to take advantage of the work opportunities available here.

Puerto Ricans arrived in New York City in substantial numbers and found housing in the traditional areas where poor immigrants first settled. Williamsburg was one of those places and had the advantage of having local work sites available for them. Roman Catholic Churches (see figure 5) dot the area and were mostly founded and built during the second half of the nineteenth century. The Germans, Irish, Italian and Eastern European populations, who attended services there, were replaced by the Puerto Ricans. In 1952, Transfiguration Church attracted a young priest named Bryan Karvelis who joined the community and quickly became a charismatic leader among the Puerto Ricans. He learned Spanish and rapidly fitted into the community of devout Latino Catholics by living among them, refusing the greater comfort and convenience of the Rectory. He eventually moved into the Rectory and invited the homeless to live with him, often cooking their meals. Over the nearly fifty years of service, he was instrumental in spiritually organising members of the parish's lay community, encouraging them to believe that they deserved the same dignity and respect as any other American and that they had the right to fight for available resources to improve their lives.

Life in *Los Sures* became more difficult with the withdrawal of government services and private capital in the 1970s. As the manufacturing industry closed up shop, abandoned buildings and lots were left to the vermin that found shelter there. Due to the easy access that the Williamsburg Bridge, BQE and subway commuters had to Williamsburg, the illicit drug trade was able to flourish there. The consequences of the presence of illegal drugs in the community were dramatic, especially among the young. Youths

Figure 5: Transfiguration Roman Catholic Church one of the central institutions supporting the Latino community. Photo by the author.

formed territorial associations, 'gangs', to protect drug trade turf. Gangs were formed in an age grade system among children and youth who grew up together on a particular street. As one community leader still recalls, 'We had teenagers dying every day; it was a killing field!'

Seeing what was happening in his community, Father Karvelis found an alternative to the gangs by organising the youth around spiritual and productive activities. Those who experienced this time remember how each group of youths the priest organised had their own identifying sweaters. They cultivated an identity that otherwise gang membership would give them. This was a time when monolingual Spanish-speaking parents who may also have been illiterate were raising their children in an atmosphere where Puerto Rican identity was perceived by white society and the media as being as bad as African American. Children experienced the limitations of living with racism and xenophobia and of being identified as members of a racial minority. The young were seeking a positive self-identity. They were not quite American nor quite Puerto Rican.

Among a number of institutions that Father Karvelis was instrumental in building, the one that has the most relevance in this chapter was the struggle for housing. Karvelis was aware that if he wanted to keep his flock in the community and improve their lives, housing had to improve. Puerto Ricans were moving out of dilapidated housing and unsafe streets to better housing and neighbourhoods whenever they could. He mobilised the youths to help neighbours fix their apartments. While landlords abandoned buildings or refused to fix buildings in ill-repair, teenaged boys who Father Karvelis organised fixed toilets, repaired walls, restored boilers, fixed roofs and so on.

From such beginnings, those who were most enthusiastic about improving their neighbourhood, refusing to permit housing to be lost that would cause more people to leave, went into the business of repairing homes. In 1972 Southside United HDFC, or *Los Sures*, was organised.[1] This was truly a community-based organisation that involved many members of the community. It was responsible for obtaining contracts from the city and the federal government to refurbish buildings, build new housing and manage housing units. *Los Sures* also helped many Puerto Ricans gain control over their buildings, cooperativise them and teach residents how to manage their buildings. While initially some of the expertise to carry out this work came from VISTA volunteers and non-Puerto Ricans who lived in the community or became allies in this struggle, most of the people employed were neighbours, family members or friends, often those people who attended the churches involved in the creation of this organisation. They remain the heart and soul of the organisation.

Churches United

By the 1990s, more people who were priced out of Manhattan's real-estate market started to move into buildings that were zoned for manufacturing. Artists squatted or rented low-cost spaces in Williamsburg's Northside, as did young urban professionals working in this area. By 2005, city government successfully re-zoned the waterfront area for luxury residential housing (see figure 6). This is when the second phase of housing-based organising and mobilisation began.

Father Jim O'Shea of the Passionist Order of Roman Catholic priests, who lived and worked in North Brooklyn, recognised in 2003 that the people in the community with whom he worked to improve their lives needed affordable housing. The incremental growth of young people moving into the area was having an impact on the area's working-poor and middle-class Latinos. The rate of their displacement was accelerating and affecting the very people with whom he developed close spiritual and friendship relationships. He decided to organise the Latino community by opening discussions from the pulpit of Catholic churches in the area. His wisdom and his organising skills gained through his training as a social worker helped him generate a powerful grass-roots movement against the avarice of luxury housing developers and the power of city government to drive its policies into poorly organised communities, and for participation in a decision-making process to determine who will be allowed to remain in the community and who by necessity will have to leave.

Father Jim sought ways to keep parishioners in affordable housing, which also meant keeping families together or keeping them from living in too small, over-crowded apartments. For the priests in the area who were also responsible for managing churches, it was in their self-interest to maintain their laity, whose numbers were dwindling. Cimino (2011) discusses the relationship between religion in North Brooklyn, gentrification and sustaining of a religious commons. One of the signs of this demographic shift was the closing of parochial schools and Church consolidations and closings. If a movement to stabilise and perhaps even grow the

Figure 6: First phase of the Domino Sugar luxury/affordable housing project. Photo by the author.

Latino population could not be initiated, Catholic churches may have to face their closure due to the loss of population. While a longer discussion on how he was able to mobilise churches is not possible here, the short of it is that he was successful.

His success as a leader in the affordable housing movement was celebrated but short lived. Due to the internal politics of Brooklyn and the decision of the Bishop of Brooklyn and Queens, Nicholas DiMarzio, to ally himself with the then Assemblyman and Democratic Party strongman, Vito Lopez, of North Brooklyn, Father Jim fell out of the Bishop's good graces and was not only asked to step down from the leadership of Churches United, Corp., which he was instrumental in creating, but was told to leave. He resigned from Churches United but refused to leave in order to carry on his work in his community, a matter that remains a thorn in the Bishop's side.

There was some confusion in the community about what had happened with the organisation. The members of the Board of Churches United, Corp., split up between the religious leaders

Figure 7: El Puente High School painted mural. Photo by the author.

who had to obey the Bishop, the lay members who felt they needed to retain their allegiance to the Bishop or the Assemblyman, and the lay members who were outraged by what had happened. Among the latter group, three young men – Rob Solano, Juan Ramos and Esteban Duran – set out to carry on what Father Jim had started. They identified themselves as members of the lay portion of Churches United, Corp., renamed their group, 'Churches United for Fair Housing', and formally incorporated a month after Father Jim resigned in 2009. Having learned their lesson about episcopal oversight, they created a new board made up exclusively of lay members. Soon thereafter I worked out relationships with Rob Solano, who became executive director of Churches United for Fair Housing, to have my students carry out community service under his supervision. By participating in this organisation's grassroots initiatives, college students are folded into the community through a structured reflection process with experiential and practice-based learning opportunities, as in the following case.

Transformative Learning and Participatory Research in Williamsburg

Through Cornell's Urban Semester Program, undergraduates who come to New York City participate in internships they have chosen, together with community service and participation. These experiences, combined with reflective writing and seminars, constitute a holistic approach, grounded in ethnographic research methods. As a result, students begin to integrate what they learn in one field of experience to other fields, as in the case of community service and participatory research at Churches United for Fair Housing (CUFFH) in North Brooklyn and their respective internships.

CUFFH is a 501(c)(3) faith-based, nonpartisan grassroots organisation seeking to create a sustainable living community responsive to housing, open space, education, health and economic development needs in North Brooklyn. It organises community-wide campaigns to ensure the growth of affordable housing. CUFFH has made it possible for low- and moderate-income people of colour to continue to live and raise their families in Williamsburg. As of 2013, CUFFH had an executive director, one full-time and two part-time staff members. A cadre of volunteers can be called on at any moment. Where it lacks budget and personnel, its strength lies in its capacity to mobilise, organise and lead community coalitions through alliances with churches and community organisations. CUFFH also monitors and ensures that city government agencies fulfil commitments made to build affordable housing as part of the 2005 Greenpoint–Williamsburg re-zoning of North Brooklyn properties. CUFFH also works to ensure that tax-abated luxury housing projects provide a minimum of 20 per cent affordability.

In developing a relationship with CUFFH, its executive director, Rob Solano, and I worked out an understanding based on a handshake. The first is that our relationship will be long-term; second, the relationship is based on general reciprocity; third, that students will make significant contributions to CUFFH as members of this community-based organisation; fourth, that CUFFH members would act as 'teachers' of their knowledge, wisdom and experience, with the idea that students would learn; and fifth, that students would make contributions based on what CUFFH needed, not on the research or learning agenda of the course instructor.

Organising a course along these lines contradicts much of how we normally organise university courses. There are a number of difficulties built into such an approach; the most central is that students doubt that an eight-hour contribution each week to CUFFH work has any merit since it seems so little time spent in an activity. Second, they doubt that the work they contribute, sometimes clerical work, such as data input, is significant to the workings of the organisation; and third, they feel that they are not learning much, if anything, and they do not necessarily 'feel good' about making such contributions.

Central to the community service and participation part of the curriculum and pedagogy is transformative learning (Mezirow et al. 2009). This is a critical thinking approach to teaching, with the expectation that experience-based learning promotes change. By participating in environments beyond their normal experiences, students come to question and assess the veracity and soundness of their deeply held beliefs and worldviews, particularly about poverty, race and ethnicity, and neighbourhoods of colour. The fundamental elements inherent in this approach to learning are individual experiences, critical reflection, dialogue, understanding (sociocultural, historical and political economic) context, and the nature and qualities of practice.

The majority of students, from relatively homogenous and affluent communities and households, experience a degree of culture shock as they take subways into North Brooklyn and involve themselves with CUFFH, located in a neighbourhood defined as low-income and populated by Latinos and African Americans. They discuss this most often as 'living outside of my comfort zone'. However, as students participate in CUFFH and get to know the neighbourhood and interact with people as they struggle to gain access to affordable housing, they begin to understand a condition of 'living in the world' very differently from what they have experienced in their lives.

For transformative learning to succeed, students need a safe environment in which open and honest reflection and dialogue may take place. This requires the formation of trust between instructor and students and building trust among participating students for peer learning to take place. This non-normative approach to teaching and learning usually takes six weeks of relationship building to take place. Students are not accustomed to highly individualised and non-competitive and in-context approaches to learning and must undergo an unlearning of attitudes and behaviours. The experiential learning approach also has an inherent difficulty because students feel more confident and comfortable about reflecting on experiences 'out there', rather than how their experiences change how they think or the meaning they draw from them through self-reflection.

Students participate with CUFFH and in the process the goals we set for them are to incorporate a sense of responsibility for CUFFH and its mission, to develop an authentic sense of membership in and behave as participants of a community of practice (Wenger 1998), and critically deepen their understanding of service. To accomplish this, Rob takes on the role of 'instructor', bringing with him his own personal history, values, and wisdom that he comfortably communicates to students.

One aspect that he brings to the students is the idea of accountability in leadership development. Rob acts as a role model for this sense of accountability and leadership. The nature of the relationship he builds with them is referred to as 'reciprocal accountability' best articulated by DuFour et al. (2006: 1): 'Leaders who call upon others to engage in new work, achieve new standards, and accomplish new goals have a responsibility to develop the capacity of those they lead to be successful in meeting these challenges'.

Rob assigns tasks to students that allow them to discover how to accomplish them. One student was assigned the task of organising a youth group to play basketball while managing three teenaged volunteers. Students are encouraged to ask Rob questions. However, he encourages them to come to him with solution scenarios that were either tried or are being thought of as possibilities. In this process, students develop a firm grasp of CUFFH's mission by participating and by taking on CUFFH responsibilities. They begin to identify with the organisation. By the end of the programme, they leave without the feeling of outsiders coming to help, an act of charity, but as members of the organisation making their contribution to improving people's lives. This is a framework that Lave and Wenge identified as 'Legitimate Peripheral Participation' (1991). Service in this sense is not a 'feel good' charity but serving in action because 'it is the right thing to do', a moral act and a behaviour associated with membership in the organisation with which they identify.

Instead of out-of-context learning, the Urban Semester Program places students in contexts of lived experience, in action and as members of a community of practice, through which ' [m]eaning arises out of a process of negotiation that combines both participation and reification' (Wenger 1998: 135). Much of CUFFH work involves students preparing and managing workshops that take place in churches, gathering data on intake forms, digitising the data, analysing these and presenting their findings to the community. In this sense, the students are participating in and identifying with the social movement for affordable housing. Participation is not merely carrying out tasks but taking responsibility for carrying out actions and being accountable for them in relationship to the organisation's mission. Meaning occurs through acts of reflection, either by writing journals or through orally recounting experiences in weekly seminars and informal interactions.

Students, whose life experiences are typically suburban, learn that in one of the most modern, urbanised and developed cities in the world, people in North Brooklyn are organising to protect and manage a resource they cherish: their sense of community, a 'cultural commons' (Nonini 2007). Roman Catholic Church leaders up until recently played a significant role in leading the Latino movement in Williamsburg as well as community-based organisations to defend the commons established by Puerto Ricans and later Dominicans in the post-Second World War period. Students are encouraged to contribute to CUFFH's struggle to reproduce a Latino cultural commons by organizing, advocating for and obtaining affordable housing. Together, they are devising long-term strategies to sustain their community institutions, even as powerful forces are ready to displace them.

Acknowledgements

My involvement in North Brooklyn started with my friendship with John Mulhern and Father Jim O'Shea, in trying to learn about the complexities of politics at the community level and its relationship to city government and to be able to teach this knowledge to my students during site visits in the community. I continue to work with Father Jim as a founding board member of the Vernon Avenue Program, Inc. (VAP), a new organisation he created to support the youth in the community. This effort spun off a subsidiary, Reconnect, an organisation dedicated to integrate 'disconnected' youth into society by involving them in entrepreneurial activities. I wish to recognise and thank a number of other individuals who have helped me understand North Brooklyn: Rob Solano, Juan Ramos, Marty Needelmann and Marianne Cocchini. I thank Carl Maida for his encouragement, insights and editing. Any errors are my own.

SAM BECK is Senior Lecturer at Cornell University where he directs the Urban Semester Program. He has dedicated himself in the last twenty years to an activist role as an anthropologist carrying out research in North Brooklyn. As such he is an active Executive Board member in local community-based organisations that insist on being recognised with dignity and respect, and struggle for community sustainability. He is a member of the Vernon Avenue Project and its spinoff Reconnect Industries, Churches United for Fair Housing, The Grand Street Boys, and Brooklyn Legal Services A. He has received multiple awards for his community service work and as a teacher.

Notes

1. *Los Sures* refers to the area of Williamsburg where the Latino community forged its identity, not to be confused with the Los Sures HDFC.

References

Anasi, R. (2012), *The Last Bohemia* (New York: Farrar, Straus and Giroux).
Basch, L. G., L. W. Saunders, J. W. Sharff and J. Peacock (eds.) (1999), *Transforming Academia: Challenges and Opportunities for an Engaged Anthropology* (Arlington, VA: American Ethnological Society Monograph Series, Number 8).
Butin, D. W. (2010), *Service-learning in Theory and Practice: The Future of Community Engagement in Higher Education* (New York: Palgrave Macmillan).
Caro, R. A. (1974), *The Power Broker: Robert Moses and the Fall of New York* (NY: Knopf).
Cimino, R. (2011), 'Neighborhoods, Niches, and Networks: The Religious Ecology of Gentrification', *City and Community* 10, no. 2: 157–81.
Coy, M. W. (1989), *Apprenticeship: From Theory to Method and Back Again* (Albany: State University of New York Press).
Cranton, P. (2006), *Understanding and Promoting Transformative Learning: A Guide for Educators of Adults* (2nd ed.) (San Francisco: Jossey-Bass).
Dewey, J. (1916), *Democracy and Education: An Introduction to the Philosophy of Education* (New York: Macmillan), http://en.wikisource.org/wiki/Democracy_and_Education (accessed on March 20, 2016).

DuFour, R., R. Dufour, R. Eaker and T. Many (2006), *Learning by Doing: A Handbook for Professional Learning Communities at Work* (Bloomington, IN: Solution Tree Press).

Echeverria, D. (1984), *Los Sures* (film about Williamsburg, Brooklyn Puerto Ricans and Dominicans).

Finucane, J. (2007), *When the Bronx Burned* (Lincoln, NE: iUniverse).

Florida, R. (2002), *The Rise of the Creative Class... And How It's Transforming Work, Leisure, Community, & Everyday Life* (New York: Basic Books).

Freire, P. (1970), *The Pedagogy of the Oppressed* (New York: Continuum Press).

Freire, P. (1973), *Education for Critical Consciousness* (New York: Continuum Press).

Freire, P. (1996), *Pedagogy of Hope* (New York: Continuum Press).

Gadotti, M. (1996), *Pedagogy of Praxis: A Dialectical Philosophy of Education* (Albany: State University of New York Press).

Goldstein, P. A., C. Storey-Johnson and S. Beck (2014), 'Facilitating the Initiation of the Physician's Professional Identity: Cornell's Urban Semester Program', *Perspectives in Medical Education* 3: 492–500.

Kranzler, G. (1961), *Williamsburg: A Jewish Community in Transition* (New York: Feldheim Books).

Kranzler, G. (1995), *Hasidic Williamsburg: A Contemporary American Hasidic Community* (Northvale, NJ: Jason Aronson, Inc.).

Lave, J. and E. Wenger (1991), *Situated Learning: Legitimate Peripheral Participation* (Cambridge: Cambridge University Press).

Mahler, J. (2005), *Ladies and Gentlemen, the Bronx Is Burning* (New York: Farrar, Strauss and Giroux).

McKenna, B. (2013), 'New Techno-peasants of the Latifundia: The Predatory Pedagogy of On-line Education', *Counterpunch*, 3 June, http://www.counterpunch.org/2013/06/03/the-pedatory-pedagogy-of-on-line-education/ (accessed on March 20, 2016).

McLaren, P. L. (1995), *Critical Pedagogy and Predatory Culture: Oppositional Politics in a Postmodern Era* (New York: Routledge).

McLaren, P. L. (1996), 'Beyond Humanistic Education: A Discussion with Moacir Gadotti', in *Pedagogy of Practice: A Dialectical Philosophy of Education*, (ed.) M. Gadotti (Albany: State University of New York Press), ix–xvii.

Mezirow, J. (1991), *Transformative Dimensions in Adult Learning* (San Francisco: Jossey-Bass).

Mezirow, J., E. W. Taylor and Associates (eds.) (2009), *Transformative Learning in Practice; Insights from Community, Workplace, and Higher Education* (San Francisco: Jossey-Bass).

Moses, P. (2005), '"Discovering" Williamsburg', *The Village Voice,* 19 April.

Nonini, D. M. (2007), *The Global Idea of 'The Commons'* (Brooklyn, NY: Berghahn Books).

Rubin, I. (1997), *Satmar: Two Generations of an Urban Island,* 2nd edition (NY: Peter Lang).

Schön, D. A. (1983), *The Reflective Practitioner: How Professionals Think in Action* (NY: Basic Books).

Schön, D. A. (1990), *Educating the Reflective Practitioner: Toward a New Design for Teaching and Learning in the Professions* (San Francisco: Jossey-Bass).

Sennett, R. (2008), *The Craftsman* (New Haven: Yale University Press).

Strathern, M. (ed.) (2000), *Audit Cultures: Anthropological Studies in Accountability, Ethics and the Academy* (London: Routledge).

Tabb, W. K. (1982), *The Long Default: New York City and the Urban Fiscal Crisis* (New York: Monthly Review Press).

Wenger, E. (1998), *Communities of Practice: Learning, Meaning, and Identity* (Cambridge: Cambridge University Press).

Zukin, S. (1989), *Loft Living: Culture and Capital in Urban Change* (Rutgers, NJ: Rutgers University Press).

Part 3

Organizing for Sustainability

Knowing Sustainability
Building Communities of Practice in Urban Ecology at High Tech High

Carl A. Maida

This chapter describes a community of practice comprised of students and adult mentors, with the goal of *knowing* sustainability through socially defined competence and habits of mind developed in carrying out urban ecology projects that integrate a holistic perspective of Earth's natural and human systems. To this end, project-based learning, involving students as collaborators in the creation of curricular goals and outcomes, takes place at High Tech High, San Diego, California, where a project uses San Diego Bay as an outdoor laboratory to understand regional urban ecology.

Over a decade, High Tech High's San Diego Bay Study has introduced high-school juniors to original research in ecological assessment, engaged writing and reflection on the Bay and its estuaries. The school's proximity to the Bay affords easy contact with several wetland and bay habitats. Students study the complexity and fragility of the urban-bay ecosystems to gain an understanding of the interconnections between human activities, notably fishing, boating and military exercises, and local marine life. Teachers and students design their learning experiences and develop strong local partnerships with academic, industrial and non-profit sector stakeholders in a multi-year community-based conservation programme on behalf of the Bay, thereby expanding the community of practice. Student researchers use photography, interviewing, mapping, drawing and journaling, together with

ecological surveys and DNA barcoding for identification of species, including invasive species, to develop an understanding of
their surroundings and self-awareness of their place within them.
Through learning in the field and the classroom, students begin to
make connections about the complexity of the local environment,
and the need to care for it.

Swords to Ploughshares

In the aftermath of the Cold War, national elites abandoned a mili-
tarised domestic economy in the various post-war defence production areas, and moved towards 'swords to ploughshares' regional
economies, embracing high technology and biotechnology industries. The federal government enacted a Base Realignment and
Closure (BRAC) process that shutdown operations at hundreds of
military installations, providing funds to finance environmental
restoration and mitigation activities, while altering the economies
of surrounding communities. Change within advanced industrial
manufacturing regions, the closing of the auto, rubber and steel
plants, followed by the reduction of jobs in the aerospace sector,
brought about a new set of capitalist economic relations, together
with deleterious environmental conditions, as many industrial
plants left communities facing toxins from their heavy metals seep-
ing deep into the soil and the aquifer. Workers displaced by large
producers were re-employed in medium-sized manufacturing operations, trucking and warehousing. Young women with at least
high school and some post-secondary training found screen-based
office work; young men followed their fathers and uncles into
the mid-sized manufacturing operations and trucking fields, and
the various semi-skilled trades. New immigrants found work in
auto dismantling; granite and marble shops; and the landscaping,
home building and renovating areas, including painting, roofing,
flooring and stone masonry. The shift towards computer-assisted
office work, light manufacturing, building trades and regional
transportation, each dependent on non-renewable resources, had
divergent impacts on the natural and built environments after
those of the heavy industries that they replaced.

Twenty-first century schooling gradually began to adopt project-based learning pedagogies, in part because of the skill demands of knowledge work in firms that put down roots in abandoned industrial production regions, often in suburban locations. Those wishing to compete as knowledge workers require a degree in engineering or bioscience at the professional level, or a mix of technology, software application and social skills for technoservice occupations. The new skill sets are now taught in public charter schools, magnet schools and public school academies with competitive entrance requirements. Urban areas caught up in neo-liberal solutions are experiencing significant institutional changes, including rearranged class relations, retooled educational systems for social reproduction, and a system of local-level politics to adapt to the knowledge economy. Underlying the new economy and its transformative dynamics are the global financial and climate crises placing the life chances of youth at stake. Social class disparities are rife in regions opting for knowledge work to replace older technologies, and there remain white flight and suburbanisation movements, as more affluent families continue a half-century trend of abandoning the cities in search of educational opportunities that will make their children competitive. As the knowledge economy moves forward, with computerised methods that make skilled and semi-skilled work more efficient, the challenge of sustainability remains.

This post-Cold War transformation of Liberty Station, the former Naval Training Center in San Diego, as a new neighbourhood in Point Loma (at the marine–urban interface) within two hundred meters of San Diego Bay, is instructive in this regard. The place was converted from a single-use military area to a mixed-use area, with both a cultural and an educational district, including schools developed within a larger regional economy of high technology and biotechnology (Comer-Schultz 2011). Surrounded by green landscaping, Liberty Station is now an urban village with service, retail and commercial businesses, parks, residential units, hotel sites, marine science laboratories and an urban waterfront. A hilly peninsula bordered on the west and south by the Pacific Ocean, Point Loma is a seaside community of 38,000 within the city of San Diego. The peninsula is comparable to an island because of the aquatic borders and the urban landscape to the north. The southern one-third of the peninsula is entirely federal land, with residential uses comprising about 90 per cent of non-federal land. The soundscape includes military and commercial aircraft, Coast Guard and Navy activity, vehicular traffic and the operation of a nearby water-treatment plant. San Diego Bay is a major port of entry, especially for ships traveling north from Mexico. The Navy operates several bases with direct access to the Bay including Naval Base Coronado, Naval Base San Diego and Naval Base Point Loma with associated submarine bases. The U.S. Coast Guard also actively uses the bay for daily operations and manoeuvres. Water quality is affected by the industries around the bay, and by commercial, governmental, private, national and international ships and boats. The City of San Diego operates a nearby Wastewater Treatment Plant that treats 180 million gallons per day of sewage and deposits the treated effluent four miles offshore at a depth of four hundred feet. Meanwhile, the area contains multiple species of wildlife, both in the federal lands at the southern end of the peninsula, managed in part as an ecological reserve, and in the developed suburban areas. More than three hundred species of birds have been observed in Point Loma, which lies on the Pacific Flyway migration route.

From the 1940s, San Diego was a key shipbuilding and aircraft assembly region dominated by the defence industry, with General Dynamics, General Atomics, Rohr and National Steel and Shipbuilding bound to massive federal government contracts (Lotchin 1992). The San Diego Bay is home to one of California's five major ports and is the base for the U.S. Navy Pacific Fleet. The Naval Electronics Laboratory moved into Point Loma after the war, and expanded its radio communications and sonar work to include basic research on electromagnetic energy and sound in the ocean. In 1956, the Pentagon awarded Convair (later, a division of General Dynamics) the contract to build the Air Force's first intercontinental ballistic missiles; with 32,000 employees in the mid-1950s, Convair was San Diego's largest employer. The aerospace and defence industry grew throughout the post-war decades, together with the regional population, with the County growing from 556,000 in 1950 to 2,498,000 in 1990. However, in the mid-1990s, during the wave of post-Cold War consolidation, General Dynamics shut down its Kearny Mesa plant, together with the 27-acre Missile Park that provided recreational activities for employees and their families, and sixty thousand workers lost their jobs within 18 months of the closure.

The signal event – a plant closing of this magnitude – had a profound effect on the region's business culture, so closely tied to defence contracting and the broader military economy; as a result of decades of federal largesse, San Diego had virtually no access to venture capital funding or equity banking to support science-based innovation or entrepreneurship. Two decades after the end of the Cold War, San Diego reinvented itself as a high-technology hub, with both academic research and industrial production in telecommunications and biotechnology. The region's 1,500 high-technology companies, together with the University of California, San Diego, Scripps Institution of Oceanography, Sanford-Burnham Medical Research Institute and Salk Institute for Biological Studies, on the Torrey Pines Mesa, form a network of regional science and technology-based innovation clusters that fuels a knowledge economy focused on commercial applications of dynamic fields, such as genome sequencing, climate and oceanography and information technology (Zucker et al. 1998). Considerable collaborations between San Diego's business and research communities formed over these decades fostered a web of relationships and co-investments that facilitated access to capital (Sable 2007). Science and engineering professionals and technoservice workers moved into the North County suburbs, where new industries were transforming a military-, tourist- and real-estate-based economy into a global high-technology and biotechnology production region.

Students of Consequence

Schooling began to change as a consequence of the skill demands of knowledge work in firms that put down roots in post-Cold War San Diego. Beginning in 1998, the San Diego Unified School District introduced a seven-year systemic reform effort to improve student's literacy skills. The district's *Blueprint for Student Success*, while focusing initially on implementing new programmes in literacy and mathematics, initiated a broader instructional reform effort that brought about dramatic changes in school-based leadership and teacher professional development to improve student outcomes (Betts 2009). With the goal of social justice and equity in mind, the district-led reform policies were based on the assumption that instructional practice and student achievement growth were linked. Although some opposed the whole-district content-driven reforms, the San Diego Chamber of Commerce, the Chamber's Business Roundtable for Education, the San Diego *Times-Union*, together with local philanthropies and educational researchers, endorsed the *Blueprint*. The Business Roundtable also spearheaded the San Diego Charter School Consortium to foster the introduction of public charter schools to the area, such as High Tech High School in Point Loma that was designed with the new knowledge economy in mind (Kerchner 2012). According to Rob Riordan (personal communication), a co-founder of High Tech High:

> The Business Roundtable discussions led to starting a charter school, but also for a local, pragmatic reason: at the time, there was a cap on work visas for technicians from abroad, and there was a dearth of local talent for the emerging high tech industry. While there was recognition of the need for change in local business and school administrative circles, the top-down reforms generated a great deal of resistance on the ground. Moreover, the reforms prioritised basic skills and standardisation, such as the literacy initiative, over essential skills, such as collaboration and communication, and teacher autonomy. The charter avenue allowed High Tech High to sidestep dysfunctional labour-management dynamics and focus on collaborative design and execution of authentic work.

High Tech High opened in September 2000 in a newly renovated 38,500 square foot facility, formerly a U.S. Navy technical training centre, at Liberty Station, with substantial support from Gary Jacobs, at the time a software engineer and senior education specialist of Qualcomm, Inc., a semiconductor and telecommunications equipment company in San Diego. According to Larry Rosenstock (personal communication), a co-founder of High Tech High:

> Without question, High Tech High would not exist without Gary Jacobs. Gary was deeply engaged for years in an initiative that began with his insight to make the case that San Diego very much needed a new kind of school. He organised meetings with several key civic leaders who met and planned for years. He and his wife, Jerri-Ann, gave the first critical and substantial financial support to the first High Tech High (which is named after them). But it does not stop there. Gary Jacobs has chaired the board that overseers the thirteen High Tech High schools. He is also on the board of the High Tech High Graduate School of Education. Gary Jacobs has provided steady, and visionary leadership to both organisations. In short, there would be no High Tech High were it not for Gary Jacobs.

Since the original school's founding, there are six additional schools at the same location, creating a 'village' of three high schools, two middle schools and two elementary schools. One of 48 high schools in the San Diego Unified School District, High Tech High has 589 students, with a 67 per cent minority enrolment; 31 per cent of the students are economically disadvantaged. The school's 23 seminar rooms, seven labs, and a large high-ceilinged open area, known as the 'Great Room', were designed to support educational pro-gramme elements, including team teaching, integrated curriculum, project-based learning, community-based internships, frequent student presentations, and exhibitions (Pearlman 2002). The build-ing's flexibility allows students to work individually and in large and small groups. Vast expanses of glass contribute to the sense of transparency; classrooms and common spaces are bathed in natural light to create a sense of 'visible learning'. Wall and ceiling spaces are dedicated to exhibiting student projects, reinforcing the students' 'ownership' of the milieu. The building's design features inform High Tech High's culture of learning based upon a set of educational design principles, namely equity, personalisation, au-thentic work and collaborative design (Rosenstock 2017).

At High Tech High, students work together in projects that integrate science, mathematics, the arts and humanities (Behrend et al. 2014). Integration is frequently accomplished through the use of important or essential questions. Throughout, students are encouraged to develop *habits of mind*, including evidence, perspective, connection, supposition, relevance or significance; and then to reflect critically on their learning and personal growth through this lens. As a form of active inquiry, the five habits of mind, or 'thinking dispositions', originally put forward by Ted Sizer (1996), can also be framed as questions for both learning and assessment (Duckor and Perlstein 2014: 7):

How do you know what you know? (Evidence)

From whose point of view is this being presented? (Perspective)

How is this event or work connected to others? What causes what? (Connection)

What if things were different? (Supposition)

Who cares? Why is this important? (Relevance)

Each student has a faculty advisor who provides ongoing support and helps the student to develop a customised learning plan. Students connect to the world beyond school through field studies, community service, junior and senior-year internships, and consultation with outside experts; they exhibit that work in professional venues. Assessment is performance-based, with all students developing projects, solving problems and presenting findings to community panels. High Tech High students are required to complete a substantial senior project and a personal digital portfolio to archive and share their learning; and make annual presentations of learning in lieu of exams (Stephen and Goldberg 2013).

High Tech High teachers employ a variety of approaches to accommodate diverse learners, acting as programme and curriculum designers (Caillier and Riordan 2009). They work in interdisciplinary teams to design the courses they teach and teachers have ample planning time to devise integrated projects, common rubrics for assessment and common rituals, such as a presentation of learning, by which all students demonstrate their learning and progress towards graduation. High Tech High's curriculum is a hybrid of teachers' expert knowledge and what is referred to as *indigenous invention* (Heckman and Montera 2009), namely, a school culture that is created through local knowledge and experience, and where the learning environment and styles of inquiry are place-focused and rooted in community action. Based upon new conceptions of learning, cognition and development, curriculum and standards for school and enrichment programmes are co-created by teachers and other local individuals with a stake in children's learning. Project-based learning, especially in high school, will often involve the students as collaborators in the creation of curricular goals and outcomes, derived from their *lived experience* (Riordan and Rosenstock 2013).

High Tech High students engaged in a long-term project that used San Diego Bay as an outdoor laboratory to understand regional urban ecology, as the school is located in the ongoing redevelopment of Liberty Station. The school's proximity to the bay affords easy contact with several wetland and armoured bay habitats. Ninety per cent of the bay's historic wetlands have been filled in, drained or diked. Seventy-four per cent of the shoreline has been armoured, providing habitat for open-coast hard substrate species in a traditionally soft-substrate estuary. As the city's redevelopment efforts continue to progress, the students' study of the complexity and fragility of urban-bay ecosystems contribute to the city's ongoing discussion and decisions. Teachers and high-school juniors developed strong local partnerships with academic, industrial and non-profit sector stakeholders in a continuing community-based conservation programme on behalf of the bay. Using this setting as a field laboratory, students began to understand the interconnection between human activities, such as fishing, boating and military exercises, and local marine life, and then provided decision-makers with a set of perspectives, recommendations and original research findings from their field studies.

The study's faculty designer, Jay Vavra, grew up in San Diego and returned home after a range of experiences in biology abroad and throughout California. He graduated from Stanford University and has a Ph.D. in Marine Biology from the University of Southern California. Vavra also worked as a biologist in the fields of biotechnology and zooarchaeology, and as an environmental consultant. He led High Tech High students on two expeditions to Tanzania to carry out projects on global conservation, specifically the African bushmeat trade, using DNA barcoding techniques to help local wildlife-protection officials fight poaching. Vavra also worked in Mozambique on biodiversity assessment with Edward O. Wilson, and contributed to Wilson's digital biology textbook, *E.O. Wilson's Life on Earth* (Ryan, McGill and Wilson 2014). In co-designing the study, the first cohort of high-school juniors placed all of the components necessary to understand the bay on the floor, organised them with the class and then linked them with thread. The activity involved each of the students, who were required to communicate with one another what they knew about the bay from various perspectives. From this original schematic, photographed from above and archived digitally so that subsequent cohorts could carry out a similar design process, students set out to understand the bay as a mix of both human construction and nature's slow reclamation of the marine ecosystem.

In its first eight years, *High Tech High San Diego Bay Study* (Vavra 2009) introduced 450 high-school juniors to original research in ecological assessment and engagement in writing and reflection regarding their urban ecology. The first study focused on describing the wildlife and reflecting on nature at the nearby *Boat Channel*, and then expanded to include detailed field studies of the entire San Diego Bay that would result in a series of published field guides. Inquiry-based research projects served to integrate a holistic perspective of Earth's natural and human systems, specifically the complexity and fragility of the urban-bay ecosystems to understand the interconnections between human activities and local marine life better. Student researchers use photography, interviewing, mapping, drawing and journaling, together with ecological surveys of species biodiversity and DNA barcoding for identification species, including invasive species, to develop an understanding of their surroundings and self-awareness of their place within them. Through learning in the field and in the biology classroom, students begin to acquire, according to Vavra (personal communication), 'the ability to make fundamental connections, an awareness of complexity, and the necessary compassion to understand and care for the environment'.

In their humanities classes, students produced illuminated journals, reviewed and produced nature photography, poetry and reflective writing to investigate historical perspectives on the environmental crisis, and debated issues related to stewardship and conservation; their readings included Thoreau's *Walden* and John Steinbeck's *The Log from the Sea of Cortez*. As they reflected on their interaction with the bay, Vavra and Tom Fehrenbacher, their humanities teacher and co-designer of the project, posed the following questions to the students: 'What is our place in nature? Is civilization inherently harmful to nature? Can we repair our broken relationship with our environment? Can we accept ourselves as part of nature?' Considering that these are overarching questions about humanity's place in nature, Fehrenbacher (2015) understood that the humanities were essential in cultivating students' insights concerning these larger issues, and in helping to answer questions raised in their field studies and reflective journals. In his words:

> In working with Jay, I found out that addressing climate change requires contributions not only from those who study nature, but also from those who study humanity. After all, WE are the species causing it. In humanities, with climate change a settled fact, our Socratic Seminars focused more and more upon the nature of humanity itself. We asked an essential question about climate change: 'How can we, as a species, while knowing this is happening, leave it largely unaddressed?' If we had not done so, I could not have looked Jay in the eye. Had humanities students not engaged in relevant social study, neither Jay nor I would have found their work authentic. And, by taking up social analysis, students found that our history, our literature, and the best in our culture can tell us a great deal about life, about living simply, and about sustainability.

From their studies and reflections, students produced a series of books on specific topics about the San Diego Bay, including the historical ecology and conservation practices; each volume integrates cartography, humanities, biology and art. Four books were produced that focused on the issues that reflect San Diego's most pressing environmental priorities including those that students identified as most meaningful to their generation. These books – *Two Sides of the Boat Channel: A Field Guide* (2005), *Perspectives of*

San Diego Bay: A Field Guide (2006), *San Diego Bay: A Story of Exploitation and Restoration* (2007) and *San Diego Bay: A Call for Conservation* (2008), were praised by local residents, marine scientists, conservation advocates and policymakers alike. A fifth volume, *Biomimicry: Respecting Nature Through Design* (2014) discusses sustainability and provides case studies of biomimetic design as a way to craft solutions to environmental problems. The students used mathematics to test their biomimetic designs for sustainability and reflect upon the implications of these designs for such topics as 'natural capitalism', 'tenets of sustainability' and 'the biological basis of morality'. The books, available through major online booksellers, contain forewords by scientist-advocates Jane Goodall and E. O. Wilson, and endorsements by the National Audubon Society, Sierra Club, Wildlife Conservation Society and Blue Ocean Institute, as well as local stakeholders, or 'Stewards of the Bay', who have taken up the cause of San Diego Bay conservation and restoration.

Students also used the bay as a site for naturalist and scientific observation, focusing on benthic marine invertebrates. Student teams collected and analysed different taxonomic groups and tried to identify all species within their assigned taxa. They also collected samples for DNA barcoding work done in their lab. DNA barcode sequences were uploaded to GenBank and Bold, both *Encyclopedia of Life* (Blaustein 2009; Wilson 2003) content partners. The students also created documentaries, combining video footage of interviewees and their original research with multimedia and graphic arts skills acquired in art classes. This community of practice among students and their adult mentors holds the promise of 'knowing' sustainability based upon socially defined competence and habits of mind grounded in a sense of accomplishment and responsibility. Integrating the arts, humanities and social sciences with active engagement in documenting and restoring an urban ecosystem can help avert the disenchantment and sense of helplessness that frequently accompanies studies of environmental degradation and the adverse effects of climate change. Fehrenbacher (2015) sums up the sense of knowing that comes from adults and students working within a community of practice that is open-ended with respect to both the discovery process and the integration of the 'consequences' of interdisciplinary experiential learning:

> With our students we looked for connections, sought relevance and asked questions no matter where they led. In the field guide's uncharted territory, our students found a place to raise their own questions and express their own ideas. We learned a lot from them. What started as a simple look at the local Boat Channel turned into a study of the Bay's ecological history, which then became a consideration of the environment itself. In some sense, there was nothing planned about it.

Engaging students in helping to create these outcomes through a mentored process that provides enhanced foundational scientific knowledge, critical skills for success in group settings and inspirational community-based experiential activities, significantly enriched what youth learned through traditional curricula. Etienne Wenger (2010: 180) sees communities of practice as enacted through a 'dual process of meaning making', namely through personal participation in social activities and the production of physical and conceptual artefacts that reify experiences. Rob Riordan (personal communication) understands this dual process as enacted in the San Diego Bay Study:

> This dual process, facilitated by Vavra and Fehrenbacher, is precisely what was going on in the San Diego Bay project, where the social relations of production took the form of multiple drafting and peer critique as students engaged in observation, documentation, analysis, and the collaborative creation of the artefacts (photos, essays, calendars, guides) by which they articulated and shared their findings. In other words, there was an instructional technology that supported the intertwining of the relational and creative processes, as Vavra and Fehrenbacher, invoking larger purposes, moved toward the two overarching student outcomes to which High Tech High aspires: self-directed learning, and relational agency (the ability to navigate systems and relationships). The immediate pedagogical roots of that technology, for Fehrenbacher, reside in the writing process re-

forms that emerged in the 1960s; the broader older professional roots (for High Tech High) may be seen in the architect's studio as prototype.

The San Diego Bay Study case demonstrates varieties of informal learning outside of school that take place in face-to-face venues, which offer mentoring, apprenticeship and participation in projects as fledgling artists, engineers, planners, writers, teachers and scientists. Youth in communities of practice developed over a decade on behalf of San Diego Bay conservation efforts were eager to explore out-of-classroom learning activities that introduced urban environmental issues, such as water quality and wetlands restoration, through student collaboration with peers and mentors on applied projects. This approach especially appeals to adolescents, who are more conscious of their community, by using it as an environment to demonstrate scientific principles.

Another Way of Learning

Structural transformations took place in San Diego since the end of the Cold War that, although regional in scope, clearly impact the local and global commons, as each is key to the Pacific Rim economy. New forms of enclosure and displacement came with rapid population changes and urbanisation pressures, affecting housing and services. Planning regimes, such as the *New Urbanism* design movement in the affluent suburbs of Point Loma, accommodated according to these pressures. Geographic mobility, together with the location of new industries, altered local ecosystems, notably plant and animal species, including marine fisheries in the San Diego Bay. In the socioeconomic sphere, long-held urban institutional arrangements gave way to new configurations of work, family and community life, with increased costs in housing, transportation, fuel and communication technologies. The region experienced organised forms of resistance to the consequences of these social, economic and ecological transitions, ranging from grassroots civic engagement to ballot measures and land trusts.

The educational arena changed in the San Diego area, as schooling regimes adapted to the needs of the new local industries, although federally funded systemic change initiatives, such as 'No Child Left Behind' and 'Race to the Top', established benchmarks and timelines for accountability, which influenced school district decision-making. As a corrective to these schooling regimes, project-based learning that is experiential, hands-on and student-directed challenges youth by acknowledging their roles as participants engaged in producing knowledge (Maida 2011). Through an amalgam of knowledge, skills, teamwork and communication, inquiry-based learning helps to develop habits of mind associated with personal and occupational success in the global economy

As a critical pedagogy, project-based learning is an educational praxis that bridges 'action and reflection' in the creation of challenging conditions for youth within and outside the classroom (Monchinski 2009: 1). Moreover, in bringing together students, teachers, parents, administrators and the wider community to engage with and through project-based learning activities – thereby creating a 'crossroads' phenomenon – the ensuing experiences and relationships among these diverse stakeholders can breach any number of boundaries and result in challenges to traditional schooling. The challenges typically encountered when this form of learning works in practice fit Paulo Friere's (1985: 155) image of people 'as beings of praxis, [who] in accepting our concrete situation as a challenging condition […] are able to change its meaning by our action'. Reflective activities associated with project-based learning, which take into account any number of occupational techniques and world images, move students towards greater understanding of themselves and their world. This is not unlike Ira Shor's (1999: 1) view of 'critical literacy' as a praxis that 'connects the political and the personal, the public and the private, the global and the local, the economic and the pedagogical, for rethinking our lives'. As 'public pedagogies – spaces, sites, and languages of education and learning that exist outside the walls of the institution of schools' (Sandlin et al. 2010: 1), project-based learning activities also take place beyond the school – in shops, offices, labs and in wetlands, mountains and forests; all can serve as 'living laboratories'. Whether in the school or beyond, according to Henry Giroux (2010: 495), students who engage in project-based learning encounter a public sphere where they may 'connect their experiences to specific problems that emanate from the material contexts of everyday life'. As a result, according to Peter McLaren (2010: 650–651), youth become protagonists engaged in 'the struggle for knowledge, a place where consciousness can discover itself, a place where knowledge gives way to creative purposiveness'. However, to create the conditions where an epistemic paradigm shift – towards project-based learning – could occur within education, educational progressives a century ago would need to look beyond their classrooms in order to explore the "new model" organisations, especially in the local governmental, labour and non-profit service sectors that were coming into being in their communities.

For youth attempting to make a place for themselves in the recent configuration of capitalist economic arrangements, new forms of education, experiential learning, project-based learning and work practice activities, such as apprenticeships, potentially increase their life chances, as these are forms of deeper learning (Farrington 2013) that may serve as a corrective to the master narrative of advanced capitalism as it plays out in schooling regimes. Increasingly, educators working in large urban communities are adopting this style of organising learning work, as a non-mechanistic approach, beyond schooling. Under neo-liberalist regimes, schooling has become more mechanistic, driven by standardised tests, ratings and consumer satisfaction scores, and on teacher evaluations and administrative routines. There are still limited opportunities for youth to actually engage in deeper learning activities with mentors, which are consciously designed as communities of practice for skill acquisition. These forms of learning are typically found in certain experientially based programmes, such as apprenticeships, in the more progressive high schools, or in experimental co-curricular activities designed by universities and other non-profit organisations. Robert Halpern (2009) advocates for high-school apprenticeship as the style of learning that may provide the best chances for the youth. Halpern's approach requires buy-in outside the school, from industry, trade unions and practice communities and then within these worlds, from adults who are willing to go the distance with the youth, including dealing with their steep learning curves, their often chaotic home lives, and the false starts and setbacks in their education. These work-practice experiences expose youth to a culture of artisanship. Building on Lave and Wenger's (1991) idea of a community of practice, Julian Orr (1996: 147) observed how a culture of artisanship exists among technicians through an informal community of practice based upon 'becoming and remaining a competent practitioner'; within the community, seasoned practitioners employ stories to celebrate their own competency and to instruct novices about the nuances of their craft. The occupational community is maintained through technicians' 'war stories' about confronting and overcoming problematic situations that arise in technical work, and these stories 'preserve and circulate hard-won information and are used to make claims of membership and seniority within the community' (Orr 1996: 126).

A major task, then, is the redefinition of craft and its associated modes of thought, through a local lens, and action that will need to take place in a more equitable manner than in the past, when only certain social classes were permitted access to craft knowledge and its modes of social transmission (Sennett 2008). Cognitive psychologists and anthropologists are discovering what artisans have always known, namely the value of experiential and project-based learning, including apprenticeships, in gaining and retaining craft knowledge. Craft refers to any particular type of skilled work: music, carpentry, surgery, handicraft, writing, drafting, experimental science, cartography, animation, photography, filmmaking, sound engineering are older crafts transformed and made more efficient through digital computer technology. The professional and service sectors use the digital screen as a supportive device to map information on behalf of their practices, including information, data, record keeping, billing, appointments and the maintenance technicians require to keep hardware running. However, it is the strategic learning, beyond schooling, that characterises who works where, uses what, lives near and succeeds or fails within the new economy. Those holding the new craft knowledge, namely the gatekeepers who educate or train others in the skill set, also control entry into the skilled work arena. Those with mastery maintain the occupational boundaries of their craft, controlling both entrance and training opportunities, and the sum of the various crafts selected by the new economy, and the practitioners, themselves, influence the current urban landscape. Residential patterns, schooling, politics, and more, follow the path of these new crafts within a region. Clearly, there is a need to reorient both those maintaining the boundaries and those seeking entry.

Beyond craft skills, youth require practice in learning how to meet the new exigencies that impact their daily lives. The litany of complexity includes: thinking statistically about risk, such as the probability of getting into an accident when you get into a motor vehicle, or ride in an airplane; having some knowledge of biochemical terms, for example contraindications and side effects of prescribed drugs, and nutritional content on food packaging; thinking strategically in the sense of being active consumers by negotiating health care for themselves, their children, their aging parents; understanding the complexities of the legal system; and making sense of income tax forms. Moreover, managing a household involves considerable skill in budgeting, maintaining records, banking, understanding contracts and following through with payments to creditors. However, educating youth in solving these more complex problems requires a more equitable and inclusive educational experience, from the admissions process; through the curriculum, the programme and the school culture; and beyond the classroom through fieldwork, service learning and internships (Kluver and Rosenstock 2002).

Setting out to improve the life chances of youth in the new economy requires a mode of collaborative and continuous learning on behalf of knowledge-based work, specifically through pedagogies of practice found in urban community-based organisations, and in museum outreach, after school, out-of-classroom, internships, community service, and high-school apprenticeship programmes. These practice-based pedagogies surfaced within a new economy based upon innovative technologies and their products, and new ways to deliver services. These styles of learning clearly fit within Hannah Arendt's (1968) view of education as a way of providing future generations with tools for 'setting right' a world that is 'out of joint' and perhaps 'wearing out' as a result of prior generations' demands and uses. To accomplish this goal, accessible spaces will then need to be created to promote learning beyond schooling where individuals are exposed to what Thomas Bender (2007) calls urban knowledges, namely professional, creative and social forms of knowledge that help to define a new metropolitanism that is socially inclusive.

The intent is that the youth will carry with them the tools and experiences gained through this style of learning as they enter college and beyond. Linked is the goal of instilling a different perspective on their lives and life chances by creating the conditions for a transformed identity associated with academic interest and success. An effective way of integrating traditional and modern views of education, work and career, and gaining parental buy-in, is to connect cutting-edge contemporary pedagogical and work practices to familiar aspects of older generations' culture and community, notably the culture of artisanship and the role of the craftsman. In California's ethnically diverse urban regions with their mix of immigrant and second-generation families, many youth are often the first to complete an academic programme in high school and go on to college. For these adolescents, success in navigating school and family worlds in the critical last two years of high school will often require them to demonstrate some connection to the artisanal tradition, broadly understood, to meet the challenge of cultivating in their parents, and often in their grandparents, an acceptance of the need to *let go*, for a time, as they enter demanding, and somewhat heartless, contemporary university and work settings.

High-school-based communities of practice, as found at High Tech High, offer youth opportunities to develop the requisite social and emotional skills, together with the hands-on experiences and perspectives fostered by project-based learning and reflective activities. Following from John Dewey's (1916) understanding of the primacy of lived experience and reflection as fundamental to learning and effective self-direction, the case of High Tech High's San Diego Bay Study considers how informal, inquiry-based learning experiences could improve the life chances of youth living in low- and middle-income communities. A sense of 'knowing-in-action' derives from the students' participation in mentored internships and apprenticeships in skilled work during the passage to young adulthood – a time for the assimilation of occupational knowledge and values. Learning encounters between High Tech High youth and their mentors are dialogues through which the mentoring relationship is constructed and negotiated. Social neuroscience views mentoring encounters as ways to enhance the social interaction essential to learning, which, in turn, is supported by neural circuits linking perception and action for close coupling and attunement between youth and mentor, and for synaptic plasticity (Meltzoff et al. 2009). High Tech High's emphasis on work-practice experiences encourages youth to move beyond outmoded class reproduction practices and embrace newer forms of learning where they can express their educational and occupational talents and speak for themselves on behalf of their futures.

Acknowledgements

This chapter, dedicated to the memory of Jay Vavra, is based on a long-term ethnographic study of High Tech High, part of a larger study of project-based learning in high school carried out by researchers at UCLA and University of California, Davis, and funded by the Sally and Dick Roberts Coyote Foundation. I would like to thank Richard Adler, Sam Beck, Paul Heckman, Llon King, Jean Kluver, Brian McKenna and Dick Roberts for spirited discussions of project-based learning. I also wish to thank the following teachers who graciously shared with me their work with their students in their classrooms during and after school hours, on exhibition night and during their students' presentations of learning: Mark Aguirre, Stacey Caillier, Amy Callahan, Tom Fehrenbacher, Jeff Robin and Jesse Wade Robinson. I am also grateful to the many students at the Gary and Jerri-Ann Jacobs High Tech High and at the HTH Graduate School of Education who generously shared their projects and reflections on their learning. I am especially grateful to Larry Rosenstock and Rob Riordan who spent many hours with me sharing their visions of twenty-first-century learning.

References

Arendt, H. (1968), 'The Crisis in Education', *Between Past and Future* (New York: Viking).

Behrend, T. S., M. R. Ford, K. M. Ross, E. M. Han, E. P. Burton and N. K. Spillane (2014), 'Gary and Jerri-Ann Jacobs High Tech High: A Case Study of an Inclusive STEM-focused High School in San Diego, California' (OSPrI Report 2014-03), *George Washington University, Opportunity Structures for Preparation and Inspiration in STEM*, https://ospri.research.gwu.edu/sites/ospri.research.gwu.edu/files/downloads/OSPrI_Report_2014-03.pdf

Bender, T. H. (2007), *The Unfinished City: New York and the Metropolitan Idea* (New York: The New Press).

Betts, J. R. (2009), 'The San Diego Blueprint for Student Success: A Retrospective Overview and Commentary', *Journal of Education for Students Placed at Risk* 14, no. 1: 120–129.

Blaustein, R. (2009), 'The Encyclopedia of Life: Describing Species, Unifying Biology', *BioScience* 59, no. 7: 551–556.

Caillier, S. L. and R. C. Riordan (2009), 'Teacher Education for the Schools We Need', *Journal of Teacher Education* 60, no. 5: 489–496.

Comer-Schultz, J. (2011), 'History and Historical Preservation in San Diego Since 1945: Civic Identity in America's Finest City', (dissertation, Arizona State University).

Dewey, J. (1916), *Democracy and Education* (New York: Macmillan).

Duckor, B. and D. Perlstein (2014), 'Assessing Habits of Mind: Teaching to the Test at Central Park East Secondary School', *Teachers College Record* 116, no. 2: 1–33.

Farrington, C. A. (2013), 'Academic Mindsets as a Critical Component of Deeper Learning', *University of Chicago: Consortium on Chicago School Research*, Paper prepared for the William and Flora Hewlett Foundation, http://www.hewlett.org/wp-content/uploads/2016/08/Academic_Mindsets_as_a_Critical_Component_of_Deeper_Learning_CAMILLE_FARRINGTON_April_20_2013.pdf

Fehrenbacher, T. (2015), 'Logs from San Diego Bay', *UnBoxed*, 13. http://www.hightechhigh.org/unboxed/issue13/logs_from_san_diego_bay/

Freire, P. (1985), *The Politics of Education: Culture, Power, and Liberation* (South Hadley, MA: Bergin and Garvey).

Giroux, H. A. (2010), 'Neoliberalism as Public Pedagogy', in J. A. Sandlin, B. D. Schultz and J. Burdick (eds), *Handbook of Public Pedagogy: Education and Learning Beyond Schooling* (New York: Routledge), 486–499.

Halpern, R (2009). *The Means to Grow Up: Reinventing Apprenticeship as a Developmental Support in Adolescence* (New York: Routledge).

Heckman, P. E. and V. L. Montera (2009), 'School Reform: The Flatworm in a Flat World: From Entropy to Renewal through Indigenous Invention', *Teachers College Record* 111, no. 5: 1328–1351.

Kerchner, C. T. (2012), *The Emperor's Clothes: Traditional and Avant Garde at High Tech High* (Claremont, CA: Claremont Graduate University).

Kluver, J. and L. Rosenstock (2002), 'Choice and Diversity: Irreconcilable Differences', *Principal Leadership* 3, no. 8: 12–18.

Lave, J. and E. Wenger (1991), *Situated Learning: Legitimate Peripheral Participation* (New York: Cambridge University Press).

Lotchin, R. W. (1992), 'The Political Culture of the Metropolitan-Military Complex', *Social Science History* 16, no. 2: 275–299.

Maida, C. A. (2011), 'Project-based Learning: A Critical Pedagogy for the Twenty-first Century', *Policy Futures in Education* 9, no. 6: 759–768.

McLaren, P. (2010), 'Afterword: Public Pedagogy and the Challenge of Historical Time', in J. A. Sandlin, B. D. Schultz and J. Burdick (eds), *Handbook of Public Pedagogy: Education and Learning Beyond Schooling* (New York: Routledge), 648–651.

Meltzoff, A. N., P. K. Kuhl, J. Movellan and T. J. Sejnowsky (2009), 'Foundations for a New Science of Learning', *Science* 325, no. 5938: 284–288.

Monchinski, T. (2008), *Critical Pedagogy and the Everyday Classroom* (New York: Springer).

Orr, J. E. (1996), *Talking About Machines: Ethnography of a Modern Job* (Ithaca, NY: Cornell University Press).

Pearlman, B. (2002), 'Designing, and Making, the New American High School', *TECHNOS-BLOOMINGTON* 11, no. 1: 12–19.

Riordan, R. and L. Rosenstock (2013), 'Changing the Subject', *Edutopia*, https://www.edutopia.org/blog/21st-century-skills-changing-subjects-larry-rosenstock-rob-riordan

Rosenstock, L. (2017), 'High Tech High Design Principles', https://www.hightechhigh.org/about-us/

Ryan, M, G. McGill, and E.O. Wilson (2014), *E.O. Wilson's Life on Earth* (Durham, NC: E.O. Wilson Biodiversity Foundation).

Sable, M. (2007), 'The Impact of the Biotechnology Industry on Local Economic Development in the Boston and San Diego Metropolitan Areas', *Technological Forecasting and Social Change* 74, no. 1: 36–60.

Sandlin, J. A., B. D. Schultz and J. Burdick (2010), 'Understanding and Exploring the Terrain of Public Pedagogy', in J. A. Sandlin, B. D. Schultz and J. Burdick (eds) (2010), *Handbook of Public Pedagogy: Education and Learning Beyond Schooling* (New York: Routledge), 1–6.

Sennett, R. (2008), *The Craftsman* (New Haven, CT: Yale University Press).

Shor, I. (1999), 'What Is Critical Literacy?' *Journal of Pedagogy, Pluralism & Practice* 4, no. 1: 1–26.

Sizer, T. (1996), *Horace's Hope: What Works for the American High School* (Boston, MA: Houghton Mifflin).

Stephen, D. and E. Goldberg (2013), *PROFILE: High Tech High Network – Student-centered Learning in Action* (Quincy, MA: Nellie Mae Education Foundation). https://www.nmefoundation.org/getmedia/aa1d06 c3-dd1d-460b-b99f-5b283d03e008/PROFILE-HighTechHighNetwork-NMEF

Students of the Gary and Jerri-Ann Jacobs High Tech High (2004), *The Two Sides of the Boat Channel: A Field Guide* (San Diego, CA: BuenFeVA Press).

Students of the Gary and Jerri-Ann Jacobs High Tech High (2005), *Perspectives of the San Diego Bay: A Field Guide* (Providence, RI: Next Generation Press).

Students of the Gary and Jerri-Ann Jacobs High Tech High (2007), *San Diego Bay: A Story of Exploitation and Restoration* (El Cajon, CA: Sunbelt Publications).

Students of the Gary and Jerri-Ann Jacobs High Tech High (2009), *San Diego Bay: A Call for Conservation* (El Cajon, CA: Sunbelt Publications).

Students of the Gary and Jerri-Ann Jacobs High Tech High (2014), *Biomimicry: Respecting Nature Through Design* (San Diego, CA: High Tech High).

Vavra, J. (2009), 'The San Diego Bay Study: Community-based Conservation', *Proceedings of the Pacific Division, American Association for the Advancement of Science Volume 28, Part 1* (Ashland, OR: American Association for the Advancement of Science, Pacific Division), 72.

Wenger, E. (2010), 'Communities of Practice and Social Learning Systems: The Career of a Concept', in C. Blackmore (ed.), *Social Learning Systems and Communities of Practice* (London: Springer), 179–198.

Wilson, E. O. (2003), 'The Encyclopedia of Life', *Trends in Ecology & Evolution* 18, no. 2: 77–80.

Zucker, L. G., M. R. Darby and M. B. Brewer (1998), 'Intellectual Human Capital and the Birth of U.S. Biotechnology Enterprises', *The American Economic Review* 88, no. 1: 290–306.

Inventing Eco-Cycle
A Social Enterprise Approach to Sustainability Education

Sandy Smith-Nonini

In June 2011 several colleagues and I opened a non-profit creative-reuse retail shop that houses a community centre for sustainability education in a bungalow near downtown Rushton,[1] a small city near Raleigh, NC. The idea was for income from the shop (called Eco-Cycle[2]) to subsidise costs for a meeting space and weekly educational events. We incorporated as a federal-registered non-profit, and to date we have sponsored over 350 educational workshops, films, talks and panel discussions, fieldtrips or cultural events, mostly on topics related to environmental sustainability, community economics/social justice or practical 'skill-shares' (how-to) workshops. Since 2013 we have partnered closely with Research Triangle Transition,[3] a grassroots group working to promote a shift to a low-carbon future.

Given my academic background (researcher and part-time university teacher), I think of Eco-Cycle as an engaged community-university project. As the founder and volunteer coordinator, I am hardly in a neutral or objective position to evaluate the venture, but no one else involved can offer a history of its origins. I undertook the project in the hopes of establishing a model that could be emulated, and I am too familiar with the fragility of our day-to-day budget to declare our experiment a success to date. Nonetheless, a period of community-building and fund-raising to buy our building in the last year, coupled with new initiatives, makes me optimistic we are on the right track. So I offer this ethnographic 'memoir' in the hope it assists advocates in other places that need community institutions for grassroots/alternative education.

My Path to Sustainable Community:
Crossing Disciplinary and Social Divides

I began this path out of a deep curiosity and alarm about the future that emerged from my job as an assistant professor of anthropology at Elon University in the early 2000s. I assigned my students a (now classic) reading titled 'The End of Cheap Oil' (Campbell and Laherrère 1998) which they (and I) found alarming and hard to believe. I also led several student groups to visit an off-the-grid ecovillage whose residents had radically changed their lives to learn to be sustainable without fossil fuels. To evaluate these ideas I joined a new meet-up group in late 2005 called NC Powerdown focused on 'peak oil', renewable technologies and climate change.

In retrospect, theoretical assumptions from my background shaped my responses to the new findings. I had done engaged research on social activism, initially on health work during civil conflict in El Salvador, and later on labour organising among immigrant farm labourers. Both movements were influenced by Marxist understandings of capitalist exploitation and by Christian liberation theology, which championed a morality guided by needs of the poor (Smith 1991). Both were also shaped by radical critiques of development that emphasised community-based democracy and a pedagogy of reflexive engagement and hands-on learning (Chambers 1983; Freire 1982; Giroux 1988). I had internalised these concepts but also had observed the variety of forms of leadership and constant experimentation that characterises successful movements as they adapt to new situations (Smith-Nonini 2009, 2010).

My premises about sustainable development fit best with the perspective of political ecology which Byrne and Glover (2002) contrast with more liberal moderate reformist approaches to capitalist development or ecological economics, which fails to take a stand on the breach between price and values. As an anthropologist who teaches economic globalisation, I had been influenced by Harvey's (2005) analysis of late capitalism, and was receptive to the idea that access to fossil fuels had helped enable British and later U.S. hegemony. Since I had prior training in biology, I found it curious that most accounts of globalisation had little to say about energy. In our meet-up group I was also struck by the dissonance between the scientists or technocrats in the room and the social-change activists – who brought different assumptions to the table and often talked past each other. Likewise, I found widely separated discourses on ecology in the social science literature, with little cross-fertilisation.

In 2005 I decided to downshift from full to part-time teaching to enable more writing and community-based work than was possible working fulltime at a liberal arts college with a high teaching load. I had built a small property renovation and management business since 1992 which gave me the financial security to make the shift. Also, I won a year's grant support to write a book that year which gave me more time flexibility to become involved in local sustainability initiatives.

The first of these was Clean Energy Triangle (CET[4]), a network of energy committees based in neighbourhood associations led by a dynamic woman with former non-profit experience. CET's focus was reducing the carbon footprint of buildings. Participants engaged in demonstration projects to learn about and teach their neighbours how to save energy, with a focus on weatherisation, efficient lightbulbs, appliances and solar hot water – all of which could be shown to save money, as well as energy for homeowners. Initially CET's focus was middle-class homeowners, but several committees were formed in poorer African-American neighbourhoods, and gradually CET engaged with local officials.

Meanwhile, I teamed up with UNC physicist Gerald Cecil (another meet-up member), and other friends, to carry out a 'sustainable enterprise project' funded by a $6,000 (U.S.) grant from the UNC Business School to study efficiencies of solar hot water for homes. This led to a joint project with our neighbourhood CET committee and two high-school classes to survey our area for houses with sufficiently sunny roofs for solar. The solar roof survey led me to seek funds for green projects for teens. I sought feedback from students, and we dubbed the fledgling effort 'YIKES!'

for Youth Involved in Keeping Earth Sustainable. High-school teachers convinced me that the crowded public-school curriculum left little room for topics like climate change and renewable energy. YIKES! joined another UNC-funded project to teach teens about climate change and how to lobby on public policy. Due to a recent drought, rain barrels were newly popular, so we designed kick-off events in two towns for students to paint rain barrels with fun designs to attract them to the workshops. This turned into a lesson on the importance of hands-on approaches, as the rain barrel painting was far more heavily attended than the climate sessions that followed! For months I received invitations to bring our painted rain barrels to sustainability and science fairs. This planted the seeds for Eco-Cycle.

I withdrew from the CET activism partly because of its focus at that time on (relatively privileged) homeowners, and because CET did not prioritise work with youth. In fall 2007, a biodiesel company with a non-profit educational affiliate offered us warehouse space for YIKES! activities, and I worked with their tiny staff on joint proposals for grants to fund environmental education, most of which were not successful. But in partnership with others we received small grants to assist an African American church to build a community garden, and for projects with the N. C. School of Science and Mathematics to build a solar space heater and do research on oil seed crops. Students painted nature murals on our warehouse walls, and a church group built us a stage. We hosted monthly educational events in the warehouse space that we dubbed 'The EcoLounge', using the NC Powerdown meet-up site to spread the word.

We continued to experiment with rain barrels, which appealed from multiple perspectives – they were made of recycled materials, they could be used to teach water conservation, painting them was a great hands-on activity to engage new people, and they could be sold for revenue. In 2009 I read a book by Tom Szaky called 'Revolution in a Bottle' about how he built a company called Teracycle that got its start recycling food waste and marketing worm 'poop' plant food in used soda bottles. Terracycle went on to market hundreds of products made from waste 'upcycled' into new products. The potential for upcycling as a creative, educational and potentially revenue-generating activity lit a fire for me.

Our area has long been home to a creative-reuse non-profit called the Scrap Exchange, which collects and recycles industrial waste to benefit artists and school projects. So I organised a meeting at the Scrap Exchange to form an upcycling club which we named Eco-Cycle. This group of crafty people (mostly adults) with green inclinations began meeting weekly in our warehouse space to make and paint rain barrels. We experimented with upcycling worn surfaces of frames and pots with broken ceramic mosaic and rebuilding broken lamps in innovative ways. Many in our group were underemployed. Some were trained artists but lacked opportunities to use their talents in day-to-day working life. Others were more interested in environmental issues. Most were not as interested in sustainability education as I was, but they joined me in hosting rain barrel painting water conservation events for community groups, and we were hired by the city to do a series of workshops at a new Parks and Recreation facility in a marginalised neighbourhood.

Goodwork, a local community development non-profit organisation, assisted us to organise ourselves better as a cooperative. We paid an unemployed member a piece rate to convert industrial food-grade polyethylene barrels into rain barrels. Everyone else was a volunteer. Earnings from sales or events went towards rent, gas, supplies and components of a booth for craft fairs.

Where Do Sustainability and Social Justice Meet? – Promoting Green-collar Jobs

Eco-Cycle's early days overlapped with my involvement in new political activism in Rushton to create green jobs. Many observers have noted the conservative trend among large environmental organisations which found their base among middle-class whites and neglected to develop programming relevant to people of colour. An exception was the Environmental Justice Movement which focused on pollution and landfills disproportionately affecting poor and black neighbourhoods (Adamson et al. 2002). The Green Job movement was spurred by new interest in urban gardens and by Van Jones' book *The Green Collar Economy* (2008), published just as the mortgage crisis landed us in a prolonged recession. Jones advocated solving two problems at once – our fossil fuel dependence and minority unemployment – through creating new jobs in sustainable industries.

North Carolina Central University (NCCU), a nearby historically black college, held a green jobs conference out of which grew a new initiative called the 'Black, Brown, Green Alliance (BBGA)'. The group was supported by NCCU and three Triangle-area social justice non-profits. The BBGA seemed well-positioned to address the challenges of grounding activism for sustainability in the grassroots reality of a profoundly unequal society, and I joined with enthusiasm. From 2008 to 2010 we held regular meetings designed to build an environmentalist rainbow coalition around green jobs. The BBGA was blessed with experienced community leaders who kept us democratic and committed to a long-term process of building trust across racial and class boundaries. As someone who is typically allergic to endless meetings and eager to get on with projects, I learned a great deal from submitting to this process.

Our focus on green jobs brought many social entrepreneurs to meetings who sought help to start initiatives, from community garden projects to house deconstruction businesses. We looked for a central project around which we could work together. This quest led to conflicts as backers of potential projects sparred with each other for attention, with some members dropping out. President Barack Obama's stimulus funding became the golden ring, and I took on a major role chairing a group to develop a grant proposal for a green-job training programme that would draw on strengths of several non-profit organisations in the group. We benefited from advice from Majora Carter, founder of the Sustainable South Bronx, but unfortunately because we had to apply through a municipal agency, the proposal became watered down by city grant writers who sought to divert funding to existing town services. The project was not funded. But before we even knew the outcome, a well-loved black leader who had helped hold the BBGA together died unexpectedly from health problems. In her absence, tensions erupted between other activists in the project, one of whom had taken on debt to support her community work and had been counting on the grant. Gradually the BBGA began to splinter.

I dwell on the BBGA experience here because of how formative it was in shaping my thinking. I am reminded of Alfred O. Hirschman's essay, 'Principle of Conservation and Mutation of Social Energy' (1983) where he observed how political consciousness forged in activists tends to continue even when a given movement loses energy. One positive outcome from the BBGA was that an African American woman leader (who I had recruited into the group) revised our grant proposal and gained funding for a smaller 'green tracks' training project as part of a non-profit programme she ran for unemployed people. The two-week green tracks trainings continued with different cohorts of adult students for roughly five years, taught by instructors from Eco-Cycle and other non-profit groups that came together through the BBGA.

I also came away from the BBGA somewhat wary about dependence on grant projects, and a more realistic sense about prospects for green jobs as an answer to unemployment. Most projects Van Jones featured in his book were grant supported, raising questions about long-term economic sustainability. Many local food projects have sprung up in our region, but they tend to have low profit margins and limited hiring potential.[5] Meeting other green entrepreneurs, however, and my personal experience running a small business renovating and managing rental houses, led me to consider social entrepreneurship to support environmental education. Bornstein (2004) describes social entrepreneurs as agents of change that draw on skills and models of business to solve social problems. Most of the projects he discusses draw on premises and values that closely resemble non-profit-oriented approaches to community development.

The Shift from Informal Community Group to Place-based Non-Profit

Eco-Cycle's planning for events in our warehouse space was constrained by extremes of the weather due to limitations of the building, which was sweltering in the summer and frigid in the winter (despite our weatherisation upgrades). Our workshop was hidden away in a high-crime, post-industrial landscape which, while a good location for organising in the black community, presented problems for rain barrel customers and event participants who had trouble finding us, if they were brave enough to try. To solve this problem I often did deliveries myself with my Acura Integra hatchback.

In spring 2010, with support from Goodwork, I attended the annual conference of the Business Alliance for Local Living Economies (BALLE) in Charleston, SC. BALLE is a network of green entrepreneurs and non-profits, and one of the conference challenges was a 'back of the napkin' contest in which participants outlined a social enterprise idea. I did not win the modest cash award, but my design for a site-based project with a retail shop supporting educational activities was the prototype for the hybrid business/non-profit that Eco-Cycle grew into.

This idea took shape later that year when I met a fabric crafter who was organising venues for herself and other artisans to exhibit their goods. I began to attend and collect their business cards. That fall I taught an environmental class at UNC with a service-learning component. Ten of the thirty-five students opted to do a project with Eco-Cycle and came up with a plan to hold a competition for upcyclers – who would submit products to be judged. An anonymous donor offered us funding that we used to cater for the event and offer cash prizes. Thus was born the 'Re-Hashed Trash Bash' held at UNC in December 2010. Other students in the class did a project with an African American neighbourhood group opposing expansion of the Chapel Hill landfill, so we invited their leader, along with a municipal solid waste expert, and the head of the UNC sustainability office to speak. The judges included waste specialists, green activists and artists, and our prizes reflected both environmental and artistic criteria, plus a best product for green job creation award (which happily went to an artistically painted Eco-Cycle rain barrel!). We filled the room with exhibits of upcycler crafters and local green businesses.

This event led me to consider a place-based venture to serve crafters' needs for both a market and place for educational and how-to workshops. For a while I had had my eye on a boarded up bungalow on a busy road near our neighbourhood that was once an antique store. I took the owner out to lunch, and after a presentation of our plan she agreed to rent it to us at a very reasonable cost, given the location and the building's commercial zoning. A bonus was a small apartment in the rear that we could rent out for steady income to supplement the shop's earnings.

My husband Don Nonini, an anthropology professor, and Anthony Watts, a long-time environmentalist friend, joined me to form a board and we applied for federal non-profit status for the educational wing of our enterprise. We invested in a computer, a point-of-sale programme, a website and tasked our compatriots with helping us source furniture and displays. I later calculated that our spending on the project came to roughly $13,000 (U.S.) in the first two years. Eco-Cycle opened in June 2011, with two rooms used only for retail, one for an upcycling workshop and one that we dubbed the 'EcoLounge' which doubled as retail for books and a meeting space. In addition to upcycled crafts and small furniture, the shop carries vintage, free trade items, sustainability products, educational toys, books and an eclectic selection of thrift and donated items. We started with one event a month, but realising the synergy between educational workshops and promotions of the shop, we moved rapidly to two and then four a month promoted by a weekly email newsletter. Promotion on list serves, meet-up sites and online calendars has helped populate events and bring people to the shop. We built a 'friends list' from customers and events participants who receive the newsletter (over 900 people at present) which goes out each Tuesday, leading with the event of the week at the top.

Our events take place either Friday evenings (for films, talks, etc.) or Saturday afternoons (for how-to workshops). A survey of 290 events we have held since January 2012 revealed that slightly more than half were films, talks or discussions, and the other half were how-to workshops or cultural/social events. Thematically, 32 per cent were on environmental or sustainability themes and 22 per cent were on politics or community economics (including critiques of mainstream economics). Another 33 per cent were 'how-to' events (most with sustainability aspects),[6] and 11 per cent were cultural or social events. In 2013 and 2014, we collaborated with Research Triangle Transition on five to six events a year in larger venues that seated 50–100 people. We pass the hat at all events and our suggested donation is $5 (U.S.), although a few how-to workshops cost more if we need to pay an instructor. We decided our initial EcoLounge room was too small, so in mid-2013 our rear tenant, a former Greenpeace staffer who had construction skills, removed a wall to expand the EcoLounge. The larger room can seat around twenty-five, and gave us space to develop a coffee/tea bar and to expand the shop's book inventory.

Slouching Towards a Cooperative Venture

There are trade-offs in the shift from a grassroots group to a place-based non-profit. It is common for a non-profit organisation to turn inward and focus on programming and grant-seeking rather than outreach and community-based projects. Also, we are at risk for founder's effect – when a community project struggles to build enough support and capacity to survive even if its founders withdraw. I also knew that as an intellectual acclimatised to writing and research, my personality was not the ideal type for nurturing social consciousness. I drew cautious optimism from readings and past research on social movements which argued that effective leadership can come in a variety of packages.

Much like good private entrepreneurship, I feel that social enterprise for community development must be adaptive, always watching for potential synergy with allies and ways to grow through experimentation. Before we opened, Eco-Cycle volunteers and some of our new upcycling crafter friends held meetings to brainstorm. The initial idea, based on a women's craft cooperative in nearby Chapel Hill, was to offer attractive terms for vendors to sell their wares in the shop in return for them putting in four volunteer hours each month running the shop, doing promotions and other tasks. Our crafters who volunteered split sales with the shop 70:30, in the crafter's favour.

This plan did not work all that well, mainly for lack of enough reliable volunteers. We held many meetings in the first eighteen months aimed at sharing ideas and responsibilities for cooperative management. Some crafters were intent on developing a reputation as an artist, leading them to insist on higher prices. But the higher-priced products did not sell well, and the bottom line for many crafters was that they did not earn enough in the shop to justify the volunteer time. One vintage vendor (employed fulltime elsewhere) has routinely earned $60–100 (U.S.) per month with us and has remained a steady volunteer for four years; likewise other retired crafters and supporters have lent their time generously. Others have been active during bouts of unemployment. Overall, vendors showed little interest in a cooperative structure, which most doubted would work well. Their preference, as several said outright, was for a direct one-on-one relationship with management (which meant me by default), although I initially resisted the role.

Most vendors had only a vague or loose identity with environmentalism, despite a preference for working with recycled/reused materials – a practice that had become fashionable. I understand this, and I had to admit myself that what we were doing was symbolic, in that we were drawing on an aesthetic to draw people to the shop and our events. We noted that few crafters attended the Friday night events, with one exception – a crafter unhappily employed in a science lab, who joined our board and took a leadership role managing our volunteers for most of a year but then pulled back when she found a new job teaching for a green nonprofit organisation.

About nine months after we opened I gave up trying to run the shop with volunteers and hired a part-time person. Until recently, that position was filled by Max, a UNC graduate who studied anthropology and sustainability, and helped coordinate the 2010 Re-Hashed Trash Bash. He also managed our friends list and some promotions. Henry, our Eco-Cycle rain barrel maker, continued with us, earning $18 (U.S.) per converted rain barrel. One limitation has been our inability to keep the store open full-time on weekdays due to costs of staff. Our sales and event donations in 2014 average $1,100 (U.S.)/month (with much seasonal variation), of which 18–20 per cent is paid out to vendors. Over time we grew a new pool of volunteers, most of whom are motivated by our environmental education work.

The newsletter production and much of the programming became my responsibility, with occasional assistance from the board,
and, after 2012, from members of Research Triangle Transition. We
rely on volunteers to staff booths at outdoor sustainability fairs
and an annual alternative gift fair. Through a new collaborative
grant effort with the Rushton Public Library we have a contract
to teach summer sustainability workshops to minority teens. In
winter/spring 2015 we hosted two small courses that met weekly –
one on watersheds taught by another organisation, and a 'reading
group' class discussing J. K. Gibson-Graham's book *Take Back the
Economy*. We also advised a university class of students who did
studies and write-ups on local green projects to produce educational materials.

Our location on a busy artery near a bohemian shopping district close to a university campus is not bad for retail. But for
purposes of building a diverse community it was a far cry from
the poor, mostly black neighbourhood of Eco-Cycle's former warehouse. Thus we feel we always need more outreach to people of
colour. Research Triangle Transition's work on hunger (see below)
and our community economics events have helped cross that di-
vide. We have a popular African-American radio host and crafter/
sustainability advocate on our board, and we have had several
instructors from minority communities give workshops, which
often bring in new people.

Our partnership with Research Triangle Transition has helped
tie Eco-Cycle more tightly to social needs of the community. The
group's initial work was outreach to link up social justice groups
working on hunger with sustainable food advocates. During summer 2015 the Transition Food Committee put together a series of
well-attended events on how to end hunger in Rushton. In the
last year our Energy Committee held a series of events on renewable energy (especially solar) and controversies over state energy
policy, collaborating closely with NC WARN, a renewable energy
advocacy non-profit. In fall 2015 I led a climate change reading
group studying Naomi Klein's new book *This Changes Everything*.
The group sponsored an area premier screening of the new film by
the same title which sold out a 200-seat theatre in Chapel Hill, providing a venue for a panel discussion by activists. Our third focus

has been community economics, with dozens of events so far on issues of debt, cooperatives, alternative currencies, participatory budgeting and social justice topics.

Recent events in fall 2017 included a demo of electric cars by their owners, showing of the film "We the People 2.0" on en-vironmental and community rights, and two events in collaboration with NC WARN (a local nonprofit) on advocacy for solar energy in North Carolina. Most Friday nights, participants in the week's event gather afterwards at a nearby café for drinks or a late meal.

One of our greatest challenges was in 2014 when our landlord told us she needed to sell the house. Suddenly we faced a test of the concreteness of the sociality implied by "community build-ing." She offered us a good price, given the location and the ar-ea's current rapid gentrification. But investigating costs of a loan and the high down payment needed for a commercial purchase made me nervous about our chances. Tours of rental properties ended in sticker shock, but a new student volunteer helped us put together a video for an Indiegogo online fundraising campaign, and we held meetings with board members, Research Triangle Transition and our wider circle of friends, asking them how to move forward and soliciting input on what they wanted Eco-Cycle to become.

It turned out we had a wider circle of supporters than we thought. In roughly three months, with donations or peer-to-peer loans from twenty-eight individuals and one unsolicited $1,000 (U.S.) grant (from the Triangle Community Foundation), we raised over $33,300 (U.S.) towards the down payment. Also, sev-eral people offered volunteer help, including one who loaned her time helping run the store and our small EcoLounge Café for eight months, and two who joined our board. To meet our mortgage payments we made the difficult decision to rent out our workshop room where we had done repair and upcycling projects and stored supplies. Since then, we have built outdoor storage space and a greenhouse from used windows on the rear of the building which will enable us to raise organic starter plants for the shop and to engage in new educational projects.

The good news as of late 2017 is we expect to end the year with a surplus for the first time. We plan to use some of the funds to begin offering an annual award for environmental activism. And after nearly ten years collaboration with eco-activists, our motley coterie of volunteers and collaborators is beginning to feel a lot like community. We have survived for five years, and we have a twenty-year mortgage, so we are 'all in' now.

Can this model work somewhere else? I think it can. The challenge we all face is how to create hybrid models that form a bridge between the economy we are in and the one we want to build. Getting there requires some good sense, some donated time (all entrepreneurship does) and some capital (not necessarily a lot); but if you want to build community the most important piece of advice I can give is spend a lot of time studying groups you admire and listening to leaders and colleagues. Think about synergies – between your talents/skills and a service that is in demand; and between your ideas for social change and practices that inspire others. Look for points of commonality that a small group can cohere around. Once you have a social nucleus and an idea, try a project. If it does not work, sit down with others and try to figure out why. Then try again.

Sandy Smith-Nonini is an adjunct assistant professor of anthropology at the University of North Carolina, Chapel Hill. She is the author of Healing the Body Politic: El Salvador's Popular Struggle for Health Rights – From Civil War to Neoliberal Peace (Rutgers University Press, 2010), and is currently doing research on the political economy of petroleum.

Notes

1. Rushton is a pseudonym.
2. Eco-Cycle is a pseudonym.
3. Research Triangle Transition is a pseudonym.
4. Clean Energy Triangle is a pseudonym.
5. In contrast, thanks to attractive state tax incentives and a requirement that our major electric utility company purchase solar power at a higher than market rate, solar jobs have grown rapidly in North Carolina. The downside is the field favours jobseekers moving horizontally

from other technical fields, over minority jobseekers. Weatherisation seemed a promising green job creator, but we found that most middle-class homeowners are unlikely to invest heavily in weatherisation in the current economy, and public funds to retrofit low-income homes are very limited. Deconstruction and specialised recycling (supplementing municipal services) may hold the most potential for job creation.

6. Examples include crocheting with plastic bag strips, building solar ovens, lamp repair, sewing, terrarium building, home energy saving, grey water projects, rain barrel making and painting, fireplace inserts, composting, raising chickens and beekeeping.

References

Adamson, J., M. Evans and R. Stein (eds.) (2002), *The Environmental Justice Reader: Politics, Poetics, and Pedagogy* (Tucson: University of Arizona Press).

Bornstein, D. (2004), *How to Change the World: Social Entrepreneurs and the Power of New Ideas* (New York: Oxford University Press).

Byrne, J. and L. Glover (2002), 'A Common Future or Towards a Future Commons: Globalization and Sustainable Development since UNCED', *International Review for Environmental Strategies* 3, no. 1: 5–25.

Campbell, C. and J. Laherrère (1998), 'The End of Cheap Oil', *Scientific American* March: 78–83.

Chambers, R. (1983), *Rural Development: Putting the Last First* (New York: John Wiley and Sons).

Freire, P. (1982), *Pedagogy of the Oppressed* (New York: Continuum).

Giroux, H. (1988), *Teachers as Intellectuals: Toward a Critical Pedagogy of Learning* (Portsmouth, NH: Greenwood Publishing Group).

Harvey, D. (2005), *A Brief History of Neoliberalism* (Oxford: Oxford University Press).

Hirschman, A. O. (1983), 'The Principle of Conservation and Mutation of Social Energy', *Grassroots Development Journal* 7, no. 2: 2.

Jones, V. (2008), *A Green Collar Economy: How One Solution Can Fix Our Two Biggest Problems* (New York: Harper One).

Smith, C. (1991), *The Emergence of Liberation Theology: Radical Religion and Social Movement Theory* (Chicago: University of Chicago Press).

Smith-Nonini, S. (2009), 'Inventing a Public Anthropology with Latino Farm Labor Organisers in North Carolina', *NAPA Bulletin* 31: 114–28.

Smith-Nonini, S. (2010), *Healing the Body Politic: El Salvador's Struggle for Health Rights: From Civil War to Neoliberal Peace* (Rutgers, NJ: Rutgers University Press).

Szaky, T. (2009), *Revolution in a Bottle: How TerraCycle is Eliminating the Idea of Waste* (New York: Penguin Group).

Confronting Tyranny
in a Public Health Agency
Crafting a 'Philosophy of Praxis'
into a 'Community of Resistance'

Brian McKenna

> Gramsci's philosophy of praxis is a theory of learning and
> education.
>
> (Jean Lave, anthropologist 2012: 159)

Introduction

In June 1998 I was hired by the Ingham County Health Department
in Lansing, Michigan to 'turn the Public Health into the Peoples'
Health'. Government officials selected me to lead 'The Ingham
County Environmental Health Assessment and Improvement Project' where I would research and write an 'energised description'
of the local environment (complete with maps, photographs and
graphics) while establishing contacts throughout this 550 square
mile county in Mid-Michigan. The purpose was to catalyse the local citizenry to 'stand up and take notice' and then to 'take action'
to resolve the most serious environmental problems in the region.
They told me, 'do not be afraid of offending anyone – even General Motors – [the city's most powerful company] if the data leads
you there' (McKenna 2010).

While they were talking I noticed a blue and white bumper
sticker pasted onto the Health Director's door which pronounced,

'Lansing Works, KEEP GM', referring to a movement on the part of government officials to court General Motors and prevent them from leaving for Mexico or other environs as had happened in Flint, Michigan in the 1980s.

I had access into the inner sanctums of the public health world and absorbed the rhythms and tensions of this secretive governmental culture. It was a deep immersion with a very sharp learning curve. I knew that I would be sorely tested as I informed governmental officials that we would have to countenance multiple controversial topics. They agreed and were not concerned. I would conduct the research with a pre-selected community group of twelve environmental experts, called 'The Roundtable', (where I was a member) who would have the ultimate authority in producing the studies. This state-of-the-art project was a strategic innovation that would assist in redesigning the Health Department's mission. Officials said that they were aware that nobody had ever stepped back to take a look at the big picture, to assess the area's overall environmental health and rank the issues according to some criteria, like the most urgent problems, and then help to resolve them. They requested 'a holistic analysis'. So they hired a medical anthropologist with organising and journalism skills (McKenna 2010).

I follow a Gramscian 'philosophy of praxis', pursuing knowledge wherever it takes me (Hale 2008; Thomas 2009). As Lave describes it, a philosophy of praxis is 'a very broad vision of the production of social life ... not just of the *mind*, or of a *historical institution*, or of *language* [my emphasis]as a thing in itself [but] ... the participation of ... [all] three in producing persons in practice' (Lave 2012: 156). As a critical theorist (Adorno 1966) I analyse the evolving history (unravelling the reified data), the essences (behind the illusory appearances) and the contradictions (the oppositions, conflicts and paradoxes) of the objects under investigation – in this instance local environmental health, local corporations, my government employer and myself.

A few months into my research, a restaurant inspector, Carol (pseudonym) privately approached me, and arranged to meet me at a place outside of work. When we met she shared a suitcase with me. Inside was a large batch of files, discs, charts, photos and documents. I learned that the Health Department had assigned her to conduct an environmental health assessment in 1995, three years previously. No one had informed me of this. Carol told me that she had gotten far in the assessment but as she began making interesting and controversial finds she was suddenly removed from the project and it ceased altogether. She was ordered to be silent and never discuss the project with anyone or else 'suffer severe consequences'. She told me to be very careful: 'You are in danger'. Later I learned that many of her colleagues spoke of Carol as though she was crazy and about to 'go postal' at any moment. Carol was openly shunned and derided but I found her to be a very honest and capable colleague. Indeed the environmental health data Carol gave me, at risk to herself, was extremely valuable, both in its content and in the leads it gave me. She saved me several months of research (McKenna 2010).

Carol's revelation was highly disturbing. In essence, the former project director was telling me that her governmental superiors (the same people who hired me) had suppressed her work, threatened her livelihood and ordered her silent for doing the same work I was now hired to do. This revelation was environmental health data as much as any local pollution data. I developed a friendship with Carol and decided that I would recruit her as part of my community of resistance if I encountered similar problems down the line.

Crafting a Philosophy of Praxis

The philosophy of praxis ... is the expression of subaltern classes who want to educate themselves in the art of government and who have an interest in knowing all truths, even the unpleasant ones, and in avoiding the impossible deceptions of the upper class, and even more their own.

(Antonio Gramsci, quoted in Peter Thomas 2009: 291)

My critical ethnography of a governmental health department permitted me to identify certain truths that would have never have come to light if I had just studied public health theory or academic texts in isolation. I required a situated learning environment and a critical community of practice (Lave 2012). My research methodology is highly influenced by the theories of Paulo Freire, Antonio Gramsci and John Dewey – I learn by doing. More so, I act (research/do) and then self-consciously reflect on what I do. In other words, in this government job I was acting and studying 'up, down and sideways' (Stryker and González 2014) in expanding circuits of discovery and re-discovery, propelling myself up the funnel of a swirling tornado so to speak, becoming a practitioner of a pedagogical art (McKenna and Darder 2011) and a threatening science (Price 2004) in a gnosiological cycle of knowledge formation (Freire 1970; Hale 2008). I approach social science as a craft (Lave 2012; Mills 1959) to *reveal* reality (Ingold 2000). And so, I became a 'walking fieldnote' (Sanjak 1990) in the everyday world of local government. Of course I was dialectically divided into three contradictory subject positions: (1) an employee, (2) a professional and (3) a citizen whose identities overlapped and conflicted (McKenna 2010). Following this holistic epistemology I absorbed a great deal of knowledge about environmental issues and the state apparatus. I was committed to share my discoveries with the public as a cultural broker, critical pedagogue and anthropologist.

A year later I learned that the kind of organisational tyranny that Carol was suffering had a name: mobbing (Davenport et al. 1999). I was surprised to learn that one of the three authors of *Mobbing: Emotional Abuse in the American Workplace* was an anthropologist, Noa Davenport. In the book's forward the women note that, 'This book came about because all three of us, in different organisations, experienced a workplace phenomenon that had profound effects on our well-being. Through humiliation, harassment and unjustified accusations, we experienced emotional abuse that forced us out of the workplace' (Davenport 1999: 14). I wondered, 'What kind of government bureaucracy is this?'

The Official 'Community of Practice'

This particular bureaucracy – the fourth largest public health department in Michigan – was trying something new and daring, they told me. Officials admitted that its environmental bureau was too narrow and specialised and they wanted to innovate. As I came to discover, environmental workers there spent decades dedicated to the same task: water well permits, lead remediation, storage tank inspections. As I learned by shadowing them in the field, they did their jobs well. But programmes were often haphazardly connected to episodic funding sources. Administrators planned to reorganise to adapt to the changing landscape of environmental health concerns. They organised an external 'Environmental Health Roundtable', an external advisory group given independent authority to direct the research and organise community participation in the appraisal. I was directed to lead it. Health Department administrators selected the Roundtable members. Three of the twelve members, including myself, my manager and the Environmental Health Director, were Health Department employees. They were an 'internal eye' on the proceedings. The nine other members included a physician, a Michigan Department of Environmental Quality official, two members of Public Sector Consultants, an influential think tank and MSU academics in Resource Development, Agricultural Economics and two Environmental Toxicology professors. Two of the most influential environmentalists in the state of Michigan from opposite poles of the political spectrum were in the group, Dr Michael Kamrin and Dave Dempsey (McKenna 2010).

The Roundtable wanted to do a wide-ranging thorough assessment. It was agreed that we would also consider 'emotional health' (surveying citizens to see how they feel about the environment) and would analyse indicators of sustainability and adopt the broad-based World Health Organization's definition of environmental health as a guide. I would be responsible for researching hundreds of indicators regarding health exposures and health effects, environmental history and 'shadow knowledge' uncovering, 'what we know, what we kind of know, and what we don't know'. I was to pursue knowledge across several disciplines – sociology, ecology and anthropology – and employ several conflicting epistemologies – positivist, hermeneutic and critical – in this effort. Using a wide-range of quantitative and qualitative skills, I immersed myself in the data, made widespread ethnographic observations, contacted experts, forged relationships with activists and read widely. With the oversight of the Roundtable who met monthly between September 1998 and January 2000, I eventually filled the equivalent of five filing cabinets and placed scores of electronic files on my hard-drive with data and background perspectives on twenty-two targeted areas of inquiry. Environmental topics included: pesticides, water quality, urban sprawl, indoor and outdoor air pollution, citizen perceptions, enforcement status, food quality, land application of sewage sludge, lead poisoning, asthma, toxic wastes and occupational health. I dug deeply, FOIA'd (Freedom of Information Act) state documents, visited top pollution sites and factories, traced leads, read local environmental history, and within two years crafted our first report, a 135-page narrative (with thirty-two colour graphics and pictures) describing the state of water resources in the county, 'The Story of Water Resources at Work, Ingham County, Michigan'. I carried the investigation where the data (and the Roundtable) led me, and this meant, of necessity, that we confronted several controversial issues. Predictably, as with most innovative projects of this kind, a number of unanticipated obstacles arose that slowed the pace of research. For example, I had to review the literature on how to conduct environmental health assessments; explore the numerous 'sub-issues' within each of the topical areas; determine how thoroughly we should inquire into the epidemiological and toxicological literature to estimate risk; and conduct detective work to uncover particularly difficult to find data (e.g. determining the number of homes that had had a carbon monoxide incident). I learned how to make geographic information maps (GIS), SPSS, Quattro Pro Paradox. I supervised two research assistants, promoted the project to community groups, constructed a slide show, a poster and eventually designed over 30 graphics for publication, working closely with two professional graphic artists (McKenna 2010).

Some Critical Findings

I have written extensively about the hundreds of environmental health findings in numerous reports (PEER 2001a), newspaper articles (McKenna 2002) and scholarly journals (McKenna 2010). Below I highlight five discoveries in order to help the readers gauge the significance of concern:

- General Motors owned the area's worst leaking underground storage tank plume, located at the Townsend Street plant. GM has had fourteen toxic underground LUST (Leaking Underground Storage Tanks) releases, more than any other local corporation. According to the DEQ, it was 'an immediate threat to health, safety or the environment'. This LUST is particularly dangerous because if untreated, it could destroy portions of Lansing's aquifer, the source of the area's drinking water (PEER 2001a).

- Asthma has reached epidemic proportions among African American youth in Lansing, particularly in zip code 48915 where two General Motors plants were located. The rate of preventable hospitalisations for black males, aged one to fourteen, was particularly high, amounting to 64.8 per 10,000 hospitalisations. This greatly exceeded the [federal] Healthy People 2010 goal of 10 per 10,000. Despite this, a local hospital, Sparrow Hospital, will not share emergency room disease data directly with the public or local health professionals (see McKenna 2010; PEER 2001c).

- *Farm pesticides.* Atrazine is a probable human carcinogenic pesticide banned throughout much of Europe (Fagin and Lavelle 1999: 20–1). It was Ingham County's number one restricted-use pesticide in 1997. According to the EPA, farm run-off of pesticides and fertilisers had seriously impaired the Grand River. Ciba Geigy, a corporation with an East Lansing plant, lobbied the EPA not to ban atrazine (Fagin and Lavelle 1999: 22; McKenna 2010; PEER 2001a).

- *Sewage sludge.* My research uncovered that sewage sludge, created from human urine and faeces and banned throughout much of Europe, has become the Lansing area's preferred mode of waste disposal. In 1999, 65 per cent of Ingham County's 6,345 tons of sewage sludge was trucked to local farms in the surrounding counties (PEER 2001a: 94–5).

- *Wetland loss.* New subdivisions and development have contributed to wetland loss. Ingham County has lost nearly 90
  per cent of its wetlands, compared to the state average of 50
  per cent. Seventeen species are endangered including gold-
  enseal, ginseng and the spotted turtle (McKenna 2010; PEER
  2001a).

In 1999, the Public Employees for Environmental Responsibility (PEER), based in Washington DC, published the work of
government whistleblowers across the country. In 1998, PEER
mailed surveys to all 1,462 employees of Michigan's Department
of Environmental Quality. PEER received 609 responses (a 41.6
return rate). When asked if employees 'experienced or know
of a situation(s) in which DEQ management has re-assigned or
changed the job responsibility of a staffer for doing their job "too
well" on a controversial project', 54 per cent agreed or strongly
agreed. When asked, if they feared 'the possibility of job-related
retaliation for advocating enforcement of environmental rules and
regulations', 52 per cent agreed or strongly agreed (PEER 1998). I
contacted PEER and received leads on various suppressed reports
in Michigan related to my Ingham County work, and I met with
several DEQ respondents to that survey who educated me about
the ways Michigan government coerces scientists and hides and
manipulates data.

The Official 'Community of Practice' Ruptures

For four months (March–June 2000) there was a growing political
divergence between two Health Department officials and nine
members of the Community Roundtable about the direction of
the research with some sharp exchanges between these two blocs
at the monthly meetings. The government was growing concerned
about what we were discovering and started to place pressure on
me, behind the scenes, not to 'go too far ahead of the curve'. To
help ensure this end, they began surveillance of my activities and
began pressuring me to cease exploring certain themes, despite

the Roundtable's encouragement to continue doing so (McKenna 2010).

In July 2000, two years into the project, contradictions came to a head between three levels of authority: (1) the Roundtable's authority, (2) the Health Department's authority and (3) my professional authority as an anthropologist (and lead researcher and writer). I had distributed the penultimate draft of the water report, in June 2000, to all members of the Roundtable for their final corrections and review. A week later I was shaken at the dramatic discrepancy between the responses of my Health Department bosses (government officials) and the community Roundtable (independent experts). Health Department officials crossed out almost everything that contained critical environmental health information and privately handed it to me, fully expecting me to abide by their behind-the-scenes recommendations. However, the majority of the Roundtable, which ostensibly had the ultimate authority over the 135-page publication, was in virtual agreement that it was an outstanding study. In their own careful edits they remained committed to the original plan to go where the data led us. They were unanimously excited to see it published. I was at an impasse. I could either choose to abide by the Health Department officials and self-censor most of the hard work over the previous two years or I could defer to the edits of the nine external Roundtable members. I chose the community Roundtable. This decision would come at a high price (McKenna 2010).

The Praxis Becomes Disruptive

With my decision to go forward with the Community Roundtable's leadership, I was suddenly subject to increased intimidation. Out of nowhere a host of new government officials, who had had nothing to do with the assessment, began pressuring me to ignore the Roundtable and use the government's views as I made my final edits. One, in an email, ridiculed the community Roundtable members as 'Chicken Little' professors who would frighten the public into thinking 'the sky was falling'. Serving multiple conflicting agendas, working sixty to seventy hours a week, my blood pressure, never a problem before, became dangerously high. Never had I experienced this kind of rough-and-tumble political infighting on the job. In fighting for the peoples' health, I was losing my own.

It was August and I took my planned two-week summer vacation, relieved at the break. When I returned to work on 28 August, I was just days from completing the 135-page report 'The Story of Water Resources at Work' (PEER 2001a). Within twenty minutes of arriving I was called to an ambush meeting with top management, union officials and a lawyer where I was summarily removed from the project. I was ordered to go into the government's EAP programme if I wanted to retain my job. Then I was taken behind closed doors by my supervisor who turned out the lights, drew the blinds and, pointing a finger in my face, expressly forbade me from 'saying one word about any of the environmental research' to anyone – the Community Roundtable and the public, or risk 'serious disciplinary action against you. Do you understand what I am telling you?' Ironically, that very night I was scheduled to begin teaching about this work at MSU's Anthropology Department. In effect I was being censored by the government in every sphere of civic activity: as a teacher, researcher, writer and citizen. Within days rumours began circulating within the organisation parallel to those that were used against Carol. People stopped talking to me and worse. I was being mobbed.

Theoretically speaking, the Community Roundtable's 'community of practice' had come crashing down on the iron rocks of bureaucracy. Brown and Duguid (1991) theorise about the dialectics of 'working, learning and innovating' in an organisation, illustrating how these three aspects often come into conflict with one another. My case had become emblematic. It became a 'disruptive innovation' outside of the bureaucracy's control. The project ended with government officials suppressing the full 135-page report and its findings. All but Dave Dempsey questioned the Health Department when in December 2000 they published a high-glossed 20-page whitewashed report, minus about 95 per cent of the facts, omitting me as the writer. The Health Department's official report largely sang the praises of Ingham County's water as safe and under control (Witter et al. 2000).

A Community of Resistance

I set about organising a community of resistance, strongly supported by Dave Dempsey. Over the following months, while still
employed but confined to banal tasks, Dempsey and I worked
closely with Public Employees for Environmental Responsibility
to prepare the report for eventual publication. In the ensuing two
months (February and March 2001), frustrated at the cover-up and
threats on me to stay silent, I began 'publishing' the suppressed
work (about a fictionalised place in Michigan) in about twenty
short articles for Michigan's Number One Environmental Listserv
(Enviro-Mich, see McKenna 2010). I contacted a top employment
law firm in Detroit and they agreed to take my whistleblower
case, given the overwhelming evidence in my favour. I also met
with the ACLU and they agreed to contribute an amicus brief on
my behalf as well. But contingencies obviated my desire to pursue
a legal remedy, including a family member who asked me not to
sue. With government harassment escalating to an intolerable degree, and my wife, Joyce, suddenly taking ill, I left in March 2001
to take care of her.

Over the summer of 2001 I travelled to Washington DC and
met with the Executive Director Jeff Ruch and his staff of PEER
for extensive dialogue, planning a national 'roll out', with press
releases and media coverage on 12 September 2001. Two months
after my 'constructive discharge' from the Ingham County job, I
received a phone call, in June 2001, from veteran newspaperman
Berl Schwartz, offering me the chance to write the Health and
Environment column for his new weekly, *The City Pulse*. He had
asked Jim Detjen, the Knight Chair of Environmental Journalism
at MSU, and the founder of the prestigious Society for Environmental Journalism, for candidates to write the column and Detjen
had recommended me. The opportunity to have a public voice was
one of the most remarkable turns in this ethnographic journey. I
was doing 'action anthropology' as a public writer and critical
public pedagogue (McKenna 2010). But then the tragedy of 9/11
happened and PEER told us that the rollout would have to wait
for another week. Finally on 19 September 2001 PEER published
The Story of Water Resources at Work making the information avail-

able to Michigan citizens. The story stirred a great deal of interest. The PEER website got 3,000 hits the first day. In the coming weeks PEER released two other reports on air pollution (PEER 2001c) and another on food quality (PEER 2001b). The *Lansing State Journal* did a small 500-word piece favouring PEER's perspective of the cover-up (Martin 2001: 1B). WKAR, the local public radio station associated with MSU interviewed four people, including myself, conducting an hour-long taped interview at my home. But after interviewing Health Department officials the station killed the story, saying that if they conveyed what the department said about me that the public radio station would be vulnerable to a libel lawsuit from me. There were two other print stories; one was carried by the MSU State News, a student paper, but it mistakenly reported that there were no serious concerns at the GM site (Byron 2001: 1A). The other was a feature story for EJ Magazine of MSU's Knight Center for Environmental Journalism, called 'Ducking the Truth', that supported PEER (Tuinstra 2002). In all I wrote thirty-three columns for the Pulse before leaving to assume the Executive Director's position for LocalMotion, an environmental group based in Ann Arbor. In January 2002 I won an environmental achievement award from Michigan's Ecology Center, based in Ann Arbor, for my work at the Health Department and City Pulse.

Conclusion

> We need to make familiar and recognize our own everyday possibilities for 'revolutionary praxis' and then take them up in our own research practice.
>
> (Jean Lave, anthropologist 2012: 169)

My story is a common one. In 2011, MIT-educated Marsha Coleman-Adebayo released her book *No Fear: A Whistleblower's Triumph Over Corruption and Retaliation at the EPA*. She tells how, in 1996, she secured her 'dream job' at the US EPA. The book details how Coleman-Adebay, an African-American, suffered enormous retaliation through racism, sexism and bullying in an effort to keep her quiet after about the corruption she found, as part of her job assignment. She refused. After years of struggle, and with a strong community of supporters, she prevailed in court. Noam Chomsky wrote in the book's foreword, 'Dr. Coleman-Adebayo's work ... analyzes how the government looks from the inside ... [and how it] resort[ed] to standard formulas to crush yet another whistleblower' (Coleman-Adebayo 2011: xiii).

A year after departing the public health job I wrote an article, in the press, which speculated – and theorised – why the government had taken the position it did. It was titled, 'Environmental Data Suppression in Lansing: Why Did They Do It?' (McKenna 2002). I isolated fifteen reasons for their actions. Here are five of them. One reason is that governments are neurotic. All governments are torn between the contradictory roles of supporting economic development and serving the public at large. The economy takes priority. The county probably had anxiety about offending local corporations, even though industry tends to treat the environment as its own 'tap and sink'. Ergo the fact that General Motors had the worst leaking underground storage tank in Lansing – an 'immediate threat to health, safety or the environment' according to the MDEQ – was not important enough to mention in the official report (McKenna 2002).

Another reason is that 'Being secretive is better all around'. Public Health officials want to keep contamination violations to themselves so that they can enjoy negotiating leverage with offenders like local restaurants. The meta-message to the polluter: clean up your operation or we will publicise your infractions in the press.

A third reason is that 'Attributing specific health outcomes to the environment would undermine the entire medical-industrial complex'. Doing environmental health research is a very radical proposition. If a significant portion of local diseases – cancer, heart disease, asthma – could be attributed to specific environmental toxins at given sites, then the social order might be turned upside down as massive monies shifted to the victims of toxins (via litigation, legislation or other methods). That is why in the U.S. BIO-medicine is the dominant form of medicine. It focuses on BIO-logical pathology diagnosed after the fact and pretty much ignores social, psychological and environmental etiologies to illness and disease. And if the social and psychological factors are recognised, they are seldom reimbursable.

I consulted Hal Draper's excellent *Karl Marx's Theory of Revolution, State and Bureaucracy* (Draper 1977), to characterise a more fundamental reason: Government is obsessed with bureaucracy and hierarchy, leaving little room for democracy. I wrote about Marx's view on the 'bureaucratic essence' of government:

> With the best will in the world, the keenest humanitarianism and the strongest intelligence, the administrative authorities are unable to do more than resolve temporary and transitory conflicts. ... The essential relationship is the bureaucratic relationship, inside the administrative body as well as in its connection with [in] the body administered. ... The state exists as various bureau-mentalities connected by relations of subordination and passive obedience where the chief abuse becomes hierarchy. (McKenna 2002: 17, cited from Draper 1977: 488–9)

Hierarchy was a watchword that my anthropology mentor Harry Raulet often used. A life-long Marxist, Harry despised MSU administrators for converting the university into a 'Disney Theme Park'. He relentlessly questioned authority. Harry died during my time at the Health Department, in 2000, and afterwards Harry's wife gave me his unfinished book-length manuscript, titled 'Hierarchy'. I have been practicing Harry's lessons in my life's work.

A central lesson I learned through practice is that 'holistic perspectives [– the essence of anthropology –] are loathed by administrators and governments' (McKenna 2002). As I wrote then:

> Health and environmental agencies, in particular, are dominated by a regulatory approach, focusing on one incident, one disease or one type of intervention. This prevents officials from stepping back to take a look at the big picture. Holism requires that we ask how all the broken pieces of Humpty Dumpty fit together – politics, economics, and old secrets. But all the King's horses and all the King's men can't put Humpty together again,

as the rhyme goes. Governments can crack eggs but cannot fix them because they are major players in environmental politics. When good studies are produced, governments often suppress them. Governments have too many conflicting interests to tell the straight story. It takes critical scholars, investigative journalists or enlightened citizens to do the job of researching the local environment in an honest and thorough manner. (McKenna 2002: 17)

My philosophy of praxis in the Health Department taught me how to become more attentive to the micro-processes of power, bullying and hierarchy everywhere. My identity was transformed by my *inability* to be subordinate to this corrupt hierarchy. As I teach my students, under the 'terror of neoliberalism' (Giroux 2004), anthropologists must become better educated on the methods, possibilities and risks of doing a kind of cultural activism that 'studies up' in their communities and converts private pain into a public issue, as C. Wright Mills instructed (Mills 1959). Activist anthropologists must learn how to develop communities of resistance to sustain them as they challenge authoritarianism in their own jobs.

Acknowledgements

I thank scores of anthropologists and activists for sustaining me in difficult times especially Joyce McKenna, Carl Maida, Sam Beck, Harry Raulet, Peter Rigby, Scott Whiteford, Dave Dempsey, Jeff Ruch, Eric Wingerter, Henry Giroux, Antonia Darder, Tim Wallace, Jim Detjen and Jane Sheldon. They have exemplified the truth that, 'to exist, you must resist'. Cheerful robots we will not be.

BRIAN MCKENNA is an anthropologist and journalist with three decades of experience working for non-profits, government, public health and NPR's Fresh Air. He received an environmental achievement award from Michigan's Ecology Center in 2002; was "Faculty Member of the Year" in 2009; and received the Rudolf Virchow Award, Honorable Mention, in 2014.

References

Adorno, T. W. (1977) [1966], *Negative Dialectics* (New York: Continuum).

Brown, J. S. and P. Duguid (1991), 'Organizational Learning and Communities of Practice: Towards a Unified View of Working, Learning and Innovation', *Organization Science* 2: 40–57.

Byron, S. (2001), 'Environmental Group Claims County Misrepresented Water Quality Facts,' *State News* (East Lansing, MI), 1A, 27 September.

Coleman-Adebayo. M. (2011), *No Fear: A Whistleblower's Triumph over Corruption and Retaliation at the EPA* (Chicago: Chicago Review Press).

Davenport, N., R. Schwartz and G. Elliott (1999), *Mobbing: Emotional Abuse in the American Workplace* (Ames, IA: Civil Society Publishing).

Draper, H. (1977), *Karl Marx's Theory of Revolution, State and Bureaucracy* (New York: Monthly Review Press).

Fagin, D. and M. Lavelle (1999), *Toxic Deception: How the Chemical Industry Manipulates Science, Bends the Law, and Endangers your Health* (Monroe, ME: Common Courage Press).

Freire, P. (1970), *Pedagogy of the Oppressed* (New York: Seabury Press).

Giroux, H. (2004), *The Terror of Neoliberalism* (Boulder: Paradigm Publishers).

Hale, C. R. (ed.) (2008), *Engaging Contradictions: Theory, Politics and Methods of Activist Scholarship* (Los Angeles: University of California).

Ingold, T. I. (2000), *The Perception of the Environment* (London: Routledge).

Lave, J. (2012), 'Changing Practice', *Mind, Culture, and Activity* 19, no. 2: 156–71.

Martin, T. (2001), *County Water Report Challenged*, Lansing St. J., 22 September, at 1B.

McKenna, B. (2002), 'Environmental Data Suppression in Lansing: Why Did They Do It?', *From the Ground Up* (Ann Arbor, Ecology Center) 33, December/January: 15–17.

McKenna, B. (2010), 'Exposing Environmental Health Deception as a Government Whistleblower: Turning Critical Ethnography into Public Pedagogy', *Policy Futures in Education* 8, no. 1: 22–36.

McKenna, B. and A. Darder (2011), 'The Art of Public Pedagogy: Should the "Truth" Dazzle Gradually or Thunder Mightily?', *Policy Futures in Education* 9, no. 6: 670–85.

Mills, C. W. (2000) [1959], *The Sociological Imagination* (New York: Oxford University Press).

Price, D. (2004), *Threatening Anthropology McCarthyism and the FBI's Surveillance of Activist Anthropologists* (Durham, NC: Duke University Press).

Public Employees for Environmental Responsibility (PEER) (1998), 'Preliminary Results, 1998 PEER Survey of Michigan DEQ Employees', http://www.peer.org/assets/docs/surveys/1998_mi_deq.pdf (accessed 27 June 2015).

Public Employees for Environmental Responsibility (PEER) (2001a), 'The Story of Water Resources at Work, Ingham County, Michigan, Washington, D.C., 130 pages, 19 September. News release: http://www.peer.org/news/news-releases/2001/09/19/suppressed-water-quality-report-released/ (accessed 27 June 2015). Full report: http://www.peer.org/assets/docs/mi/Ingham_co_water.pdf (accessed 27 June 2015).

Public Employees for Environmental Responsibility (PEER) (2001b), 'Food Quality Indicators, Ingham County, Michigan, Washington, D.C.', 20 pages, 26 September. News release: http://www.peer.org/news/news-releases/2001/09/26/suppressed-report-shows-nearly-a-third-of-lansing-area-restaurants-fail-inspections/ (accessed 27 June 2015). Full report: http://www.peer.org/assets/docs/mi/Ingham_food.pdf (accessed 27 June 2015). Appendix A: http://www.peer.org/assets/docs/mi/Food_Appendix_A.pdf (accessed 27 June 2015).

Public Employees for Environmental Responsibility (PEER) (2001c), 'Air Quality and Asthma Indicators, Ingham County, Michigan, Washington, D.C.', 62 pages, 31 October. News release: http://www.peer.org/news/news-releases/2001/11/01/asthma-epidemic-among-young-blacks-in-ingham-county/ (accessed 27 June 2015). Full report: http://www.peer.org/assets/docs/mi/Ingham_air.pdf (accessed 27 June 2015). Attachment 1: http://www.peer.org/assets/docs/mi/Ingham_co_air_table.pdf (accessed 27 June 2015).

Sanjek, R. (ed.) (1990), *Fieldnotes: The Makings of Anthropology* (Ithaca: Cornell University Press).

Stryker, R. and R. González (2014), *Up, Down, and Sideways: Anthropologists Trace the Pathways of Power*, foreword by L. Nader (New York: Berghahn).

Thomas, P. (2009), *The Gramscian Moment: Philosophy, Hegemony and Marxism* (Leiden: Brill).

Tuinstra, K. (2002), 'Ducking the Truth', *EJ Magazine* (Winter).

Witter, S. G., Glandon R., Godbold R., Paulson S., Kamrin M. (2000), *Ingham County's Surface and Groundwater Resources* (Lansing: Ingham County Health Department) December.

Local Trade and Exchange/Employment Systems (LETS) in Future Eco-sustainable Societies

Richard Westra

Introduction

Mainstream Green thinking on eco-sustainable social change subdivides into two broad genres.[1] One holds that eco-sustainability can be wrung out of the current economy by making prices sensitive to ecological costs (Speth 2009). This view is often paired with arguments for 'degrowth' which maintain eco-sanctity will be realised if the current economy is run in a 'steady-state' (Heinberg 2011). The second calls for more substantive change involving a global transition towards reduced economic scale or 'small', 'local' economies. Well-known proponents of the latter position include Bill McKibben (2007) and David Korten (2009).

This chapter accepts with McKibben and Korten that scale matters and averting dire impacts of climate change or transgressing environmental, 'planetary boundaries' (Rockström et al. 2009) demands we 'split things up' (to paraphrase McKibben 2011: 146–7). However, where the Green view, as such, miscarries, is in the claim, as stated by McKibben (2007: 2), that '[s]hifting our focus to local economies will not mean abandoning Adam Smith or doing away with markets'. Rather, McKibben continues (2007: 125) 'we may be able to re-create some of the institutions that marked, say, Adam Smith's Britain'. Similarly, David Korten (2009: 2) asserts: 'Ironically, it turns out that the solution to a failed [Wall Street] capitalist economy is a real-market economy much in line with the true vision of Adam Smith'. Smith, Korten proclaims, 'envisioned a world of local-market economies populated by small entrepreneurs, artisans, family farmers with strong community roots, engaged in producing and exchanging goods to meet the needs of themselves and their neighbours' (2009: 119).

As will be treated below, the chapter does not dismiss the role market operations and calculations might contribute to a sustainable future. However, grasping how market workings might be incorporated in even local economies is by no means as straightforward as McKibben and Korten assume. What this chapter argues is that, following Smith, McKibben and Korten conflate two very different meanings of 'exchange'. This conflation leads McKibben and Korten to the position that it is possible to decouple the 'market economy' per se from capitalism. Drawing upon work of anthropologist David Graeber, economic historian Karl Polanyi and political economist Karl Marx, it will be shown that 'exchange' across the precapitalist era was always of the face-to-face kind, entailed the 'exchange' of goods based on their qualitative, useful properties and imbricates in *interpersonal* social relations of various sorts. Exchange in the capitalist 'market economy', on the other hand, is predicated upon *impersonal* exchange of goods as value objects where sensuous, qualitative aspects of goods are suppressed to enable quantitative differentiation of goods in terms of market prices. The chapter concludes that if future small-scale eco-sustainable economies come to pass, to the extent market 'exchange' activities are utilised in them, the forms exchanges assume will be as local exchange/employment and trading systems (LETS). Exchange will necessarily be face-to-face or *interpersonal*, and function more akin to *sharing* rather than the impersonal, so-called 'invisible hand'-operated exchanges theorised by Adam Smith.

Historical Principles of Economy

Copious studies of economic history by David Graeber and Karl Polanyi yield similar conclusions. Graeber, for his part, pillories Adam Smith's 'myth of barter' which imputes to an unspecified society in a 'state of nature' the mechanisms of market 'exchange' akin to Smith's eighteenth-century English village (Graeber 2012: Chapter 2). Polanyi, on the other hand, refers to the 'economistic fallacy' as the Smithian 'error' imbibed by neoclassical economics of 'equating the human economy in general with its market form' (Polanyi 1977: 6). In making their case for the historical specificity of capitalism, both Graeber and Polanyi are driven to elaborate typologies of economic principles other than that of the market principle of capitalism.

Let us begin with Polanyi (see figure 1). Polanyi's hugely important intervention in debates over economic history is his point that prior to the dawn of the capitalist era it was inconceivable to refer to such a thing as an 'economy' separate from ensembles of social practices – religion, culture, politics, ideology and so forth – with which economic life was enmeshed. And that it is only in the capitalist era that the economy tends to 'dis-embed' from the social as such. Polanyi then refers to economic relations as they imbricate with the broad spectrum of precapitalist social practices in terms of two key principles of economy: reciprocity and redistribution. The former encompasses a wide gamut of activities engaged in by the most primitive societies involving some variant or degree of sharing or cooperation, including things like gift giving and 'give-and-take' in the context of kinship relations or customary/communal practices, along with what may be understood as small-m markets. The latter involve one-off 'exchanges' of goods according to their qualitative properties. Redistribution, on the other hand, occurs in more advanced, geospatially larger-scale precapitalist societies and entails the movement of goods, tribute, taxes, tithes and so forth towards the 'centre' and their reallocation according to interpersonal relations of domination and subordination of various kinds and the 'status' of layered social sectors (Polanyi 1957: Chapter 4).

David Graeber seeks to distinguish economic principles according to the 'moral grounds' that underpin them (see figure 2). He sets out baseline communism as his first. We are all essentially communists at a fundamental level, Graeber opines, as in offering a stranger a light without expecting anything in return. We are also predisposed to supporting others in the aftermath of a natural disaster. To the extent people do not perceive themselves as enemies, Graeber asseverates, Marx's principle of socialist distribution set out in his *Critique of the Gotha Program* – 'from each according to their abilities, to each according to their needs' – exists as a foundational norm of human sociality. The same logic that holds among individuals is then extended within groups: And from there to management of common resources. Graeber sees baseline communism diverging from Polanyi's reciprocity except 'reciprocity in the broadest sense' (given that there is no compulsion communistic 'giving' will be reciprocated). Next, for Graeber, are relations of hierarchy involving unequal parties. Charting this on a continuum, Graeber sees plunder and theft at one end, selfless charity at the other. Graeber observes how hierarchy often crystallises in social relations of superiority and inferiority that are regulated through webs of custom or habit. Finally, Graeber sets out two principles of *exchange*. What we may refer to as 'exchange 1' is the sort of exchange that imbricates in interpersonal relations such as gift giving, where comparing the 'value' of goods exchanged does not occur. Graeber follows up: 'Nor did anyone ever consider making such a calculation'. Then there is 'exchange 2' or 'commercial exchange' as Graeber puts it, which is impersonal and concerned with 'equivalence'; although, for Graeber, non-commercial exchange, gift giving, tit-for-tat 'games' and so on grey into barter in a fashion somewhat akin to Polanyi's notion of a small-m market activity (Graeber 2012: 102–13).

Differing from Graeber and Polanyi, Karl Marx does not offer commensurate detailed historical accounts of economic practices to back up his carving human history into grand epochs or 'modes of production' (each marked by a specific configuring of social class relations) – primitive communism, slavery, feudalism, capitalism, with socialism nigh as Marx's saw things at the end of his life (Marx 1859 [2015]). Nevertheless, Marx's far deeper elaboration upon the workings of the capitalist economy combined with a mastery of the available economic history literature of his day led him to a similar position on precapitalist economies as later work by them. Certainly one of Marx's most important corroborative insights here is his recognition that economic forms like money, wages, even profits, existed at various junctures across the sweep of precapitalist history, but the economic impact of such forms was always exogenous to the specific modalities by which human beings reproduced their livelihoods in early societies. And these modalities, according to Marx, were always characterised by the interpersonal relations of the sort captured in the more refined typologies above. Set out below is the Marx–Polanyi,[2] Marx–Graeber correspondence.

The Karl Marx – Karl Polanyi Correspondence

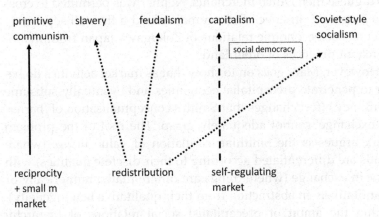

Figure 1: The Karl Marx–Karl Polanyl Correspondence.

The Karl Marx – David Graeber Correspondence

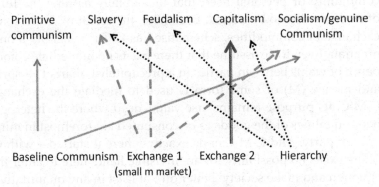

Figure 2: The Karl Marx–David Graeber Correspondence.

Further, in Part 1 of the first volume of his *Capital*, Marx notes that to the extent impersonal exchange of goods is found in the ancient world, it occurs at the borders of separate communities ([1867] 2015). A clear example of the practice by which communities sought to ensure their internal interpersonal socioeconomic relations were never infiltrated by such 'trading' activity is the creation by the Tokugawa Shogunate in 1634 of *Dejima*, or 'protruding island', in the bay of Nagasaki to accommodate first Portuguese then Dutch merchants. Neither was permitted to cross into Nagasaki. In effect, Dejima maintained a firewall separating discrete socioeconomic relations of Tokugawa Japan from that of merchant practices of other lands.

However, Marx goes on to show that as market activities do begin to penetrate precapitalist economies and eventually subsume them they effect changes that Smith's conceptualisation of 'barter' or 'exchange' cannot adequately grasp. The root of the problem Marx argues is the Smithian conflation of value in *use* (where goods are differentiated according to their discrete qualities) with *value* in exchange (where things are differentiated numerically or quantitatively in abstraction from their qualitative heterogeneity). Within the ambit of precapitalist social relations of hierarchy and baseline communism in Graeber's terms, reciprocity and redistribution in Polanyi's, or primitive communism, slavery and feudalism in Marx's, the incidence of goods taking the form of a commodity (C), a good actually *produced* for impersonal market exchange, is rare. More likely, it is goods produced in surplus of community or personal need that incidentally assume the form of a commodity to be traded. Even here, the resulting impersonal exchange of commodities, schematised as C-C is generally a one-off affair. Even if we assume that there exists no immediate coincidence of wants between parties in a precapitalist 'market' of sorts, and money (M) of some form is used to mediate the exchange C-M-C, its purpose remains 'use value' need where the heterogeneous qualities of the goods to be consumed are foremost in mind of each party. And C-M-C ends exactly where it started – with C. There exists no possibility for an 'invisible hand' here to enter the equation and make society 'better off', at least in any quantitative, objectively measurable fashion.

Indeed, we would also have to question how such a society materially reproduces itself even in a potential 'steady-state'. After all, in a local economy composed of presumably self-employed 'small entrepreneurs, artisans, family farmers' (as Korten sees it), there exists virtually no elasticity of labour supply given how each self-employed operator is tied to a concrete-specific use value skill. As McKibben and Korten leave no space for *ex ante* economic decision-making in their local community model, with each self-employed economic actor pursuing their own self-seeking proclivities a-la-Adam Smith, whether in the end each individual decision on the what, how and how much of production is valid in any 'community' sense, is only established *ex post*.[3] Because each C-M-C is simply a one-off exchange, by the time all the wants worked their way through the division of labour based on self-employed artisans, and the realisation dawned that so many wants were unsatisfied, there would be no social basis for 'efficiently' adjusting supply to demand, therefore ensuring that the society was mired in shortages. To take an example on the supply side of C-M-C, the historical record of early modern European transition to capitalism with its loosening of feudal interpersonal bonds is replete with accounts bemoaning the ethic of artisans or pre-industrial craft workers who having worked enough to satisfy their own needs simply went on vacation (Duplessis 2004: 262–6). And, in the end, any society unable to allocate basic goods to meet shifting patterns of social demand will die out.

The Historical Specificity of Capitalism

In the section of *Capital* cited above, Marx offered rudiments of his understanding of the specific *modus operandi* of the *capitalist* market. The approach Marx took opened a new world for us. Beginning with consumption and consumer preferences as did Smith and his neoclassical followers might tell us something about precapitalist barter (to the extent it ever existed in the degree claimed). But it tells us little about *capitalism*, a society where, paradigmatically, goods take the form of commodities and are produced specifically for the market. Rather, Marx's theorisation

starts with the *seller,* and initiator of all 'exchanges', for the owner
of the commodity C is interested *not* in its use value or consumption (otherwise the owner would not be going to the market), but
in its *value* or 'moneyness'. Money emerges as the social connector
in capitalist society because it can purchase *any* commodity without qualitative use value restrictions. We can point out here, as an
aside, that it is precisely the 'tension' inhering in the commodity
between its concrete-specific, qualitative attributes as a use value
and its abstract-general, quantitative property of 'moneyness',
or value, from which Marx developed the basic categories of the
capitalist commodity economy in his economic theory (Westra
2012/13).

Returning to the issue at hand, Marx schematised exchange in
the capitalist market economy as M-C-M`. M-C-M` captures the
specificity of capitalism as a society of generalised commercial exchange where goods paradigmatically take the form of commodities and exchange is no longer a one-off affair. Each purchase and
sale has benefit maximisation, as expressed in M`, as its goal. In
Adam Smith's iconic words: 'It is not from the benevolence of the
butcher, the brewer, or the baker, that we expect our dinner, but
from their regard to their own interest' (Smith [1776] 2015: Book 1
Chapter 2). Indeed, looking at capitalist market workings from the
perspective of the seller, interested in M`, we can well understand
why the social goal of capitalist society as a whole – profit-making or augmenting value – is abstract and quantitative.[4] And here
resides the deal with the devil that McKibben and Korten unwit-
tingly made with their position that the capitalist market can be
decoupled from capitalism.

First, operations of the capitalist market where economic decisions in society are made on the basis of quantitative price signals
does overcome the bottleneck of inelastic labour supply adverted
to above. But it does so at a social cost. That cost is the rendering of
the human power to labour, or labour power, itself a commodity.
Market 'efficiency' in allocating resources stems from the fact that
workers, divested of means of production and livelihood (having
in their possession neither the tools of Korten's 'artisans' nor property of his 'small entrepreneur' or 'farmer'), make their labour
power available in the market to be applied to the production of

any good in response to shifting patterns of social demand and opportunities for profit-making. Remember, Smith's iconic words quoted above advert to the *ex post* nature of the 'market economy'. It is this feature as well that McKibben and Korten lauded in their call for not 'abandoning' Smith. Smith's writing antedated the industrial revolution and formation of its urban proletariat. But, as eminent historian Christopher Hill showed, the real world example Smith could draw upon where 'self interest' actually made everyone 'better off' was not the interaction among 'baker' and 'butcher' in his village. Rather it was when greedy landlords and capitalist farmers, hiring labour displaced by the loosening of feudal bonds, fostered a range of improvements to increase profits while lowering the price of food across Britain (Hill 1969: 147ff). Of course, the industrial revolution and urbanisation would not have been possible without this transformation. But we have to be clear on the economic principle responsible for it.

Second, the very act on the part of the seller in M-C-M` of bringing the commodity to market, reflecting the interest of the seller *not* in the use value of the good but in its 'moneyness' or value, fosters an *indifference* to use value or the sensuous, qualitative properties of goods. This indifference inhering in exchange as it occurs at the most fundamental level of the capitalist market has ramifications which reverberate through the 'market economy' as a whole. For workers hired by business to produce *any* good according to shifting patterns of social demand and opportunities for profit-making, the 'market economy' fosters a disinterest in the outcome of their activity leading to the regular production of noxious and dangerous goods with potential to destroy life on the planet itself. The worker as consumer similarly manifests a studied indifference to the modalities and wherewithal of the producing of goods with both deleterious environmental and human consequences.

Finally, the indifference to use value which is part and parcel of the price mechanism that tethers human economic decisions to quantitative criteria means that in the most substantive sense, the market economy will always reproduce human economic life and satisfy human use value need as a *byproduct* of profit-making or value augmentation as captured by M`.

Eco-sustainable Human Communities of the Future

McKibben and Korten certainly struck a resonating chord with their claim that future eco-sustainable societies built around small, local economies need not abandon Adam Smith and the 'market economy'. Economy-wide *ex ante* economic decision-making, as embodied in Soviet-style planning, proved disastrous on numerous levels. Anarchists, who had been kindred spirits of socialists at the outset, broke with socialists over socialist determination to institute central planning of all facets of economic life from commanding heights of the state. Anarchist belief in the need for interpersonal sharing, mutual aid, even small-m markets, in line with Polanyi's conceptualisation of reciprocity proved justified even in the Soviet context. As James C. Scott suggested, without elements of the foregoing, including 'grey markets, bartering and [other] ... informal practices', it is not clear how the Soviet Union would have survived under its regime of state-managed collectivised agriculture (Scott 1998: 203–4). Today, in a similar vein, it is no historical accident that we are witnessing a surplus of coops, community currencies, grassroots organisations and local exchange/ employment and trading systems (LETS), proliferate across the neoliberal decades. LETS, in particular, spawned from the 1980s, instructively most in developed economies (Westra 2011: 532).

What is important to grasp about LETS is that the 'money' it utilises operates with only one of the functions of money in the capitalist 'market economy' – money as means of exchange – excluding the second and third functions respectively, money as measure of value and money as store of value. This anchors value in *use* and 'exchange' as an act where parties are interested in the heterogeneous qualities of goods. Unfortunately, even if we assume that LETS of one kind or another is adopted by communities predisposed to sharing and so forth, its market 'exchange' activities will not realise the notion of Smithian exchange idealised by McKibben and Korten. Nor will LETS on its own be able completely to surmount the inelasticity of labour-supply problem of the economy of 'small entrepreneurs, artisans, family farmers', touched on above, with only *ex post* economic decision-making. Even advocates of LETS often do not appreciate what is at stake here (Greco 2009).

Both Graeber and Polanyi claimed that across the divergent really existing historical human economies, no single economic principle – reciprocity, baseline communism or redistribution or hierarchy or 'market economy', commercial exchange – is able to reproduce material life on its own. Marx, for his part, argued how in all forms of society one economic principle 'predominates', with its specific relations assigning 'rank and influence' to other principles (Marx [1857] 2015). Meeting the challenges of the future will require an 'uncommon nimbleness' to quote McKibben (2011: 147). Hence, my position falls in between that of McKibben/Korten and Marx.

As elaborated in greater detail elsewhere, the argument quite simply is that such nimbleness in communities of practice will be given life by organisational forms that combine economic principles not for ideological reasons but to enhance human flourishing (Westra 2014: Chapter 6). Variants of reciprocity (in the broadest sense) and baseline communism including LETS of different sorts and involving sharing, mutual aid, small-m markets and other community economic activities long advocated by anarchists must certainly form the mainstay of rich, eco-sustainable community material life. But, redistribution will need to be applied by communities to ensure basic goods are produced in correct amounts and quality to meet social demand. Similarly, to build progressive communities necessitates redistributive practices in relation to things like education, health care, provision of services to youth, the aged, the physically challenged and so forth, though a balance may be found here between community service need 'exchanges' and redistribution. However, put succinctly, there is no escaping *ex ante* decision-making in our economic life.

And what is wrong with that? After all, as even Marx recognised, capitalism with its 'market economy' played an important progressive role in human history, freeing human beings from the yoke of interpersonal relations of domination and subordination characteristic of class societies antedating capitalism. Economic freedoms as such became the foundation for the political freedoms around which constitutional democracies formed. But capitalist democracies maintain one last human non-freedom. This is the view propagated since Adam Smith and crystallised in theories lauding *ex post* decision-making in economic life: that human beings can never consciously manage their material affairs but, rather, are destined in perpetuity to simply 'react' or 'conform' to the outcomes of blind economic forces as if the latter were an *extra-human* force of nature. Marx referred to this world as the 'kingdom of necessity'. On the other hand, the 'kingdom of freedom' arises when human beings ask some simple questions such as: What are we doing in our economic lives? Should we keep doing what we are doing? And, if not, what options do we have to make changes? This chapter shows that human beings *do* have choices in a set of economic principles that have proved their historical viability and now await human deployment in making progressive eco-sustainable societies of the future.

RICHARD WESTRA received his PhD from Queen's University, Canada in 2001. He has taught at universities around the world including Queen's University and Royal Military College, Canada; International Study Center, East Sussex UK; College of The Bahamas, Nassau; and Pukyong National University, Pusan, South Korea. He has been a Visiting Research Fellow at Focus on the Global South/Chulalongkorn University Social Research Institute, Chulalongkorn University, Bangkok, Thailand. Currently he is Designated Professor, Graduate School of Law, Nagoya University, Japan. His work has been published in numerous international peer-reviewed academic journals. He is author or editor of fourteen books including *Unleashing Usury: How Finance Opened the Door for Capitalism Then swallowed it Whole,* Clarity, 2016; and *Exit from Globalization,* Routledge, 2014.

Notes

1. Research for this chapter received support from the National Research Foundation of South Korea Grant NRF-2013S1A5B8A01055117.
2. Polanyi himself never made the connection between redistribution as he saw it and the workings of the economy in the Soviet experiment with socialism. An argument can be made, however, that not only did the Soviet economy engage redistribution as its core economic mech-

anism, but it bound society in relations of domination and subordination akin to that of precapitalist societies (Westra 2011: 521–4).

3. Quite simply, in the debate between proponents of 'the market' as the central principle of economy and those supportive of 'the state' as occurred over the Soviet experiment with socialism, *ex ante* decision-making refers to planning in advance. It has always been inveighed against by market proponents as cumbersome and insensitive to varied, conflicting interests marking modern, complex societies. *Ex post* refers to the after-the-fact fashion by which 'the market' purportedly adjudicates among varied conflicting interests through its price mechanism without the 'visible', interpersonal hand of government planners.

4. Of course, 'consumption' takes place in capitalist economies. But the prime activity of capitalism and the metric upon which economic decisions are predicted is profit-making as reflected in M`.

References

Duplessis, R. S. (2004), *Transitions to Capitalism in Early Modern Europe* (Cambridge: Cambridge University Press).

Graeber, D. (2012), *Debt: The First 5,000 Years* (New York: Melville House).

Greco, T. (2009), *The End of Money and the Future of Civilization* (White River Junction: Chelsea Green).

Heinberg, R. (2011), *The End of Growth: Adapting to Our New Economic Reality* (Gabriola Island, BC: New Society Publishers).

Hill, C. (1969), *Reformation to Industrial Revolution* (Harmondsworth: Penguin Books).

Korten, D. C. (2009), *Agenda for a New Economy: From Phantom Wealth to Real Wealth* (San Francisco: Berrett-Koehler).

Marx, K. [1857] (2015), *Grundrisse*, http://www.marxists.org/archive/marx/works/1857/grundrisse/ch01.htm (accessed January 5 2015).

Marx, K. [1859] (20145), *A Contribution to the Critique of Political Economy*, http://www.marxists.org/archive/marx/works/1859/critique-pol-economy/index.htm (accessed January 5 2015).

Marx, K. [1867] (20145), *Capital*, Vol. 1, Afterword to the Second German Edition, http://www.marxists.org/archive/marx/works/1867-c1/ (accessed January 5 2015).

McKibben, B. (2007), *Deep Economy: The Wealth of Communities and the Durable Future* (New York: Henry Holt and Company).

McKibben, B. (2011), *Eaarth: Making Life on a Tough New Planet* (New York: St. Martin's Griffin).

Polanyi, K. (1957), *The Great Transformation* (Boston: Beacon Press).

Polanyi, K. (1977), *The Livelihood of Man* (London: Academic Press).

Rockström, J. Steffen, K. Noone, Å. Persson, F. S. Chapin, III, E. Lambin, T. M. Lenton, M. Scheffer, C. Folke, H. Schellnhuber, B. Nykvist, C. A. De Wit, T. Hughes, S. van der Leeuw, H. Rodhe, S. Sörlin, P. K. Snyder, R. Costanza, U. Svedin, M. Falkenmark, L. Karlberg, R. W. Corell, V. J. Fabry, J. Hansen, B. Walker, D. Liverman, K. Richardson, P. Crutzen, and J. Foley et al. (2009), 'Planetary Boundaries: Exploring the Safe Operating Space for Humanity', *Ecology and Society*, 14, no. 2, http://www.ecologyandsociety.org/vol14/iss2/art32 (accessed December 3 2014).

Scott, J. C. (1998), *Seeing Like a State: How Certain Schemes to Improve the Human Condition Have Failed* (New Haven, CT: Yale University Press).

Smith, A. [1776] (2015), *An Inquiry into the Nature and Causes of the Wealth of Nations*, http://www.econlib.org/library/Smith/smWN1.html#B.I,%20Ch.2 (accessed January 5 2015).

Speth, J. G. (2008), *The Bridge at the Edge of the World: Capitalism, the Environment, and Crossing from Crisis to Sustainability* (New Haven: Yale University Press).

Westra, R. (2011), 'Renewing Socialist Development in the Third World', *Journal of Contemporary Asia*, 41, no. 4: 519–543.

Westra, R. (2012/13), '*Capital* as Dialectical Economic Theory', *Journal of Australian Political Economy*, Special Issue on *Capital* against Capitalism: New Research in Marxist Political Economy, 70: 233–250.

Westra, R. (2014), *Exit from Globalization* (London: Routledge).

Index

NOTE: Page references with an *f* are figures.

A

activism: glocal, 34; political, 178; Sulukule Platform, 99–101; urban rights (in Turkey), 94–108
Adaptamos e resistimos (We adapt and resist), 116*f*, 117*f*
adult literacy (Brazil), 79
Afonso, Ana Isabel, 13
African heritage (Brazil), 87
agriculture, 109, 118. *See also* civic ecology (Lisbon, Portugal)
air pollution, 195
AK Party (Turkey), 96
Alexander, Jacqui, 70
Alves da Silveira, Ana Lúcia, 81
Anthropocene, 4, 5
anthropology, 194
apprenticeships, 166
Arendt, Hannah, 168
Argentina (Salta), 43–59. *See also* Calchaquí Valley
artisanship, 167
Asamblea de Unidad Cantonal de Cotacachi (AUCC), 28
Ascendent, 27
Asociación Agroartesanal de Café cultures Río Íntag (AACRI), 24, 25, 30–32, 38
assessment, High Tech High (San Diego, California), 158
Associação para a Valorização Ambiental da Alta de Lisboa (AVAAL), 111, 112, 113, 117, 118–20, 121, 122
asthma, 196, 202

B

Banco do Brasil, 75
banking (transferring knowledge), 125
bartering, 208, 212
Base Realignment and Closure (BRAC), 152
Bellagio Principles (1997), 3
Bender, Thomas, 169
biodiversity, 160
biodiversity conservation, 4
Biomimicry: Respecting Nature Through Design, 162
biomonitoring, 9
Black, Brown, Green Alliance (BBGA), 179, 180
Blueprint for Student Success (San Diego Unified School District), 156
body-burden, 9
Bono de Desarrollo Humano (BDH), 26
Brazil: African heritage, 87; collective identity, 85; educational system of, 79, 86; library research, 77; nationhood, 89; social inclusion in, 75–93
bricolage, definition of, 9, 10
Bronfman, Vásquez, 54
Brooklyn. *See* Williamsburg, Brooklyn
Brooklyn Legal Services Corporation A, 126*f*
Brooklyn Queens Expressway (BQE), 129, 134
Brundtland Report (World Commission on Environment and Development 1987), 3
bullying, 201

Business Alliance for Local Living
  Economies (BALLE), 181
Business Roundtable, 156
buyers, tea, 67

C
Caetano, Luiz, 79
Calchaquí, 44
Calchaquí Valley (Salta, Argentina),
  43–59; actors, perspectives
  and emerging problems,
  49–54; changes in lifestyle in,
  44–47; research strategies, 47–48;
  workshops, 52, 53
Camaçari, Brazil, 80
Camaçarian, Brazil, 81
Cancela, Jorge, 112, 121
capitalism, 210, 213, 217; eco-
  sustainable societies, 213–15
Captial (Marx), 212
Carter, Majora, 179
Catholic churches (Brooklyn), 133,
  134, 138
Cecil, Gerald, 176
Centre for Latin American Research
  and Documentation (CEDLA),
  77
certification, fair trade, 67
chemicals, exposure to, 9
Chomsky, Noam, 202
Churches United, Corp., 139, 140
Churches United for Fair Housing
  (CUFFH), 140, 141, 142, 143, 144
El Churkal, 49
Cidade do Saber (CDS): communities
  of practice at the, 75–93
circuits of discovery, 193
citizen science, 8, 9
citizenship, 7, 12, 80, 81, 89
The City Pulse, 200
civic ecology (Lisbon, Portugal),
  109–24; institutional conflicts
  and *clandestinidade*, 113, 114–18;
  shared understandings of, 113–14;
  sustainability, 118–20
civic engagement, 3
clandestine garden *(horta
  clandestina)*, 111, 114, 115f

clandestinidade, institutional conflicts
  and, 113, 114–18
Clean Energy Triangle (CET), 176,
  177
COART, 81, 84
CODEL, 81, 84
coffee: fair trade, 31; shade-grown,
  32; sustainability through, 30–32
Cold War, 152, 155
Coleman-Adebayo, Marsha, 201, 202
collaboration, 187
collaborative peer networks, 11
collective bargaining, fair trade, 62
collective identity (Brazil), 85
Colomé, 49
commercial exchanges, 217
commodities, 214
common-pool resources, 6
commons, restoration of, 8–11
communication resources, 10
communism, 209, 210
communities: frameworks,
  2; relationships between
  environments and, 43–59;
  sustainability, 175–78; where
  relationships are built, 11
communities of practice, 1–19; at
  the *Cidade do Saber* (CDS), 75–93;
  defining, 77–78; and marginality,
  79–82; official ruptures (Lansing,
  Michigan), 197–98; public health,
  193–95; social dimensions of, 110;
  Sulukule Children's Art Atelier,
  101–4; Sulukule neighbourhood
  commons *(müshterekler)*, 99–101;
  sustainability, 81–85, 151–73;
  urban renewal (in Istanbul), 95–99;
  urban rights activism (Turkey),
  94–108
community-based projects, 183
community development, social
  enterprise for, 183
community of resistance, 200–201
Community Roundtable (Lansing,
  Michigan), 194–98, 199
community service, 128
Comunidades Unidas de Molinos
  (CUM), 45, 48

conscientização (consciousness raising), 83, 84
consciousness raising (*conscientização*), 83
conservation (Ecuador), 27
Constitution of Monticristi (2008), 23, 28
cooperatives, 183–87
Coordinadora de Mujeres de Íntag (CMI), 25, 35, 36–37, 38
Cornell University, 128; Urban Semester Program, 140, 143
Correa, Rafael, 23
Cotacachi Assembly for County Unity. *See Asamblea de Unidad Cantonal de Cotacachi* (AUCC)
Cotacachi-Cayapas Ecological Reserve, 26
Cotacachi County (Ecuador), 25, 26, 28
countryside, sustaining the, 12–13
craft knowledge, 167
crafts, communities of practice, 1
Creating a Food Forest workshop, 186
critical literacy, 165
Critique of the Gotha Program (Marx), 210
Crivos, Marta, 12, 13
Culture and Art (Brazil), 81

D
D'Amico, Linda, 12
Darjeeling, India, 60–72
Davenport, Noa, 193
DECOIN, 30, 38, 39
defence industry, 154
deforestation, 5
delocalisation, 3
democracy, 36
Dempsey, Dave, 199, 200
Department of Environmental Quality (Michigan), 197
Detjen, Jim, 200
development, 4, 30
Dewey, John, 169, 193
Diaguita, 44
DiMarzio, Nicholas, 139

discovery, circuits of, 193
disruption of public health, 198–99
DNA, 160, 162
dollarisation of the Ecuadorian economy (2000), 23
domain, 11
domestic work, 35
Domino Sugar luxury/affordable housing project (Brooklyn), 138f
Draper, Hal, 203
Duran, Esteban, 140

E
EBATECA *(Escola do Ballet do Teatro Castro Alves)*, 86
Echeverria, Diego, 131
Eco-Cycle, 174–89; cooperatives, 183–87; green-collar jobs, 178–80; place-based non-profits, 180–83; sustainable communities, 175–78
ecológia civica (civic ecology), 111. *See also* civic ecology (Lisbon, Portugal)
ecology, 194
EcoLounge, 182, 183
economic globalisation, 175
economies: historical principles of, 208–13; market, 217; transition of military installations, 152–55
eco-sustainable societies, 207–20; capitalism, 213–15; of the future, 216–18; historical principles of economy, 208–13
Ecuador, 23–42; conservation, 27; social assistance programmes (for the poor), 24. *See also* Intag, Ecuador
Ecuadorian Cloud Forests, 12
education: communities of practice (Istanbul, Turkey), 94–108; cooperatives, 183–87; green-collar jobs, 178–80; place-based non-profits, 180–83; sustainability, 174–89; sustainable communities, 175–78. *See also* learning
educational institutions (Argentina), 49

Elon University, 175
El Puente High School (Brooklyn),
    139*f*
emancipatory social movements
    (Wlliamsburg, Brooklyn),
    125–47; churches united, 137–40;
    gentrification, 131–33; overview of
    Williamsburg, Brooklyn, 129–31;
    participatory research, 140–44;
    Southside (*Los Sures*), 133–36;
    transformative learning, 140–44
'The End of Cheap Oil' (Campbell
    and Laherrère), 175
engagement, mutual, 110
entrepreneurship, 187, 214
environment: exploitation of, 5;
    measuring impacts, 9
Environmental Health Roundtable,
    194, 195
environmentalism, 4, 24
Environmental Justice Movement,
    178
environmental stewardship, 12
environments, relationships between
    communities and, 43–59
E.O. Wilson's Life on Earth (Ryan,
    McGill and Wilson), 160
Erdoğan, Recep Tayyip, 96
European Roma Rights Center
    (ERRC), 98
exchange of goods, 208, 210

F

fair trade, 60–72; certification, 67;
    coffee, 31; collective bargaining,
    62; enthusiasts, 66; practice of,
    62–68; processes, 63; tea, 60; and
    women, 64
farms: in Ecuador, 26; pesticides,
    196
Fehrenbacher, Tom, 161, 162, 163
feudalism, 210, 213
filters, 8
financialisation, 6
Flint, Michigan, 191
Foggo, Hacer, 98
FOIA (Freedom of Information Act),
    195

food: security, 35, 36; urban
    gardeners, 109–24
forest ecosystems, stewardship of, 24
Freire, Paulo, 26, 27, 84, 165, 193

G

gardens (Lisbon, Portugal), 109. *See
    also* civic ecology
General Atomics, 154
General Dynamics, 154, 155
General Motors (GM), 190, 191, 196,
    201
gentrification (Williamsburg,
    Brooklyn), 131–33
geographic information maps (GIS),
    195
Gezi Park protests (2013), 95, 96
Gibson-Graham, J. K., 185
Gidden, Anthony, 9
Giroux, Henry, 166
global change, consequences of, 3
global citizenship, 12
globalisation, 175
global sustainability, 1–19
glocal activism, 34
Gogol Bordello, 100
Goodall, Jane, 162
Graeber, David, 208, 209, 210, 211,
    212, 217
Gramsci, Antonio, 193
green agriculture, 118
The Green Collar Economy (Jones), 179
green-collar jobs, 178–80
Green Job movement, 179
Greenpeace, 183
Guerrón Montero, Carla, 13

H

habits of mind, 158
Halpern, Robert, 166
Harper, Krista, 13
Harvey, David, 7, 99, 100
Hasidic Jews, 130, 130*f*, 132, 133
health commons, 7
Health Department (Lansing,
    Michigan), 190, 191, 192, 197,
    198, 199, 201, 204; Environmental
    Health Roundtable, 194, 195

health institutions (Argentina), 46,
  49, 50, 53
hegemonies, 176
Our heritage has a trade (*El
  Patrimonio tiene Oficio*), 45
Hernandez, Efrain, 128*f*
Higher Education Programme
  (Argentina), 48
High Tech High (San Diego,
  California), 151–73; learning
  strategies, 164–70; skill demand
  changes, 155–64; transition of
  military installations, 152–55
High Tech High San Diego Bay Study
  (Vavra), 160
Hill, Christopher, 215
Hirschman, Alfred O., 180
historical institutions, 191
Holocaust, 130, 132
Horta Acessível, 112
horta clandestina (clandestine
  garden), 111, 114, 115*f*
hospitals, 53. *See also* health
  institutions (Argentina)
household income (in Ecuador),
  26

I

inclusion in Brazil, 75–93
India (Darjeeling), 60–72
indigenous invention, 158
indigenous organic cultivation, 66
industrialisation, 6
information sharing, 76, 77. *See also*
  communities of practice
Ingham County Health Department
  (Lansing, Michigan), 190
institutional conflicts and
  clandestinidade, 113, 114–18
institutions, historical, 191
Intag, Ecuador, 23–42; *Coordinadora
  de Mujeres de Íntag* (CMI)
  surveys, 36–37; glocal approach
  to sustainability, 26–29; glocal
  expressions of sustainable
  development, 30; *Periódico
  Intag* (2000–2011), 32–34; social
  and ecological contexts, 25–26;

sustainability through coffee,
  30–32; women's rights, 34–36
Intag River's Association of Small
  Scale Coffee Farmers, 25
Intag Women's Coordinating
  Committee. *See Coordinadora de
  Mujeres de Íntag* (CMI)
intercontinental ballistic missiles
  (ICBMs), 154
interdisciplinary experiential
  learning, 163
interpersonal social relations, 208
Interpretation Centre and Museum
  Indalecio Gómez (Argentina), 48
Istanbul, Turkey, 94–108. *See also*
  Turkey
Istanbul Chamber of Architects, 98
Istanbul Chamber of City Planners,
  98
Istanbul European Capital of
  Culture Agency, 101
Istanbul Technical University (İTÜ)
  Turkish Music State Conservatory,
  95, 101

J

Jacobs, Gary, 156, 157
Jacobs, Jane, 3
Joint Body, 63, 64, 65, 66, 68, 69
joint enterprises, 110
Jones, Van, 179

K

Kakan language, 44
Kamrin, Michael, 194
Karagümrük neighborhood
  (Turkey), 94
*Karl Marx's Theory of Revolution, State
  and Bureaucracy* (Draper), 203
Karvelis, Father, 135, 136
kentsel yenileme (urban renewal),
  95–99
knowledge: connection to learning,
  77; economies, 1
knowledge production
  (Wlliamsburg, Brooklyn),
  125–47; churches united, 137–40;
  gentrification, 131–33; overview of

Williamsburg, Brooklyn, 129–31;
participatory research, 140–44;
Southside (Los Sures), 133–36;
transformative learning, 140–44
Korten, David, 207, 208, 213, 214,
216

L

Lansing, Michigan, 190, 196
Lansing State Journal, 201
Latino populations (Brooklyn),
134–40, 144
Lave, Jean, 190
Law number 5366 (Turkey), 97
lead poisoning, 195
learning, 125, 126; communities
of practice (Istanbul, Turkey),
94–108; connection to knowledge,
77; interdisciplinary experiential,
163; project-based, 159, 166,
167; strategies (High Tech High
[San Diego, California]), 164–70.
See also knowledge production
(Wlliamsburg, Brooklyn)
learning energy, 2
Liberty Station, 153, 156
library research (Brazil), 77
life politics, 8–11
Lisbon, Portugal: civic ecology,
109–24; institutional conflicts
and clandestinidade, 113, 114–18;
sustainability, 118–20; urban
gardening case study, 111–13
literacy, 82, 83; Intag, Ecuador, 23–
42; sustainability, 5
literacy (Brazil), 79, 83, 86
lived experience, 159
local environment stewardship, 109
local exchange/employment and
trading systems (LETS), 207–20;
capitalism, 213–15; eco-sustainable
societies, 216–18; historical
principles of economy, 208–13
local production, 118
The Log from the Sea of Cortez
(Steinbeck), 161
Lopez, Vito, 139
Los Sures (Southside), 132, 133–36

LUST (Leaking Underground
Storage Tanks), 196

M

Maida, Carl, 14
Mainstream Green, 207
Manu Chao, 100
marginality, communities of practice
and, 78–81
market economies, 217
Marsh, Adrian, 98
Martínez, María Rosa, 13
Marx, Karl, 203, 208, 210, 211, 212,
214, 217, 218
McCay, Bonnie, 8
McKenna, Brian, 14
McKibben, Bill, 207, 208, 213, 214, 216
McLaren, Peter, 166
Meireles, Olivia, 86
Mexico, 191
Michigan: Department of
Environmental Quality, 197; Flint,
191; Lansing, 190
military installations, transition of,
152–55
Mills, C. Wright, 204
Mining Law (2009), 23, 24
Missile Park (San Diego, CA), 155
Mobbing: Emotional Abuse in the
American Workplace (Davenport et
al.), 193
Mohanty, Chandra, 70
Molinos Department, 44, 45, 48
Molinos Township populations, 46
money (as social connector), 214
Monteiro, António, 112
Mother's Association, 75
müshterekler (commons), 99–101
mutual engagement, 109

N

National Institute of Agricultural
Technology, INTA (Cieza), 45
National Science Foundation, 3
National Steel and Shipbuilding, 154
nationhood (Brazil), 89
nature, rights of (Ecuador), 28
Naval Base Coronado, 154

Naval Base Point Loma, 154
Naval Base San Diego, 154
Naval Electronics Laboratory, 154
Naval Training Center (San Diego, CA), 153
N. C. School of Science and Mathematics, 177
Needelman, Marty, 126*f*
neoliberalism, 153, 204
networks, collaborative peer, 11
New Urbanism design movement, 164
New York City, New York, 129. *See also* Williamsburg, Brooklyn
New York Mercantile Exchange, 32
No Fear: A Whistleblower's Triumph: Over Corruption and Retaliation at the EPA (Coleman-Adebayo), 201
non-governmental organisations (NGOs), 4, 27, 45, 60, 62
Nonini, Don, 182
North Brooklyn, 137, 140, 141, 142, 143, 144
North Carolina Central University (NCCU), 179

O
Open Society Foundations, 98
Oral, Funda, 13
organic cultivation, 66
Orr, Julian, 167
Orthodox Jews, 130
O'Shea, Jim, 128*f*, 137, 139
Otavalo County (Ecuador), 25
Our Common Future (UN Brundtland Commission), 30
Our Lady of Montserrat Roman Catholic Church (Brooklyn), 133
Özal, Turgut, 96, 97

P
Pacific Ocean, 153
Parque Agrícola, 116, 117, 121
Parque Agrícola da Alta de Lisboa (PAAL), 112
parques hortícolas, 112
participatory action research (PAR) partnerships, 110

participatory research, 140–44
Partido do Trabalhadores (Workers' Party), 79
Passionist Order of Roman Catholic priests, 137
El Patrimonio tiene Oficio (Our heritage has a trade), 45
pedagogies, 165, 169
Pedagogy, 81
Pequeña Agricultura Familiar programmes, 45
Periódico Intag (2000–2011), 32–34, 37, 38
Perspectives of San Diego Bay: A Field Guide, 161–62
pesticides (farm), 196
philosophy of praxis, 190. *See also* praxis (philosophy of)
Photovoice research, 109–24; shared understandings of civic ecology and urban gardening, 113–14
Pinheiro, Raimundo, 79
Plan de Vida 2007–2011 (Life Plan), 35
plantation labour act, 61
Point Loma (California), 153, 154
Polanyi, Karl, 208, 209, 210, 211, 212, 217
policies, public (Argentina), 50
political activism, 178
politics, 7, 8–11
pollution, 5
populations: Ecuador, 23; Latino populations (Brooklyn), 134–40, 144; Molinos Township, 46; Puerto Rican population (New York City), 134; Williamsburg, Brooklyn, 129, 131, 132
Portugal, Lisbon. *See* Lisbon, Portugal
practice, 11; fair trade, 62–68
praxis (philosophy of), 190–212; crafting, 192–93
"Principle of Conservation and Mutation of Social Energy" (Hirschman), 180
processes, fair trade, 63
professions, communities of practice, 1
profits, 215. *See also* capitalism

project-based learning, 159, 166, 167
Public Employees for Environmental
 Responsibility, 200, 201
Public Employees for Environmental
 Responsibility (PEER), 197
public engagement, 94; Intag,
 Ecuador, 23–42. *See also* activism
public health, 190–212; communities
 of practice, 193–95; community
 of resistance, 200–201; crafting
 a philosophy of praxis, 192–93;
 critical findings, 195–97;
 disruption, 198–99; official
 ruptures (Lansing, Michigan),
 197–98; policies, 43
public pedagogies, 165
public policies (Argentina), 50
Puerto Rican population (New York
 City), 134

Q
Qualcomm, Inc., 156
quality-of-life, 3, 7
Quattro Pro Paradox, 195
Quechua language, 44
quilombolas (or maroon)
 communities, 79

R
racism, 201
rain barrels, 184
Raleigh, North Carolina, 174
Ramos, Juan, 127*f*, 140
Rappaport, Roy, 9
Raulet, Harry, 203
Reconnect Industries, 128*f*
Redclift, Michael, 4
reflective activities, 165
Re-Hashed Trash Bash, 181, 184
relationships: between communities
 and environments, 43–59; between
 human and natural systems, 7
Remorini, Carolina, 13
research: participatory, 140–44;
 Photovoice, 109–24
Research Triangle Transition, 174,
 183, 185, 186
resources: common-pool, 6;
 communication, 10; water, 24

Revolt's Destruction *(Tahribad-ı
 İsyan)*, 102, 103
Rice, Max, 184
rights, women's, 34–36
Río Intag Coffee, 32
Riordan, Rob, 156
rituals, 110
Rohr, 154
Roma gypsies, 13, 94–96, 102, 104
Roman neighbourhoods (Turkey),
 94, 96
Rosenstock, Larry, 157
Ruch, Jeff, 200
rural areas, Calchaquí Valley (Salta,
 Argentina), 43–59
Rushton, North Carolina, 174, 178

S
Salk Institute for Biological Studies,
 155
Salta, Argentina, 43–59. *See also*
 Calchaquí Valley
San Diego, California, 151–73. *See
 also* High Tech High (San Diego,
 California)
San Diego Bay, 164
San Diego Bay (California), 153, 159
San Diego Bay: A Call for Conservation,
 162
*San Diego Bay: A Story of Exploitation
 and Restoration*, 162
San Diego Bay Study, 162, 163, 169
San Diego Unified School District,
 155, 157
Sanford-Burnham Medical Research
 Institute, 155
Save Our Streets (SOS), 127*f*
school gardening programs
 (Portugal), 119*f*
Schoon, Danielle V., 13
Schwartz, Berl, 200
Scott, James C., 216
Scrap Exchange, 178
Scripps Institution of Oceanography,
 155
Second World War, 129, 144
Sen, Debarati, 13
service, community, 128
sewage sludge, 196

sexism, 201
shade-grown coffee, 32
shamanic traditions, 66
situations, 8
Sizer, Ted, 158
skill-shares, 174
slavery, 210
Smith, Adam, 207, 208, 209, 213, 215, 216
Smith-Nonini, Sandy, 7
social class disparities, 153
social engagement, 1
social enterprise for community development, 183
social inclusion (in Brazil), 75–93
socialism, 210
social learning, 2
social permaculture, 118
social suffering, 9
Sociedade de Gestão de Alta de Lisboa (SGAL), 111
sociology, 194
soladarities, 60–72, 62, 69
Solano, Rob, 140
Southside (Los Sures), 132, 133–36
Spanish encomienda, 44
Sparrow Hospital (Lansing, Michigan), 196
species biodiversity, 160
Sports and Leisure, 81
stakeholders, 165
Stanford University, 159
stewardship: of forest ecosystems, 24; local environment, 109
STOP (Sınır Tanimayan Otonom Plancilar, or Autonomous Planners with No Frontiers), 98
stories, 110
subsistence farmers, 24
Sulukule Children's Art Atelier, 94, 101–4
Sulukule neighbourhood (Istanbul, Turkey), 94; commons (müshterekler), 99–101; urban renewal in, 95–99
Sulukule Platform, 99–101, 103
Sulukule Renewal Project (2007), 97
Sulukule Roma Association, 98
Sulukule Volunteers Association, 101

surveys: Calchaquí Valley (Salta, Argentina), 47; Coordinadora de Mujeres de Íntag (CMI), 36–37
sustainability, 114, 151–73; and collaborative anthropological practice, 11–12; communities, 175–78; communities of practice, 81–85; concept of, 3; cooperatives, 183–87; Coordinadora de Mujeres de Íntag (CMI) surveys, 36–37; development, 30; Eco-Cycle, 174–89; eco-sustainable societies, 207–20; environmental, 109; global, 1–19; glocal approach to, 26–29; green-collar jobs, 178–80; Intag, Ecuador, 23–42; learning strategies, 164–70; literacy, 5; organising for, 14; Periódico Intag (2000–2011), 32–34; place and the commons, 3–8; place-based non-profits, 180–83; skill demand changes, 155–64; sustaining the countryside, 12–13; through coffee, 30–32; transition of military installations, 152–55; urban, 94; urban gardeners (Lisbon, Portugal), 118–20; urbanism, 13; women's rights, 34–36
Sustainable South Bronx, 179
symbols, 110
Szaky, Tom, 177

T
Tahribad-ı İsyan (Revolt's Destruction), 102, 103
Take Back the Economy (Gibson-Graham), 185
tea: buyers, 67; fair trade, 60
Teixeira, Susana, 84
Teves, Laura, 13
The Story of Water Resources at Work (PEER, 2001), 200
Tohumcu, Zeynep Gonca Girgin, 95
TOKİ (Turkey's Mass Housing Administration), 97
tourism, 60
toxic underground releases, 196
transactions, solidarities, 62

Transfiguration Roman Catholic Church (Brooklyn), 133, 135*f*
transformative learning (Brooklyn), 140–44
Transition Food Committee, 185
transition of military installations, 152–55
Triangle Community Foundation, 186
Turkey: Sulukule Children's Art Atelier, 101–4; Sulukule neighbourhood commons (*müshterekler*), 99–101; urban renewal (in Istanbul), 95–99; urban rights activism in, 94–108
Two Sides of the Boat Channel: A Field Guide, 161
2000 Ecological Ordinance (EO), 28
2007 Plan, 36

U
UN Brundtland Commission, 30
UNESCO, 98, 99
United Nations Millennial Development Goals (2000), 30
universities as centers of learning, 125
upcycling projects, 186
urban ecology, 151–73; learning strategies, 164–70; skill demand changes, 155–64; transition of military installations, 152–55
urban gardeners (Lisbon, Portugal), 109–24; institutional conflicts and *clandestinidade*, 113, 114–18; shared understandings of, 113–14; sustainability, 118–20
urbanisation, 6
urbanism, sustainability, 13
urban renewal (*kentsel yenileme*), 95–99
urban rights activism (Turkey), 94–108
Urban Semester Program (Cornell University), 128, 140, 143
urban sustainability, 94
Urban Transformation Law (2007), 97

USAID, 32
U.S. Coast Guard, 154
U.S. Navy Pacific Fleet, 154

V
Vavra, Jay, 159, 160, 163
voluntary acts of solidarity, 61
voluntourism, 60, 61, 63

W
wage labour jobs, 44, 45
Walden (Thoreau), 161
water resources, 24
We adapt and resist (*Adaptamos e resistimos*), 116*f*, 117*f*
welfare payments (Ecuador), 26
Wenger, Etienne, 1, 2
wetland loss (Ingram County, Michigan), 197
Williamsburg, Brooklyn, 125–47; churches united, 137–40; gentrification, 131–33; overview of, 129–31; participatory research, 140–44; Southside (*Los Sures*), 133–36; transformative learning in, 140–44
Williamsburg Bridge (Brooklyn), 134
Wills, Henry, 178
Wilson, Edward O., 160, 162
Winona State University, 38*f*
women: empowerment, 60–72; fair trade and, 64; rights, 34–36
Workers' Party (*Partido do Trabalhadores*), 79
work-practice experiences, 170
workshops, Calchaquí Valley (Salta, Argentina), 52, 53
World Bank, 26
World Health Organization (WHO), 194
World Heritage (UNESCO), 99

X
XARXA de Consum Solidari, 35

Y
Youth Involved in Keeping Earth Sustainable, 177